Elena Lucrezia Cornaro Piscopia

(1646-1684)

The First Woman in the World to Earn a University Degree

Elena Lucrezia Cornaro Piscopia

(1646-1684)

The First Woman in the World to Earn

a University Degree

Francesco Ludovico Maschietto

Translated by
Jan Vairo and William Crochetiere

Edited by
Catherine Marshall

Saint Joseph's University Press

Philadelphia

Library of Congress Cataloging-in-Publication Data

Maschietto, Francesco Ludovico.
[Elena Lucrezia Cornaro Piscopia (1646-1684) English]
Elena Lucrezia Cornaro Piscopia (1646-1684) : the first woman in the world to earn a university degree / Francesco Ludovico Maschietto ; translated by Jan Vairo and William Crochetiere ; edited by Catherine Marshall.
      p. cm.
Includes bibliographical references and index.
ISBN 0-916101-57-6 (alk. paper)
1. Cornaro Piscopia, Elena Lucrezia, 1646-1684. 2. Authors, Italian--17th century--Biography. 3. Philosophers--Italy--Biography. I. Vairo, Jan. II. Crochetiere, William. III. Marshall, Catherine. IV. Title.

PQ4621.C48Z7813 2006
378.45'32--dc22
[B]
2006024821

Published by:

SAINT JOSEPH'S UNIVERSITY PRESS
5600 City Avenue
Philadelphia, Pennsylvania 19131-1395
www.sju.edu/sjupress/
Member of the Association of Jesuit University Presses

TABLE OF CONTENTS

LIST OF ILLUSTRATIONS

Not in the text. MILANO, Ambrosiana Library. Unknown (XVIII? century): Portrait of Elena Lucrezia Cornaro Piscopia.

1. The Island of Cyprus, from V. CORONELLI, *Atlante dell'isolario veneto*, I, Venezia 1696, p. 249.

2. The Island of Cyprus (detail), from V. CORONELLI, *Atlante dell'isolario veneto*, I, Venezia 1696, p. 249. At the southern point we find the castle of Piscopi, fief of the Cornaros, which gave rise to the last name of the Cornaro Piscopia family.

3. CODEVIGO, Erle House (already a Cornaro villa). View facing the public street (photo of the Consorzio for the development of the Piovese). The sixteenth-century villa built by Falconetto for Alvise Cornaro as it is currently seen.

4. CODEVIGO, Erle House (already a Cornaro villa). East wall: signs of a double window which has been bricked up to close it off permanently (photo of the Consorzio for the Development of the Piovese).

5. VENICE, Correr Civic Museum Library, Gherro collection 2978. Engraving by G. A. Battisti (1779): Portal, no longer in existence, for access to the Cornaro villa (work of Falconetto) in Codevigo.

6. PADUA, L. Uggeri collection. Engraving by M. Marieschi (1694-1743). Venice: St. Mark's Square with the old "Procuracy" (left) and the new (right) built as the official residence of the Procurators of St. Mark's.

7. PADUA, L. Uggeri collection. Engraving by L. Carlevaris (1665-1731). Venice: The new "Procuracy" (detail). For several years, Elena Cornaro Piscopia lived in an apartment on the first floor of this building with her family.

8. The city of Este (detail). Engraving by G Franchini (1775), from I. Alessi, *Ricerche storico critiche delle antichità di Este*, Padua 1776. The villa of Alvise Cornaro is visible in the center, with the greenhouse and the arched entrance to the garden (work of Falconetto, 16th century).

9. ESTE, Benvenuti Villa (already Cornaro). Renaissance arch (Falconetto) at the entrance to the garden.

10. ESTE, Benvenuti Villa (already Cornaro) is the 1848 radical transformation (architect G. Iappelli?) of sixteenth-century villa of Alvise Cornaro.

11. PADUA, Basilica of St. Anthony. G. Bonazza (active 1695-1730). Portrait bust of Elena Cornaro Piscopia placed (1727) in substitution of the funereal monument erected for her in 1684-1689 and demolished in 1727 because of its cumbersome nature.

12. VENICE, St. Luke Parish Archive, Baptisms 1633-1647, by name and by date. Elena Lucrezia Cornaro Piscopia's baptismal certificate.

13. VENICE, Loredan Palace (already Cornaro Piscopia) 12th century. Façade facing the Grand Canal.

14. Carlo Rinaldini, professor of philosophy at the University of Padua, who guided Elena Cornaro Piscopia in her philosophical studies until she obtained her degree (June 25, 1678). Engraving by M. Desbois (1630-1700) from C. PATINUS, *Lyceum Patavinum*, Patavii 1682, p. 52.

15. Professor Felice Rotondi, professor of theology at the University of Padua, taught this subject to Elena Cornaro Piscopia. Engraving by M. Desbois (1630-1700), from C. PATINUS, *Lyceum Patavinum*, Patavii 1682, p. 47.

16. The University of Padua (Main façade), by I. PH. TOMASINI, *Gymnasium Patavinum*, Utini 1654, p. 40.

17. PADUA, Civic Museum Library, Racc. Icon. III, 518. Engraver I. Frey (1681-1752). Cardinal Gregorio Barbarigo, Bishop of Padua and Chancellor of the University.

18. PADUA, Ancient Archive of the University, ms. 365, f. 25^{r-v} - 26^{r-v}. Regular record of Elena Lucrezia Cornaro Piscopia's degree granted by the College of Philosophers and Physicians of the University of Padua.

19. PADUA, Civic Museum Library, Paduan Iconography 718. Engraving by G. Langlois (1649-1712), Elena Cornaro Piscopia at the age of twenty-two.

20. Elena Lucrezia Cornaro Piscopia. Engraving by D. Rossetti (1650-1736), from M. DEZA, *Vita di Helena Lucrezia Cornaro Piscopia*, Venice 1686.

21. Elena Lucrezia Cornaro Piscopia. Engraving by Sister I. Piccini (active 1665-1692), from A. LUPIS, *L'eroina veneta, ovvero la vita di Elena Lucretia Cornara Piscopia*, Venetia 1689.

22. PADUA, Civic Museum. Elena Lucrezia Cornaro Piscopia. Portrait on canvas executed in 1673 and attributable more to Giovanni Battista Molinari (1638-1682) than to his son Antonio (1665-after 1727) barely eight at that time.

23. Elena Lucrezia Cornaro Piscopia. Engraving by A Portius (active 1686-1700), from M. Deza, *Vita di Helena Lucretia Cornara Piscopia*, Venice-Genova 1687.

24. PADUA, Civic Museum Library, Paduan Iconography 719. Engraving by C. Agostini from an engraving by G. Langlois, of Elena Lucrezia Cornaro Piscopia.

25. VENICE, Correr Civic Museum Library, cod. Gradenigo 49, p. 156. Elena Lucrezia Cornaro Piscopia. Drawing from G. GREVENBROCH, (1731-1807), *Gli abiti de' veneziani di qualsiasi età con diligenza raccolti e dipinti*.

26. Elena Lucrezia Cornaro Piscopia. Engraving by A. VIVIANI (1797-1854) from drawing by M. FANOLI (1807-1876) in L. CARRER, *Anello di sette gemme o Venezia e la sua storia*, Venice 1838, p. 697.

27. The family of Carlo Patin, professor of medicine at the University of Padua, who attempted to have his own eldest daughter graduate. Engraving from CARLA PATIN, *Tabellae selectae et explicatae*, Patavii 1691, p. 201.

28. VATICAN APOSTOLIC LIBRARY, Cardinals, sheet 6, I, 109. Engraving by R. van Audenaerd (1663-1743), Cardinal Emanuel Théodore de La Tour d'Auvergne de Bouillon (1643-1715), sent by the King of France to Venice (1677) in order to verify the cultural formation of Elena Cornaro Piscopia.

29. VATICAN APOSTOLIC LIBRARY, Cardinals, sheet 6, I, 121. Engraving by A. Clouwet (1636-1679), Cardinal Cesare d'Estrées (1628-1714), Ambassador of France, who came to Padua in 1680 to visit Elena Cornaro Piscopia.

30. PADUA, State Archive, St. Anthony, Confessor, vol. 320. Drawing by L. MAZZI (1735). Alvise Cornaro's "La Casasa Vechia" [The Old House] in the district of the Saint in Padua.

31. PADUA, Civic Museum Library, Engraving by G. Valle (1784), The Cornaro "courtyard": the loggia in the background and on the right the odeon (work of Falconetto), to the left the "casa nova" [new house] to even out the "corte."

32. G. LANSPERGIO, *Lettera overo Colloquio di Christo all'anima devota...*, a translation by Elena Lucrezia Cornaro Piscopia, Venetia 1669 (title page), the first literary work of Elena Cornaro.

33. VATICAN APOSTOLIC LIBRARY, Cardinals, sheet 6, I. Engraving by G. Vallet (1632-1704), Cardinal Francesco Barberini (1597-1679), to whom Elena Cornaro Piscopia wrote various letters.

34. VATICAN APOSTOLIC LIBRARY, Popes, sheet 7 (5), 104-105. Engraving by A. Clouwet (1636-1679), Pope Innocent XI (1611-1689), to whom Elena Cornaro Piscopia addressed a literary composition in gratitude for words of praise.

35. *La seconda corona intrecciata da vari letterati per il p. Giacomo Lubrani*, Venetia 1675 (title page), promoted and published by Elena Cornaro Piscopia.

36. ROME, Archivum Romanum Societatis Iesu. P. Gianpaolo Oliva (1600-1681), Superior General of the Society of Jesus, who exchanged frequent correspondence with Elena Cornaro Piscopia and with her father.

37. Domenico Marchetti, professor of medicine at the University of Padua, one of Elena Cornaro Piscopia's personal physicians. Engraving by M. Desbois (1630-1700), by C. PATINUS, Lyceum Patavinum. Patavii 1682, p. 39.

ABBREVIATIONS

A.A.U.   Archivio Antico, University of Padua

A.C.P.   Archivio, Curia Vescovile, Padua

A.R.S.J.   Archivio Romano, Compagnia di Gesù, Rome

A.S.L.V.   Archivio, Parrochia S. Luca, Venice

A.S.P.   Archivio di Stato, Padua

A.S.V.   Archivio di Stato, Venice

LIST OF SUBSCRIBERS TO THE ITALIAN EDITION

TO THIS VOLUME PUBLISHED ON THE OCCASION
OF THE TERCENTENARY OF THE FIRST
UNIVERSITY DEGREE EARNED BY A WOMAN

ABBAZIA DI S. GIUSTINA
ACCADEMIA PATAVINA DI SCIENZE, LETTERE ED ARTI, Padova
GRAZIELLA ALLEGRI, Università, Padova
GERMAN ARCINIEGAS, Ambasciatore di Colombia, Santa Sede, Roma
MASSIMILLA VALDO CEOLIN, Università, Padova
BANCA ANTONIANA DI PADOVA E TRIESTE
CARLA BARBIERI, Padova
SERGIO BAÙ, Venezia-Mestre
BENEDETTINE DEL SS. SACRAMENTO, Sortino (Siracusa)
EUGENIA BEVILACQUA, Università, Padova
BIBLIOTECA ANGELICA, Roma
BIBLIOTECA APOSTOLICA VATICANA, Città del Vaticano
BIBLIOTECA CIVICA, Padova
BIBLIOTECA CIVICA, Venezia-Mestre
BIBLIOTECA CIVICA BERTOLIANA, Vicenza
BIBLIOTECA COMUNALE, Treviso
BIBLIOTECA DEL MONUMENTO NAZIONALE DI S. GIUSTINA,
Padova
BIBLIOTECA DEL MONUMENTO NAZIONALE, Praglia
BIBLIOTECA NAZIONALE BRAIDENSE, Milano
BIBLIOTECA NAZIONALE MARCIANA, Venezia
BIBLIOTECA DEL PROTOCENOBIO S. SCOLASTICA, Subiaco (Roma)
BIBLIOTECA DELL'UNIVERSITÀ CATTOLICA DEL S. CUORE,
Milano
BIBLIOTECA UNIVERSITARIA, Padova
BIBLIOTHEEK, ABDIJ AFFLIGEM, Hekelgem
THE BISCAYNE COLLEGE LIBRARY, Miami, Florida
THE UNIVERSITY OF CALIFORNIA LIBRARY, Irvine, Ca.
LUCIANA BOLISANI GRIGGIO, Università, Padova
ERNESTO BRANCALEONI, Padova
E. MAXINE BRUHNS, Pittsburgh, Pa.
FLAVIA CABASINO CRESPI, Roma
MARIA CAPOZZA, Università, Padova
FRANCESCA ROMANA CARABELLESE, Roma

BRUNA CARAZZOLO, Padova
CASALINI LIBRI, Fiesole (Firenze)
OFELIA CELLI GALEOTA, Roma
FRANCESCO CESSI, Padova
CIRCOLO STORICI DILETTANTI PADOVANI, Padova
MARY COLLINS, O.S.B., Mount St. Scholastica, Atchison, Kansas
CONSIGLIO REGIONALE DEL VENETO, Venezia
LUISA TONZIG CORALUPPI, Pittsburgh, Pa.
GIOVANNI CORNER CAMPANA, Santa Lucia di Piave (Treviso)
ELENA CORNER JUNIOR, Thiene (Vicenza)
MRS. EARLE M. CRAIG, Pittsburgh, Pa.
MRS. RUTH CRAWFORD MITCHELL, Pittsburgh, Pa.
ANGELO D'AGOSTINO, S.J., Washington, D.C.
IRENEO DANIELE, Seminario Vescovile, Padova
ANITA DE SANTIS, Padova
ANGELA DEL TURCO, Treviso
NICOLA D'URSO, Roma
ANTONIO ELEMENTI, Padova
PIER GIOVANNI FABBRI-COLABICH, Padova
FRANCESCO FAGGIOTTO, Padova
GIORGIO FEDALTO, Università, Padova
PAOLA FERRABINO ZANCAN, Roma
MARIA FIDECARO, Università, Padova
CESIRA GASPAROTTO, Padova
GIOVANNI GIACOMETTI, Università, Padova
GIUSEPPINA GIULIODORI GATELLA, Osimo (Ancona)
MRS. JOHN D. GORDAN, New York, N.Y.
ENZO GROZZATO, Padova
SEN. LUIGI GUI, Presidente «Ente Nazionale Francesco Petrarca »,
Padova
OTTO HARRASSOWITZ, Library Agents, Wiesbaden
HANS HARTINGER NACHF., Buchhandlung, Berlin
HERZOG AUGUST BIBLIOTHEK, Wolfenbüttel, Germania
ISTITUTO DI LINGUE E LETTERATURE MODERNE E
STRANIERE, Università, Padova
ISTITUTO DI PALEOGRAFIA E DIPLOMATICA, Università, Padova
ISTITUTO DI STORIA ECONOMICA, FACOLTÀ DI ECONOMIA E
COMMERCIO, Verona
ISTITUTO STORICO ITALO-GERMANICO IN TRENTO, Villazzano
(Trento)
ISTITUTO STORICO GERMANICO, Biblioteca, Roma
ISTITUTO DI STORIA MEDIOEVALE E MODERNA, Università, Padova
ISTITUTO TEOLOGICO S. ANTONIO DOTTORE, Padova

ISTITUTO UNIVERSITARIO PAREGGIATO DI MAGISTERO
«MARIA SS. ASSUNTA», Roma
BENJAMIN G. KOHL, Vassar College, Poughkeepsie, N.Y.
MRS. GEORGE LABALME, New York, N.Y.
EMMA LA FACE, Reggio Calabria
TERESA LAURENTI BALDONI, Roma
LINO LAZZARINI, Università, Padova
LIBRAIRIE JUSTUS LIPSIUS, Bruxelles
LIBRERIA ALL'ACCADEMIA DI RANDI GIUSEPPE E PIETRO,
    Padova
LIBRERIA COMMISSIONARIA SANSONI, Firenze
LIBRERIA EDITRICE INTERNAZIONALE ROSENBERG &
SELLIER, Torino
LIBRERIA EDITRICE G.T. VINCENZI & NIPOTI, Modena
LIBRERIA FERRARI-AUER, Bolzano
LIBRERIA OTTO LANGE, Firenze
LIBRERIA INTERNAZIONALE SEEBER, Firenze
LIBRERIA LEDI, Milano
LIBRERIA GIÀ NARDECCHIA, Roma
LIBRERIA DEL PORCELLINO, Firenze
LIBRERIA ZANICHELLI, Bologna
ODDONE LONGO, Preside della Facoltà di Lettere e Filosofia,
Università, Padova
GUIDO LUCATELLO, Università, Padova
MARIO MANEA, Isola Vicentina (Vicenza)
MARIALUISA MANFREDINI GASPARETTO, Università, Padova
FRANCESCA MARANGELLI, Bari
EMILIO MENEGAZZO, Padova
MONACHE BENEDETTINE DELL'ADORAZIONE PERPETUA SS.
SACRAMENTO, Ronco-Ghiffa (Novara)
MONASTERO DELLE BENEDETTINE DI S. ANTONIO ABATE,
Ferrara
MONASTERO DELLE BENEDETTINE S. MARIA DELLE GRAZIE,
Orte (Viterbo)
MONASTERO BENEDETTINE «S. PIETRO», Montefiascone
(Viterbo)
MONASTERO BENEDETTINE S. RAIMONDO, Piacenza
MONASTERO S. BENEDETTO, Castelfiorentino (Firenze)
BUCHHANDLUNG ALBERT MÜLLER, Stuttgart
MUNKSGAARD, International Booksellers and Publishers, Copenhagen
LA NUOVA ITALIA BIBLIOGRAFICA, Firenze
CESARE PECILE, Università, Padova
SILVANO PEDRINI, Brescia

MARGHERITA PERATONER, Udine
PETRARCA-INSTITUT AN DER UNIVERSITÄT, Köln
PICCINELLI SILIPRANDI DAGMAR, Università, Padova
ERNESTO PEPATO, O.S.B., Monte della Madonna, Teolo (Padova)
MARIA PREST, Conegliano (Treviso)
PRIORATO BENEDICTINO, Esquipulas, Chiquimula
MRS. PETER F. PUGLIESE, Wayne, Pa.
ROMANICA, Buchhandlung, Zürich
ROMANISCHES SEMINAR DER PHILIPPS-UNIVERSITÄT,
Marburg/Lahn
LUCIA ROSSETTI, Padova
PAOLO SAMBIN, Padova
LIA SBRIZIOLO, Padova
FRANCESCA SCAPIN, Padova
GUIDO SINOPOLI, Conegliano (Treviso)
GIOVANNI SPINELLI, O.S.B., Bibiliotecario del Monastrero
Benedettino, Pontido (Bergamo)
AGNES L. STARRETT, Pittsburgh, Pa.
ALDO STELLA, Padova
FABRIZIO TESORIERI, Forlì
DANILO TOGNON, Padova
BIANCA TONINI, Udine
MARIA TONZIG, Padova
UNIVERSITÀ DI PADOVA
THE VASSAR COLLEGE LIBRARY, Poughkeepsie, N.Y.
PIETRO VENUTI, Padova
MARIA LUISA VISCIDI, Padova
VALENTINO VOLPINI, Padova
THE WARBURG INSTITUTE, University of London
ALIPIO ZANINELLO, Padova
STELLA ZANNONI, Brafenahl, Ohio
INES ZANON, Università, Padova

FOREWORD

Even in seventeenth-century Italy, news spread quickly. Thus on June 25, 1678, nobles, knights, city authorities, ladies, scholarly men, the vicar general, and the entire College of Philosophers and Physicians arrived at the University of Padua to witness Elena Lucrezia Cornaro Piscopia stand for her oral doctoral examination—the first time in history that a woman had been accorded that privilege. So great was the crowd that the event had to be moved from the University's Sacred College to the Chapel of the Blessed Virgin in the Cathedral.

The bishop's refusal to allow Elena to stand for a degree in theology no doubt increased interest in the grudgingly approved examination on philosophical subjects. Her eloquent discourse on two Aristotelian theses so impressed the examining committee that, despite her request for a secret ballot, they voted their approval *viva voce* to award her the *Magistra et Doctrix Philosophiae* degrees. She thus became the first woman in the world to earn a university degree—*la prima donna laureata nel mondo.*

After her death six years later, Padua contained only two public reminders of Elena's life: a statue at the university and a modest grave among the Benedictine monks in the burial chapel of St. Luke at St. Justina Monastery where she had worshiped as a lay oblate. The approval of her request to be buried there left unused a grand funeral monument of twelve figures already erected in the Basilica of St. Anthony. This monument was demolished in 1727; the statue of Elena, having passed through several hands, was placed at the foot of a staircase leading to the university's courtyard in 1773.

In 1896, the Benedictine Abbess Matilda Pynsent came from Rome to verify the remains of Elena Cornaro. She reinterred them in a zinc coffin and installed a new black marble gravestone commemorating her academic achievement to replace the original one provided by the monks in 1684. Abbess Pynsent returned to Rome and published, anonymously and in English, a biography of Elena Lucrezia Cornaro Piscopia.

In 1906, Vassar College in Poughkeepsie, New York, the first American college for women, commissioned a monumental stained-glass window for its Thompson Memorial Library. It portrayed Elena at her examination, surrounded by scholars and townspeople. From 1908 to 1912, a young student named Ruth Crawford studied beneath the Cornaro window and yearned to know more about the graceful lady surrounded by such an impressive array of people.

In the 1920s, the student, now Ruth Crawford Mitchell, became director of the Nationality Rooms Program at the University of

Pittsburgh. As she helped the Italian Room Committee plan its room, education, religion, and cultural notables became the focal concepts. A portrait of Elena, based on her statue at the University of Padua, was commissioned for the rear wall. The artist, Giovanni Romagnoli of Bologna, traveled to Pittsburgh to unveil his mural on May 14, 1949.

Mrs. Mitchell further honored Elena's memory in 1952, when she visited Padua with a group of University of Pittsburgh Nationality Room student guides, who placed flowers on Elena's grave. They returned to report that the gravestone was badly cracked. In 1969, Mitchell received a letter from Don Innocenzo de Angelis, the newly installed abbot of St. Justina, suggesting she come to Padua to see the chapel and discuss the restoration of the gravestone. On this visit, she discovered the stone totally shattered and the zinc coffin now removed to an adjacent underground area awaiting the installation of a new floor.

Mrs. Mitchell devised a plan: she would replace the marble stone and attract worldwide attention to *la prima donna laureata nel mondo* by organizing a Tercentenary celebration in 1978. With the steadfast collaboration of Maria Tonzig, Ph.D., a graduate of the University of Padua and a Benedictine oblate at St. Justina, Mrs. Mitchell enlisted Professor Paolo Sambin at the university's Institute of History to research and document the primacy of Elena's 1678 degrees. By 1972, responses from all universities existing in 1678 confirmed that she was the first woman in the world to earn a university degree.

In Pittsburgh, Mrs. Mitchell convinced Monsignor Nicola Fusco, P.A., who had long been fascinated by Elena, to write a profile of her life, using Abbess Pynsent's 1896 book as a reference. Upon its publication in 1975, purchasers were also required to procure a copy for a library of their choice. The proceeds provided funds for the new gravestone—a black marble replica of the marker laid by the Benedictine monks in 1684.

Inspired by the American effort, the Italian Ministry of Cultural Monuments restored St. Luke's Chapel and renamed it the Cappella Cornaro, the Cornaro Chapel. Fr. Francesco Ludovico Maschietto, a Benedictine monk at Padua's Monastery of St. Justina, began an eight-year odyssey of research which led to the publication in 1978 of the definitive Cornaro biography, *Elena Lucrezia Cornaro Piscopia, 1646-1684: prima donna laureata nel mondo.*

In 1976, Mrs. Mitchell, then 86 years old, asked me to assume the national chairmanship of the United States Cornaro Tercentenary Committee and lead the delegation to Padua for the culminating celebrations.

By 1978, the United States Cornaro Tercentenary Committee had accomplished its mandate. The Cornaro biography by Monsignor Fusco now graced 500 libraries in America and Italy. Forty-nine educational and

E. Maxine Bruhns, National Chairperson of the United States Cornaro Tercentenary Committee and Ludovico Francesco Maschietto, O.S.B., author of Elena Lucrezia Piscopia Cornaro, 1646–1684, *discuss his book in Padua, September 1978.*

religious institutions nationwide celebrated the tercentenary with ceremonies, lectures, and seminars. Syndicated news columns and other publications told the story of the world's first woman to earn a university degree. These included a feature in the *UNESCO Courier* which boasted a circulation of eight million.

On September 3, 1978, the University of Padua, the Monastery of St. Justina, and the cities of Venice and Padua began a weeklong series of events marking the 300th anniversary of Elena's landmark degree. Among street banners and posters heralding the event, Father Maschietto's book filled the display windows of Padua's bookstores. But the wealth of information it held was not accessible to non-Italian-speaking readers.

Now, more than 29 years later, the English translation of Father Ludovico's meticulously researched biography is in print. I wish to extend enduring gratitude to Torrence M. Hunt, Jr., and the Hunt Foundation, who not only funded the Cornaro Tercentenary project in 1978, but also underwrote the translation and manuscript preparation of this book. To educators Jan Vairo, who translated the text word-for-word, and William Crochetiere, who produced a more polished manuscript, we offer praise for their bilingual way with words.

Catherine Marshall, editor extraordinaire, who labored long and thoroughly to transform the translation into clear, logical and elegant English, has earned our lasting admiration and appreciation. Mary Pat McCarthy, who took on the task of final manuscript preparation, including Italian and Latin elements, produced an admirable product.

It is impossible to thank adequately the volunteers whose efforts have helped bring the volume into existence and place it in the right hands: Dr. Luisa Coraluppi, Salvatore Caito, June McSwigan, Donna Mathews, Dr. Isa Leita, Dr. Rosemary Civic, Marilyn Gindroz, Sally Stevenson, the late Artemis Manos, the late Frederick A. Hetzel, Jr., the late Betty McCance, Dick Edwards, Professor Dennis Looney, Frances Noetzel, Dr. Francesca Collechia, Vicky Mauclair, Dr. Clareece Godt, Laura Baccelli Vondas, Katie Stehle, the Italian Room Committee, the cultural attachés at the Italian Embassy in Washington, and Joseph F. Chorpenning, O.S.F.S. Editorial Director of St. Joseph's University Press.

May this history of Elena Lucrezia Cornaro Piscopia's pioneer achievement in education continue to inspire students and teachers for generations to come.

E. Maxine Bruhns
National Chairperson
Elena Lucrezia Cornaro Piscopia Tercentenary Committee, 1976-1978
University of Pittsburgh

INTRODUCTION

When I was invited to gather the broadest possible documentation for a new biography of Elena Lucrezia Cornaro Piscopia, to mark the third centennial of her doctorate (1678), I was rather perplexed. I knew that, in the span of those three centuries, much had been written about the first woman in the world to receive a university degree. But after examining several of those works, I understood that although many had hoed this field, few had plowed it deeply. There was, therefore, still something new and accurate to write on the topic.

This motivated me to undertake serious research in the state archives of Bologna, Brescia, Genoa, Milan, Modena, Padua, Reggio Emilia, Rome and Venice; in the Secret Vatican Archive; and in the Roman Archive of the Society of Jesus. I also consulted the archives of the Bishop's Curia of Padua, the Patriarchal Curia of Venice, the Parish of Codevigo (Padua), the Parish of Este (Padua), the Parish of Vestone in Valsabbia (Brescia), and almost all the parishes of Venice.

My investigations extended to numerous libraries in northern Italy, the Vatican Library, the "Vittorio Emanuele" National Central Library of Rome, the library of the Jewish community, and the Greek College of Rome. In addition, bibliographical information was kindly furnished to me by the libraries of the universities of Halle, Hanover, Leipzig, Paris, Uppsala, and Utrecht.

These consultations enabled me to make a thorough examination of the previous biographies of Elena Cornaro, which contained certain inaccuracies. The first, by Massimiliano Deza, a religious of the Mother of God, was published in Venice in 1686, two years after Elena's death; it presented the oral testimony of family members, teachers, and admirers of the deceased. Widely successful and twice reprinted (Venice 1687 and 1692), it remains a fundamental source despite its artificial, seventeenth-century style and preachy tone.

Much more precise and credible is the profile by Bacchini, the Benedictine who set the tone for Italian erudition in the early 1700s. According to Muratori, whose own style is attributable to Bacchini's school, Bacchini "admirably knew how to nourish genius so that whoever kept his company always left a much wiser man" (Epistle, V, n.1999, p. 2137). His sketch of Elena Cornaro, written in an elegant Latin style, was offered by Bacchini (Parma, 1688) to accompany her few remaining literary works and contained some information unknown to Deza.

Pompous in style, yet creative in content, is the narrative by Antonio Lupis of Messina (Venice, 1689), whom the Paduan Giovanni Scardova, at the beginning of the nineteenth century, attempted to denigrate in his unpublished writings.

The footprints of Deza are still evident in the biography by the English Benedictine Abbess Mathilda Pynsent (Rome 1896). But her moralistic-hagiographical tone precludes historic objectivity.

The research published by the Jesuit Angelo De Santi, (*La civiltà cattolica* 1898-1899) though more documented, adds little new information to what was already known.

It would be superfluous to mention other authors because they all slavishly repeat Deza.

My own investigation has yielded much previously unpublished data. Material that was of doubtful authenticity and undocumented in the earlier biographies has been carefully scrutinized.

A more realistic likeness of Elena Cornaro, freed from the pomposities of the seventeenth century and from unfounded assertions, is thus revealed. In saying this, I do not presume my work to be immune from deficiencies; I will be grateful to those who advise me of omissions and who help me to correct errors. The sole purpose of this biography is to make Elena Cornaro better known. In her own time she was considered a miracle of knowledge, the glory of Venice; she was the pride of the University of Padua which, by granting her a doctorate, marked a milestone in the emancipation of women; and as a Benedictine oblate, she set an example not only for women dedicated to scholarly pursuits, but also for all women.

In presenting to the public the result of my research, I wish to acknowledge Professor Paolo Sambin, who guided and encouraged me. I thank Professor Lia Sbriziolo for her bibliographical assistance, as well as Professor Lucia Rossetti, Professor Aldo Stella, and Professor Emilio Menegazzo, who patiently read my manuscript. I offer particular thanks to Dr. Maria Tonzig for her diligent cooperation.

Francesco Ludovico Maschietto
Padua, June 25, 1978

1

THE CORNARO LINEAGE

THE CORNARO NAME

Elena Lucrezia Cornaro Piscopia belongs to a family whose origin and splendor mingle with that of the Venetian Republic itself and which, along with politicians and men of letters, men of government, army heads and influential clergymen, precipitated significant action in the civil and ecclesiastical history of not only Venice, but of Italy and also of Europe.[1]

The work of previous authors is of little value in researching the Cornaro name. They wrote with adulation of the family's connection to the Roman aristocracy, attributing its origin to a certain Caio Cornelio, a resident of Padua who later settled in Venice; at the time of the Roman Republic he supposedly foretold Caesar's victory over Pompey, based on the flight of some birds. Even before writers took pen names, it was probably the practice of many noble Venetians, as it was elsewhere in Italy, to take a name with Roman connotations to lend prestige to their own names which were often common and, at times, of lower-class origin.

This phenomenon seems to imitate the ecclesiastical practice known as "apostolicity of the churches." Since the end of Christian antiquity, famous churches in the East and particularly in the West had attributed their origins directly to the apostles and their immediate disciples. This not only increased the fame of their bishops, but also gave particular prominence to the glory of their church and created strong support for the rights and privileges of the local churches compared to the other churches. There can be no doubt that in the apostolic era various churches had been founded by the apostles or by the disciples who were under their supervision. However, it is also evident that not all the churches that claim to have an apostolic foundation really do. To satisfy all of them, Christ would have needed among his followers not a squad but a phalanx of apostles and disciples.[2]

The origin of the Cornaro name must be sought not among the Romans but in another, more humble source: in the life of the common people. For example, a member of this family could have been particularly robust and resistant to fatigue, like a cornel tree (*corner* in the dialect of the Veneto Region), and thus nicknamed and known in the area as "the corner," that is, the strong one *par excellence*.[3] This is also the interpretation given by the painter and poet Gianbattista Maganza (c. 1513–1586), so-called Magagnò, in a poetic composition in Paduan dialect, "Per el cralissimo [chiarissimo] segnor Aloise Cornaro, pare [padre] e pàron de tutti i virtuliosi [virtuosi]" (For the honorable Mr. Aloise Cornaro, father and master of all the virtuous). In this composition he exalts the beauty, sturdiness, and usefulness of the *cornolaro* (corniolo), alluding to Cornaro, in whose shadow he saw many people resting or singing happily, and where he saw the bishop of Bitonto grow up.[4] He further declares that Ruzante (Angelo Beolco c. 1496-1542, playwright who wrote in the Paduan dialect) himself could not have produced his literary works if he had not encountered in Cornaro a splendid patron whom he could lean on as one leans on a hardwood cane in old age. Because many have had bread and protection from this *cornolaro*, meaning Cornaro, the poet concludes with the wise advice that "un puovero boàro s'attacche forte a sí bon Cornolàro" per stare "sú saldo, e forte, apè [fino] cent'agni [cent'anni]" (a poor farmhand holds tightly to such a good cornel so as to remain firm and strong for a hundred years).[5]

For another example of a humble source for the family name, consider the *corno* or horn used by the town crier or in battle, a word Italians usually pronounce as *corn*. In Latin, the verb *cornicare, corniculare* (to sound the horn) leads to the noun *cornarius* (sounder of the horn).[6] Whether it derives from the horn itself or from the person who blows the horn, the name has the primitive meaning of eminence, of elevation, and it represents power and courage, a common meaning both in Latin and in some Semitic languages such as Hebrew and Sanskrit.[7]

These are simple hypotheses, but they merit consideration. We must also remember that nicknames provide an inexhaustible source of additional names that emphasize qualities or, more often, physical or moral defects. A person's hair color, way of walking, or other typical characteristics, may precipitate a nickname which later becomes a last name.[8] Thus there are many possible origins of the Cornaros, although there are those who assert that they immigrated from Rimini and even from Rome.[9]

It is certain, however, that from the beginnings of the Venetian Republic the Cornaros participated first in its economic activity, then in politics and the military, and soon after, in ecclesiastical affairs. From that time on, the Cornaros are designated as one of the "twelve families of the most ancient tribunes of Venice," called *tribunizie* because the tribunes who cooperated in the governing of the state were chosen from these families. The title was a hereditary dignity of families, giving rise to the legendary numbering of the sixteen tribunal families, subdivided into twelve apostolic and four evangelistic ones. The Cornaros appear among this last group.[10] The parallel between the foundation of Venice and the foundation of the Church is clear. In fact, one could compare the role of the apostles in the founding of the Church and that of the four evangelists as the writers and propagators of the doctrine of Christ in the world, with that of the Cornaros as being among the first supporters and propagators of the strong and enterprising Venetian spirit in the world.

They accomplished this through trade and their participation in public life. They preferred business with the Orient over domestic enterprises, acquiring great wealth, honors, and influence without dishonoring their own nobility by taking part in mercantile activity. This was a common practice among Venetian nobles, since it provided an abundant source of tremendous earnings, a means of excelling over others, and an incentive to true competition for economic supremacy, given that nobility was no longer considered to be founded solely on blood lines but above all on economic power. There was, in short, the conviction that the noblest were the richest.[11] These courageous and intelligent merchants, completely committed to increasing their own economic power through trade, contributed decisively to making Venice one of the leading seafaring powers; rare and precious goods poured into the various markets of Europe and large profits into the state's coffers.

The fourteenth and fifteenth centuries are the golden centuries of the power of the Cornaros, the peak of their wealth and political influence. The greatest representative among them is Federico (d. 1382), known as *il Grande* for his magnanimous enterprises at the time of the war to reconquer Chioggia (June 24, 1380) in which he commanded one of the thirty-four Venetian galleys.[12] He was the richest man in Venice, and the 1379 tax assessment shows that he owned the greatest amount of property.[13] His economic power allowed him to become the wealthiest backer of the state in times of crisis and to open lines of credit to the country lords of the Aegean islands, especially to Pietro I of Cyprus, which tied them to Venetian politics and prepared the way for political conquest and the reign of Caterina Cornaro in Cyprus.[14]

Let us linger briefly on the issue of credit for the king of Cyprus, because it will lead to the founding of a new branch of the family which is of major interest to us, the Cornaro Piscopias.

In the first months of 1363, Pietro I of Lusignano, the king of Cyprus

(1359–1369) and only nominal king of Jerusalem, was a guest of Federico Cornaro for about three weeks in his beautiful palace on the Grand Canal in the parish of San Luca in Venice. He was en route to Avignon at the invitation of Urban V (not Innocent VI or Innocent VII as some have written)[15] to organize with him and Jean II of France an armed expedition against the Ottoman Turks (the expedition did not take place due to the disunity, and in part, the ineptitude of the Christian princes of Europe).[16] Cornaro provided both splendid hospitality and gracious generosity. Knowing that the king was short of money to handle the expenses of the trip, he loaned Pietro 60,000 gold ducats even though the royal house of Cyprus was notoriously insolvent and the money would prove difficult to recover. Four years before his death and fifteen years after granting the loan, Cornaro added a bequest to his will—"whenever it is pleasing to God, as I hope, that the money be collected which is owed to us by the King of Cyprus, or the greater part of it"—an obvious indication that the loan had not been repaid (his son Giovanni had no greater success in 1417).

PISCOPIA

The king equally and splendidly returned the favor, granting to Cornaro the right to add the royal insignia of the Lusignanos to his own noble coat of arms, naming him and his descendants knights of the equestrian order of Cyprus; he also granted him, in perpetual feudal tribute, Piscopi, or Episkopi (a castle with hamlets), located at the extreme southern point of the island of Cyprus.[17] This last concession seems to exceed the favor of the loan received and, more than a sign of gratitude on the part of the king, it appears to be a diplomatic gesture. Pietro tried to maintain a policy of balance and collaboration in order to deter the frequent incidents between Genovese and Venetian merchants, who were always seeking privileges, land, and jurisdictional rights on the Island of Cyprus, which had become the center of their commerce. Genoa already had colonies and consulates at Limassol and Famagusta. The king grasped this opportunity to appease the jealousy of the Venetian Republic by granting to Cornaro, under the pretext of an exchange of favors, a feudal property through which both Venice and the Cornaro family would profit.[18]

The Piscopi given to Cornaro should not be confused with a small island of the same name, the ancient Telos of the Romans, mentioned by Pliny the Younger as the producer of the perfume *telino* and of "Greek hay" (*Naturalis historia*, XIII, 2; XXIV, 120), which was located in the southern

Sporades between the islands of Nisiros and Khalki, about twenty kilometers from the shores of Anatolia and very far from Cyprus. That they had the same name probably led the Venetian cartographer V. Coronelli (Ravenna 1650–Venice 1718) to introduce it improperly as "owned by the Prosapia Cornari since the year 1572." A modern author follows him in this attribution.[19] The error, however, is easily corrected: the island of Piscopi was never under the sovereignty of the Lusignanos and therefore not at the disposal of the kings of Cyprus. Moreover, Giovanni Battista Cornaro, procurator of San Marco, in his 1680 request that the doge recognize his Cypriot knighthood, recalls that in 1363 Pietro di Lusignano had given Federico Cornaro possession of the famous castle and hamlet of the Piscopia and other hamlets of the Kingdom of Cyprus. No one knew better than he, the truly interested party, and if the family had been given an entire island, he would have said so with pride. Finally, after the Knights of San Giovanni, later known as the Knights of Malta, had reclaimed Rhodes in 1308 from Turkish domination, they had extended the insular possessions of their order to the minor islands nearby, among which was Piscopi, and they maintained them until the Turkish occupation of 1522 under Suliman II the Magnificent (1495–1566).[20]

The bonds of friendship and self-interest that tied the Cornaros to the Lusignanos not only remained unchanged but became stronger. Later, in 1377, Pietro II, king of Cyprus (1369–1382), son and successor of Pietro I, through the influence of Federico Cornaro, was able to obtain as his wife Valentina, daughter of Bernabo Visconti (1323–May 19, 1385), duke of Milan. Before leaving for Cyprus, Valentina was a guest of Cornaro's who, for the occasion, regally furnished a special room which from then on was known as "the queen's chamber."[21]

Like a good administrator and prudent businessman, Federico immediately began to improve the profitability of Piscopi, a natural layover for maritime trade between East and West (today's Episkopi Bay), whose hinterland was very fertile due to the abundant waters of the River Kouris which pass through it. With his common sense and the generous income obtained from the exploitation of the copper and salt mines, he intensified the production of wine, cotton, and sugar cane, and thus extended his influence to the other commerce of the island, exporting salt, grain, sugar, wine, and other more profitable merchandise like silk, spices, artistic leather crafts, ivory, and precious metals. Cornaro carried out this fervent activity with confidence and mastery, so much so that the fief of Piscopia, by royal concession, was governed and defended by an exclusively Venetian jurisdiction located in Famagusta.[22]

The work of Federico at Piscopi and his commercial activities were courageously continued and enlarged upon by his son and only heir,

Giovanni, who established in his will that Piscopi be directly administered for at least twenty-five years by his three sons, Fantino, Federico, and Pietro, in a fraternal partnership. They did not disappoint their father's expectations. In order to watch over their own interests, they alternated their stays at Piscopi with some of their sons; Ferigo, one of Fantino's five sons, died at the age of eighteen in Cyprus.[23]

In these overseas stays, the Cornaros attended to the family's interests, reinforcing their social contacts and friendships which at times resulted in marriages between Cornaros and Cypriot women, giving rise to Cypriot Cornaro families of Venetian origin.[24]

THE CORNARO PISCOPIAS

Fantino deserves particular attention because he was the first to add "Piscopia" to the family name, thus distinguishing his own branch of the Cornaro lineage from the other five that flourished at that time (and which later multiplied to twenty-four).[25] Furthermore, from the privileges conceded to his grandfather, Federico il Grande, he had a new coat of arms[26] sculpted and placed on the facade of the palace, and also styled himself "Knight of Cyprus."[27] Fantino must therefore be considered the founder of the Cornaro Piscopia family, to which Elena Lucrezia belongs. Fantino and his successors did not lead lives dedicated exclusively to making money. They served the Republic in a variety of public offices both in Venice and in the dominions on the mainland and overseas, setting an admirable example of dedication to the homeland while at the same time benefiting their own patrimony.

This increased noticeably when Giovanni Cornaro Piscopia,[28] great grandson of Fantino, married Chiara, daughter and sole heir of the famous Alvise Cornaro (Venice 1475?–Padua 1566)[29], author of *The Sober Life*, whose branch thus became extinct. In the nuptial contract, Alvise, together with his bachelor brother Giacomo, established a good dowry for his daughter, hoping to see his own line continued by this marriage.[30]

He was not disappointed. Chiara gave him a brood of grandsons and granddaughters, making him such a happy man that he wrote: "And so that no joy be lacking in these years of great happiness, I see in my descendants a kind of immortality. Because when I come home I find, not one or two, but eleven grandchildren... all children of the same father and mother, all very healthy."[31]

Soon, however, Giovanni was snatched away by death while still at a young age (October 21, 1559). In addition to mourning his son-in-law,

Alvise had to face the over-pious behavior of Chiara, who neglected her duties as a mother and revealed her intention to spend all her resources on "building monasteries, leaving her sons poor and requiring her daughters to become nuns with her."[32] This never happened, due to the advice of Cornelio Musso, a famous preacher and bishop of Bitonto, who had been educated and raised in the Cornaro household since he was a baby.[33]

Alvise, already elderly, undertook to raise, educate, and provide for his grandchildren, who then distinguished themselves both in public life and in the cultural sphere. Marcantonio, for example, wrote on hydrology, and Giacomo Alvise became an intimate friend of Galileo Galilei from whom he gained his passion for scholarship. He was encouraged in this also by his aversion to public life and his love for the quiet life in Padua.[34] On the other hand, Giacomo Alvise's son Girolamo[35] found a balance between cultural life and public office. The rich library which he put together and passed on to his son Giovanni Battista later became the instrument of Elena Lucrezia's studies. At the same time, Girolamo repeatedly held offices entrusted to him by the Republic. Captain and governor first in Rovigo, then in Bergamo, and finally in Verona, he always knew how to govern well and capture the hearts of those he governed; in Verona a statue was erected to him in the Piazza dei Signori.[36] These public commitments, however, did not prevent him from fulfilling his paternal duties to the ten children born to him from his marriage to Caterina Thilmans, daughter of Guglielmo, a Flemish merchant residing in Venice.[37] He wisely administered the numerous lands he inherited and acquired other real estate. By means of agrarian contracts and loans to one of his relatives, to whom by right belonged a floor of the ancestral palace on the Grand Canal, he attempted to acquire for himself and his family the entire property which had belonged to his ancestor Federico il Grande.[38] But he was not able to realize this project because he died shortly after he turned fifty, on January 12, 1625, in his house in Padua. He left his young children to the care of his wife and father-in-law. One of them was Giovanni Battista, father of Elena Lucrezia.[39]

2

A Family

Taking care of Girolamo Cornaro Piscopia's seven orphaned children, four boys and three girls from ages thirteen to four months (Giovanni Battista was eleven at the time), was almost exclusively the task of their widowed mother. She was helped by Matteo Van Losen, a Flemish cousin, designated by the deceased as guardian of the children along with the father-in-law, Thilmans, who was required because of his business interests to live in Pesaro and was thus unable to provide much help in caring for his grandchildren. Their mother, however, a courageous woman whom her husband in his will described as "very prudent and full of pious and Christian thoughts," was concerned above all with the education of the children. In this she received moral support from her five sisters-in-law who were nuns, four in Padua and one in Venice.[1] Prudenza, in Venice, oversaw the administration of the property in Codevigo, Este, and Venice and managed the household in Padua. The famous Alvise Cornaro was already living the "sober life" in the so-called "Cornaro Courtyard," composed of the buildings of the Loggia and of the Odeon, a work of Giovanni Maria Falconetto, which with its spacious gardens offered lodging better suited to the health and liveliness of the children.

As regards educational institutions, Venice did not offer good prospects at the time, especially after the forced removal of the Jesuits from all Venetian territory by decree of the Republic (1606). Nor had the Somaschan Fathers as yet opened their school at Santa Maria della Salute, which occurred only in 1670. There was an excellent school at Salò, however, attended also by foreign students, where, although still a child, Guglielmo Francesco Cornaro was sent. His mother might also have chosen Salò (a town on the mainland near Brescia) because its cultural life had been flourishing for some centuries and its economy prospered, especially after the Cyprus war. In 1564, the Academia degli Unanimi came into being, where the teaching of music was held in particularly high regard. Salò was, in short, a cultural center attractive to anyone initiating personal studies.[2] The widow Cornaro had planned to send her son Baldassare to Salò as soon as he reached the required age, something precluded by her death. Her will enjoined her son Giovanni Battista, who became Baldassare's guardian, to be faithful in executing this wish.[3]

When their mother died, the children, still all minors, were left entirely under the care of Matteo Van Losen who, rather alarmed by this responsibility and by the plague which was approaching the Veneto region, asked Thilmans if he might be relieved of the task. Prevailed upon by the old grandfather—swayed by respect for him, the memory of the deceased lady, and compassion for the orphans—he consented to continue for another year after which he definitively withdrew his services. From Pesaro, Thilmans transferred the guardianship to Sebastian de Cuyper, a Flemish resident of Venice. This was a brief guardianship because on October 27 of the same year (1631) he turned over the entirety of the administered patrimony to Giovanni Battista who, now of legal age, was the legitimate heir and sole representative of the family and, as such, became the guardian of his underage brothers. Guglielmo Francesco and eight-year-old Baldassare were both at boarding school in Salò, due to the family situation and to fulfill their mother's last wishes.[4] Although the dates are unknown, two other brothers, Giacomo Alvise and Guglielmo Francesco, were probably already deceased by late 1633. Their sister Isabella, on the occasion of her wedding, having received a dowry from her brother Giovanni Battista, willingly renounced (on December 13, 1633) all possible claims on future benefits in favor of Giovanni Battista and Baldassare. She did not mention the other two, an inexplicable action if not for their deaths.[5] Even the grandfather, Thilmans, in his last will and testament describes Giovanni Battista and Baldassare as the "only surviving heirs."[6]

Regarding the other two sisters, we have no information about Maria Chiara, but Caterina Isabella became a nun in the convent of Santa Maria di Bethlemme in Padua,[7] joining her three aunts, Paolina, Isabella, and Cornelia, the daughters of Giacomo Alvise. It is not surprising that the Cornaro family sent their daughters to this convent. In this period there were in Venice and Padua many convents which were greatly relaxed in their rules. Santa Maria di Bethlemme was, in contrast, one of the few that was noted for its exemplary lifestyle. Portenari, a contemporary historian, writes that at Santa Maria "all the nuns were most observant, and to the present have always been and still are mirrors of sanctity, and fervently attend day and night to the divine cult."[8]

At this time, Giovanni Battista was the only active representative of the Cornaro Piscopia family. He alone was required to represent the family, administer the estate, and exercise guardianship of Baldassare and his inheritance. He thus entered fully into the life of the Venetian patrician, the social class from which the Republic drew all its officials and magistrates. While this may have been a source of pride, it also constituted a form of enslavement.

A nobleman could neither leave Venice without permission from the government, nor travel to foreign lands or stay there longer than the allotted time without special permission. He could not refuse the expensive positions to which he was elected without paying a fine; he could not marry a woman of inferior status without losing his own privileges; he could not aspire to ecclesiastical dignity without compromising his own constituents. He alone was excluded from the common good of being judged in criminal cases by ordinary tribunals which, with his circle of friends, would have easily let him off with a light sentence or none at all. He was, instead, subject to the most inflexible court of the patricians, the Council of Ten. The patrician did not pay public taxes in peacetime, but in compensation had to take on many different jobs with no profit but rather with a liability. In time of war, his services were arbitrarily required; any payments he had to make were exacted with rigor.[9]

Giovanni Battista was young and eager to fulfil his family obligations, but at the same time he was aware that his obligations as a noble would probably force him to leave Venice. Recognizing that he was still inexperienced in the business of administration, he took advantage of the competency of his former guardian, de Cuyper, who continued to care for the young master's interests, especially his landholdings and property, residing for this purpose in the Cornaro home in Padua and the estate in Codevigo.[10]

At the age of twenty-three, Giovanni Battista already had a family of his own. He had grown close to a young peasant girl, Zanetta Boni, with whom he had a son, Francesco, and a daughter, Caterina, children whom he later recognized as legally his.[11] Although socially irregular at the time, this family brought great responsibilities to his private life. To these were added those inherent in public life when in 1637 he was elected Commissioner at Peschiera.

GIOVANNI BATTISTA CORNARO IN PUBLIC LIFE

The duties of a commissioner included monitoring the public streets, buildings, markets and prices, public religious displays, games, and, in part, judicial and administrative governance. It was a task comparable to that of the builders of ancient Rome. In short, the commissioner, being the only authority in the area, had to take care of everything.[12]

Peschiera was militarily important because it lay at the point where the Mincio flows from Lake Garda, which could allow an invader to interrupt communications between Bergamo, Brescia, and the Veneto region and separate the Mincio from Mantua, which constituted its strength. The registers of the commissioners of this fortress show that in 1638 Giovanni Battista Cornaro succeeded Marco Badoer and was later replaced by Vincenzo Grimani.[13] Like all the others in the Venetian Republic, the magistrate at Peschiera received a small stipend of forty ducats a month, an inadequate sum for maintenance and public expenses.[14] Still, Giovanni Battista performed his duties generously for his country's dignity and for his own, even with the preoccupations of his private life. In the end, having passed the burden to his successor, he returned immediately to Venice, where, according to the law of 1524, he gave a written and verbal report of his actions to the doge and the Senate, suggesting those regulations that to him seemed most useful to the needs of the city he had been administering.

Meanwhile, his brother Baldassare, having come of legal age, accepted, with expressions of gratitude and trust, the inheritance that Giovanni Battista had been administering for him. Baldassare, who was ready to depart for Constantinople in the retinue of the ambassador, Pietro Foscarini, named his brother as his legal representative. Five days later (August 22, 1640), the two brothers, by common agreement, were able to fulfill their father's dream by acquiring all the property of the palace on the Grand Canal in Venice.[15]

The young Baldassare undertook the trip to Constantinople with enthusiasm. It was his first trip abroad, and his destination was an embassy that was among the most important and sought after and would prepare him for future public positions. However, the trip ended immediately and tragically. Cornaro was stricken with smallpox and after being ill for ten days, expired on April 1, 1641. His embalmed body was transported to Venice the following June 8 by the ambassador, Foscarini, and buried in the family tomb in the church of San Luca.[16] Giovanni Battista thus became the only surviving male of the family, inheriting even the estate of the deceased Baldassare.

Giovanni Battista fathered his third child at this time, another girl, born to him by Zanetta. She later became a nun in a convent in the Torcello Diocese as indicated by a brief mention in a petition of Elena Lucrezia to Pope Clement X in 1674.[17] Not even this third illegitimate child compromised Giovanni Battista's position in public life. In fact, he was soon named captain of Bergamo for the biennial year 1641–1642, succeeding Giovanni Grimani and being later replaced by Pietro Contarini.[18]

He went there with very different duties from those he exercised in Peschiera. As captain he had to take care of the military administration, assisted by a cavalryman and others who formed his entourage, to maintain public order and implement the policies adopted by the Republic in the domain of the *terra firma*, that is, to preserve the privileges and the statutes of the city, the violation of which was punishable by the Council of Ten. The monthly salary was thirty ducats, an insignificant sum in relation to the expenses of the office, such that Cornaro had to supplement it from his own pocket as he had already done in Peschiera. He later remembered this on the occasion of an entreaty to the doge.[19]

At the end of this second public mission, he had acquired greater experience in dealing with the various problems of public office and had developed a wider circle of friendships with influential people in politics, cultural life, and the nobility. Giovanni Battista knew how to cultivate these friendships, with an ability above all for fueling his natural ambition. This instinct frequently characterized his behavior and provides the extenuating circumstances for some of his exaggerations. One should not be surprised. He was a nobleman, he had the prestige of his family name to uphold and to which he wanted to add his own personal contribution. He knew that upon his return to Venice his generous acceptance of civic responsibilities would open the door to the senate for him, increasing the influence he had acquired through his business experience. It was a stepping stone to higher office.

For a few years, therefore, he waited for the opportune moment to obtain a position at the highest level, one that would command great respect while permitting him to remain in Venice. He was at this time greatly concerned with the administration of his own affairs. His three children were living with their mother in the parish of San Polo together with her father. When he realized that Zanetta was once again pregnant, he decided, perhaps urged by her and her father, to take her and the children to his palace on the Grand Canal in the parish of San Luca. Here his fourth child was born, Baldassare, whom this time he had registered as his son with Zanetta Boni, "his lady friend," and for whom he ambitiously chose as godfather the nobleman Carlo della Rovere of Urbino. After only two years, however, death robbed them of the child.[20]

What plans did Giovanni Battista have regarding the future of his family? What was he hoping to achieve? Was he so engulfed in sensuality as not to realize how low he had fallen? Was he ignoring the drastic laws promulgated from time to time by the state that regulated marriages of the nobility among themselves or with persons of inferior position and that specified the arrangements in matters of titles, inheritance, and succession for the children of these marriages? Of the nine existing laws he had clearly infringed upon three. A primary one (December 28, 1376) established that whoever of whatever status was born of a nobleman and any woman, even a patrician, before marriage, could not be registered among the nobles nor serve on the Great Council. Another prescribed that if any member of the Great Council were to have married one of his slaves, having obtained her by purchase or in any other way, their children would be considered ordinary citizens and could not in any way be registered among the nobility, nor could they have membership on the Great Council. Furthermore, "if a nobleman were to have carnal relations with one of his servants or with any other woman of low status and declare to have married her, the children born of this union cannot nor must they 'in any way' be registered among the nobility nor have membership on the Great Council" (May 26, 1422). A third law even more explicitly established "that if in the future any of our noblemen marry any maidservant or farm girl or even any other woman of contemptible or low status, such a marriage inasmuch as it pertains to the benefit of nobility only for his children, cannot be accepted by the lawyers of our municipality, nor can it be introduced by them to the College nor to our councils."[21] Giovanni Battista Cornaro knew this legislation well, and he knew also that marrying Zanetta would not elevate her to nobility. He knew furthermore that the children born to them before the wedding, even if he legitimized them with a subsequent marriage, could never be registered in the Golden Book in which were inscribed the names of those who had the right to Venetian nobility and entrance to the Great Council. Zanetta would always be considered a commoner even if the wife of a nobleman, and the children legitimate but commoners as well. In any case, only males of noble birth could enter the Great Council and hold public office. He knew well the type of revolution that the Great Council of the Republic had been carrying on for a few centuries, known in history as the Lockout from the Great Council, otherwise known among the nobility as the closing of the Golden Book to new inscriptions from among the common people. Its purpose was both to exclude commoners from the government and to protect the noble caste since "the degree of our nobility is by divine grace and of such honorable nature that with every inquiry and care we must be vigilant to its preservation in its precision and purity befitting the decorum and dignity of this Council."[22]

Giovanni Battista's continuing relationship with Zanetta should be attributed not to contempt of the law, because in transgressing it he also had to bear its consequences, but rather to a very precise choice. He demonstrated that he was not seeking a title or a dowry, but a woman whom he could love profoundly and who would in turn love him for the rest of his life. Zanetta was not just a pleasant distraction for him in his free time, a respite from the intense worries that assailed him. Oftentimes, even geniuses (remember Galileo) prefer to find consoling serenity not in a woman with cultural, social, or financial aspirations but in a beautiful woman without the preoccupations of etiquette. If Zanetta had been only amusement, a youthful amorous adventure, I think that the affair would have consumed itself after the birth of the second child. Even if he kept the children, he could easily have rid himself of the woman—the common practice of noblemen who wished to end their extramarital affairs, and exactly what his grandfather Giacomo Alvise had done. Not only did Giovanni Battista not do this, but he fathered three more children, an indication of his intent to remain constant in his decision to make Zanetta his wife. If he did not immediately regularize his family situation by means of marriage, one must consider various obstacles, not the least of which was his absence from Venice. I do not intend to excuse his behavior altogether, but neither do I believe that he was a corrupt person who allowed himself "as a youth to be lured by that current of sensualism that gnawed at noble society of the time, especially Venetian society."[23] If he made some errors in his youth, he compensated for them later with an exemplary and Christian life, dedicating himself to the education of his children and the good of the state. The Republic entrusted him with still more important positions and honors, considering him a "man of great spirit and mind and of singular ability, and thought of as such by all."[24] Therefore, he should be judged in a more objective manner.

Who was Zanetta Boni with whom this Cornaro fell in love? She was a healthy, easy going, exuberant, and sincere young girl from a lower-class family. Her father was probably a *sansèr*, that is, a middleman, which was at that time (and is still today) held to be vulgar and proper to the lower classes only. It is possible that he was an artisan engaged in one of the so-called mechanical or servile crafts.[25] Hence Zanetta was called a "vulgar woman" by certain gossips of the Venetian nobility who were perhaps irritated at seeing the rich and noble Cornaro preferring this young commoner to one of their own daughters. With even more scorn they coined the nickname "Valdesabbia," or "daughter of foreigners who came to Venice to relieve their hunger." This was the cruel reality of it.[26] The Valsabbia, the valley of the River Chiese from Lake Idro to its outlet in the Po Valley, was very narrow and tortuous, formed by calcareous rocks and tufa, rarely touched by the sun, with a primitive, rural, sylvan economy. It was one of the poorest territories in the Venetian Republic, from which the inhabitants had to emigrate in order to avoid starvation. After the occupation of the valley by Venice in 1427, the population emigrated *en masse* to the major cities of the Veneto and especially to Venice, to earn their bread in humble trades, many as menial workers or in the militia where both the risks and the earnings were greater. However, not only did the strong arms emigrate from the Valsabbia, so did the brains as well.[27] In 1577 and in 1630 the Venetian senate ordered the opening of the crafts; new people could become workmen, whereas previously anyone who had not been apprenticed or otherwise tested was excluded. Therefore, many thronged to Venice from the Bergamo, Brescia, and Valcamonica regions and even from Lombardy. The Republic accorded hospitality to all, as long as this universal rule was observed: *Nihil de principe, parum de Deo*, that is, "Don't meddle at all in politics, discuss religion little." One was free as regards everything else.[28]

Zanetta descended from a family of these emigrants, even if it is not possible to determine precisely the place of origin; the surname Boni is found with great frequency at Vestone in the northern Valsabbia area and somewhat less frequently in other parts of the valley.[29] She carried in her blood the physical and moral characteristics of the Brescian people: vivacious, quick-witted, gifted, possessing almost instinctive common sense in all things. She was loyal and open, firm and constant in affairs of the heart, not with fine features, but generous and kindly.[30] Additionally, she always showed herself to be an affectionate mother, a thoughtful and trustworthy wife (*uxor optima*, the orator of her daughter Elena's funeral eulogy would call her), a wise administrator of the home. She was a woman whose worth was commonly recognized, a mother who knew how to educate virtuous and esteemed daughters (Elena, Caterina, and the "unnamed nun"), who personally practiced prudence for many years, a virtue for which her husband was infinitely grateful. He begged the children to leave all administrative duties to her because she was skilled in business matters.[31] These were all qualities by which she would always be recognized both publicly and by her husband, especially just prior to his death when he thoroughly praised her and pleaded with her to continue to govern the house with her usual love and charity. If her wifely qualities had not truly been such, Giovanni Battista would never have made this kind of speech at the last moment of his life, what we may call the hour of truth and sincerity, in which lying is of no benefit either to the survivors or to the one who is dying.

Zanetta was proud and resolute, and because of this many women of the aristocracy shunned her, as mentioned in the later and rather factious document noted above. But we cannot allow the claim of a more recent author that Zanetta was a woman of the world, or at least, a loose woman.[32] It is true that she was not of noble lineage, that she came from a common family. True also was that she initially committed an act of grave indiscretion. But to conclude that she was a woman of the world is going too far. From the dawn of time, a woman of the world, or whore, or lover, or for more refined ears, a courtesan, has always meant a vendor of love, shrewd in ridding herself of every kind of messy consequence. Is Zanetta the only woman of the world foolish enough to end up pregnant five times by the same man before she married him? Naive, yes, but no one will go so far as to believe that Zanetta is hardly ever remembered by her daughter Elena's biographers because of her plebeian origin and her tainted life as a girl. The truth is rather different. In the Venetian Republic, women, even noblewomen, were always kept very apart and in the shadows; usually their names were not even entered in the public birth registries (or were indicated with only the letter D for donna, i.e., woman), because for the state, women had no role in dynastic matters. In the ecclesiastical registries, however, personal information about women was duly noted.[33]

After his terms of public office, first in Peschiera and then at Bergamo, Cornaro spent a few years as a private citizen, waiting for the opportune moment to obtain a higher position. This opportunity presented itself in 1649. Venice had been engaged for some time in war with the Turks, a war that bled the city of men, materials, and, above all, of finances. Commerce with the Orient was no longer profitable because of competition from the other Italian states. Even more, because of the war, the resources garnered from the common citizenry and the rich were no longer sufficient, so that it became necessary to devise new means of obtaining money. Cornaro then got the idea of nominating three more procurators for San Marco, one for each of the three categories, he himself setting the terms for eligibility. Thus this dignity, which usually was conferred gratuitously as a reward for worthy service to the Republic, was, due to extreme necessity, granted for an act of financial generosity in support of the needs of the state. Cornaro immediately presented his candidacy to the doge, accompanied by a resume that cited his services to the country, and declared himself ready to contribute 20,500 ducats to the state—which he would have consented to serve even to the point of giving his life. Although eleven other patricians supposedly presented similar petitions, Cornaro's was looked upon favorably, and on June 6, 1649, he was named Procurator of San Marco *de supra*.[34]

The office of procurator was the highest dignity of the state after that of the supreme doge. Once elected, a procurator held office for life (without remuneration); had the right to one of the nine sumptuous dwellings on the Piazza San Marco, in the so-called Procuratie; became a senator by right without having to undergo annual elections; and enjoyed great prestige and moral authority. There were nine procurators, divided into three categories: *de supra* (above), *de citra* and *de ultra* (on the "one side" and on the "other side" of the Grand Canal), each with different duties. The procurators *de supra* monitored the maintenance, service, and administration of the basilica of San Marco, a ducal chapel symbolizing the unique marriage of church and state that permeated and guided all the history of the Venetian Republic and its people.[35] Those *de citra* and *de ultra* were responsible for the poor, orphans and widows, pious institutions, and the execution of wills. This enormous task was necessarily divided into two zones, each one served by three procurators. Of the three categories, the *de supra* was considered the highest and was, therefore, also the more sought after.[36]

Upon the nomination of Cornaro, a dash of pepper was sprinkled, perhaps by one of the rejected candidates: Cornaro was referred to as "the money procurator," that is, one who purchased his position rather than attaining it by merit. The phrase cannot be used against Cornaro, however, because this was part of a procedure frequently used by the Venetian Republic. In this case, it was a way to increase the number of procurators at San Marco by means of a financial donation and thus to augment a public treasury burdened by the heavy and extraordinary expenses of the war against the Turks, which threatened commerce, the Venetian dominions in the Orient, and indirectly, Christianity. The money exacted from the citizenry by every possible means was not enough; it had to be sought everywhere. A quick examination of Vatican documents of this era reveals frequent papal briefs addressed to the Republic of Venice that accompanied the remittance of financial aid *pro bello contra Turcas* (for the war against the Turks). They conceded such options as selling a few sacred objects from San Marco, designating the money for the expenses of the wars; using the goods of three suppressed religious congregations; imposing an extra tithe; using revenue from vacant churches and monasteries; or taking the goods of the suppressed Spirito Santo Congregation and using the organ, thirteen paintings, and some of its furnishings for the Church of Sancta Mariae Sanitatis.[37] In a speech to the Senate, Giovanni Pesaro, a procurator of San Marco, later acknowledged that while Venice lost her wealth and her sons, abandoned by the princes of Europe through jealousy or weakness, only the pope had shown himself to be a friend, helping out generously. Even bishops sent their own contributions,[38] as did the Benedictine monasteries of Cassino in the Venetian dominion, each according to its own means.[39]

Given these facts, Cornaro's nickname, "procurator for money," is meaningless. He certainly wasn't offended by it. He knew that he now stood upon a pedestal that elevated him above many nobles, and this stirred up his own innate love of self, his ambition, and his desire to reach the top. He felt, in other words, that he was somebody. Furthermore, the other procurators also acquired satirical nicknames, a phrase that drew attention to some defect, vice, shortcoming, or affectation. The words of Christ to Pilate (John 18:36) were applied to Giovanni Battista: *Regnum meum non est de hoc mundo* ("My kingdom is not of this world"), a biting criticism of his fervor for grandeur and domination.[40] He was not, however, merely a vain person as we are led to believe, but also an expert businessman. The various documents of the Cornaro Piscopia family reveal that he dealt not only with the inheritance, which would be easy to administer, but also with purchases, sales, exchanges, rents, and business concerning the various agricultural needs of the family property. Purchases undoubtedly presuppose a sum of money, frequently very large, which can only come from a very tightly controlled administration. Giovanni Battista Cornaro did not lack the acumen with which he, like all landowners of every age, tried to extend his own possessions according to the criteria of continuity and contiguity, eliminating the larger or smaller properties belonging to other owners. His real estate possessions were of every variety: rural and urban houses, vast country estates and small pieces of land, mills, bridges, river ferries, lagoon valleys, grazing land, and so forth, spread somewhat throughout the entire Veneto region.[41]

In 1654, with another child on the way, Cornaro decided finally to marry Zanetta and thus regularize a relationship which had lasted for twenty years and had produced five illegitimate children, including Elena Lucrezia, the last in this unseemly sequence.[42] Only from this moment could Zanetta, having become the legitimate spouse of Procurator Giovanni Battista Cornaro Piscopia, be called "procurator's wife," but she was not a noblewoman either before or after the marriage. Therefore, it is erroneous either to give 1642 as the date of this marriage, or to affirm that Elena Lucrezia was born of illustrious parents because of the dignity of the procuracy.[43]

The following year, 1655, a baby girl was born. She was named Caterina in memory of the daughter of the same name who died two years before at the age of seventeen. This Caterina would later emulate the virtue and culture of Elena Lucrezia. In 1657, the birth of a little boy, Girolamo, brought further joy to the family. This time the father was able to say with pride the phrase of noble Venetians at the birth of a son, *nato n'altro paròn* ("another master is born"). To Cornaro's joys another was added, and even though it was of a different nature, it was very great: he discovered in his daughter Elena Lucrezia an exceptional talent and a profound passion for scholarship. He deserves the principal recognition for supporting her in this passion, for furnishing her with the best possible preparation for obtaining a university degree, in that era an unthinkable achievement for a woman. His happiness was tainted, however, by the fact that his two sons were still excluded from the nobility and that their status within the Cornaro Piscopia family would be resolved permanently only with his death. It was like a thorn that pierced his heart. But being a wise man, used to giving things time, he hoped that time itself was working in his favor. In fact he knew that Venice, still immersed in the war against the Turks, its finances exhausted, perhaps soon would have to make some great concession, as in the past, just to obtain money. That is exactly what happened.

The famous *cassòn* (chest or safe) of the Republic, which held the state revenues—the loans, proceeds from the sale of common goods held by the municipality, the taxes on the clergy and the aristocracy, as well as any type of income, all of which could be touched only in cases of emergency—was already empty. Loans with a perpetual one percent rate or a 14 percent lifelong rate were requested. Even the right to enter the Great Council before the prescribed age was granted, and the Golden Book was opened to allow the inscription of the names of citizens and subjects if they paid an amount equivalent to one thousand soldiers' earnings for one year. Thus for 8 million ducats, seventy-seven families were added to the Venetian nobility. Some of the old nobility cried out against the scandal, maintaining that public properties or even a few provinces should be sold rather than noble titles. There was, however, much more to take care of at that time. The Republic did not hesitate to sell to private citizens the grandiose Procuratie Vecchie, which had been the sumptuous residence of the procurators of San Marco and with the ducal palace comprised the most prestigious buildings on the piazza. Only when the war of Crete ended and the public finances were restored was the Nuove Procuratie erected with the same purpose (1586–1640).[44]

At the time of his nomination as procurator of San Marco (1649), Giovanni Battista was living with Zanetta and their five illegitimate children in his palace at San Luca. This was universally known among the nobility. At the same time, even if the lax customs of the time would pardon his having a concubine, he probably could not have moved Zanetta and the children into the procurator's residence without a very serious scandal, and he knew it. For this reason, even though he had the right to reside in a sumptuous apartment of the Nuove Procuratie, he continued to live at San Luca with his unlawful family. He did so even after his marriage (1654), and used the apartment in the Procuratie only as a seat for his high position. In fact, the two children born after the marriage, Caterina (1655) and Girolamo (1657), were baptized in the parish of San Luca, and their father probably waited until they grew up a bit before moving to the Procuratie apartment with the entire family, except for Francesco, the first born, who married in 1655.

The first document to assert that Cornaro was living in the Procuratie was notarized March 9, 1671, having been drawn up above the living quarters at San Marco (*posita supra platea Sancti Marci*).[45] Even the two daughters Elena and Caterina, for their personal interests, drew up notarized records (one on September 17 and the other on April 30, 1672, and April 13, 1674) each indicating her own address as being on the Piazza San Marco.[46] In his will (August 5, 1690), Giovanni Battista wrote with detail, "done in the house where I reside, in Venice, in the Procuratia on the Piazza San Marco."[47] Immediately after the death of her husband on March 15, 1692, the widow, knowing that she no longer had the right to reside in the Procuratie, wrote the person renting her palace at San Luca a certified letter (March 28), asking him to vacate the premises at the end of the following August: "when I must by necessity come to stay myself, unable to do otherwise."[48] At the beginning of August she was already at San Luca where she drew up a notarized record (August 12, 1692) *domi habitationis infrascripte nobilis dominae procuratissae Corner de Confinio Sancti Lucae* ("at the domicile noted of the noble lord administrator Cornaro of the jurisdiction of San Luca").[49]

At the time of the reopening of the Golden Book of the Republic, Giovanni Battista understood that the opportune moment had arisen to obtain the registration of his two sons on the list of nobility. He presented his petition to the doge on April 4, 1659 (not August 4), with a donation of 40,000 ducats, reminding the doge of his fidelity to religion and country, his great merits, and those of his ancestors. He stressed his uncertain hopes of succession, since of the two, Francesco, married now for four years, was still without children, and Girolamo was only two years old. (He does not mention his daughters because their enrollment was included with the sons.)[50] The request was rejected, however, by a majority vote of the Senate and not even presented to the Great Council.[51] On September 1 of the same year Giovanni Battista repeated his request, raising the sum to 100,000 ducats, but to his immense regret it was again refused. The Golden Book continued to remain open and the Republic was still in need of money. Cornaro, on March 15, 1662 (not February 1664), presented a third petition in which he repeated his offer of 100,000 ducats and stated his reasons as a father and a noble patrician, mindful of the merits of his family lineage, expressed with great humility, but also with gentlemanly firmness. The opposition, though less, remained in the majority in the Senate, which on April 4, 1662 (not February), rejected him once more. On February 18, 1664, Giovanni Battista presented a fourth unsuccesful request, followed by another, on the same day, in which he raised his offer by 5,000 ducats.

On February 21–22, the Senate declared itself in favor of the application and passed the petition on to the Great Council, accompanying it with a favorable report on Giovanni Battista Cornaro. Finally, on March 1, 1664, the Great Council gave its consent to the registration in the Golden Book of Cornaro's sons Francesco and Girolamo, who were thus recognized as noble Venetians.[52] One can easily imagine the procurator's joy.

Dalmazzo is incorrect in affirming that Cornaro rejoiced in seeing his sons' names written in the Golden Book of the Venetian nobility "from which he had been removed."[53] He was never really removed from it, and notwithstanding his unlawful union with Zanetta, he continued to be counted among the nobles. If he had been removed, he could not have held high office nor become Procurator of San Marco, which was conferred only upon nobles. The consequence for a patrician who married a commoner was not the loss of his noble title, but the exclusion of possible offspring from the Golden Book.

Encouraged by this success, a few years later Cornaro addressed another petition to the doge asking that he confer upon him the title of Knight of Cyprus, an honor already accorded to Federico Cornaro in 1363 by the king of Cyprus and transferable to his descendants. This title had been used by Cornaros for several centuries but then fell into disuse. The request was not taken into consideration, and no reply was issued. In fact, being a procurator was worth much more than being a knight. There were several knights in Venice but only nine procurators in the entire state and procurator was the highest position after that of duke. His request revealed only too well Cornaro's great ambition and his jealousy of other patrician families who could add to their own names another title rightly conferred upon them by the Republic. In governing its overseas territories, especially the vast archipelago of the Aegean, the Republic had relied upon loyal subjects who, without losing their identity as mercantile patricians, had joined with the native population to create a governing authority both princely and common; they were the trusted and autonomous guardians of the homeland's power. The Sanudo, for example, created dukes of Nasso; the Dandolo, lords of Andro; the Quirini of Stampalia—all managed to reconcile their mercantile interests with those of the government of the dominated territories. Their titles, therefore, bore an investiture into royalty, since they constituted one share belonging to those so vested, with all associated responsibilities.[54] The title requested by Cornaro, however, was backed only by ambition, and the doge was not willing to indulge the frenzy of his nobles for titles, as already demonstrated by a decree of November 21, 1576, which regulated the use of titles.[55] Moreover, the Republic, by recognizing Cornaro's knighthood, would not have been able to exact any monies, notwithstanding its continued extreme need.

Giovanni Battista bounced back quickly from this disappointment after receiving on July 6, 1680, an affectionate letter from his beloved Elena in Padua. She had recovered from an illness caused by overwhelming fatigue sustained while pursuing her doctorate, and promised to return to her studies for the greater prestige of the family. In reality, she was already famous throughout Italy and Europe, and her father was well aware of it. She had received, and continued to receive, expressions of honor and praise that alone were enough to immortalize the Cornaro Piscopia household.[56]

His efforts on behalf of his family did not cause Cornaro to neglect other interests closely tied to his household, such as the right of jurispatronage over the parish of Codevigo, acquired in 1530 by Alvise Cornaro and passed on to Giovanni Battista and the male descendants of the lineage by Innocent XI. He had the right to choose the parish priest and to present him to the bishop for canonical investiture, to administer the goods of the church, to oversee its maintenance and its dignified conduct. Cornaro assumed all these tasks with precision and conviction, not hesitating to take legal action against Venetian nobles who were not fulfilling their parish duties.[57]

In the same spirit he used his ability and his prestige to resolve an unpleasant situation between the Holy See and the Republic of Venice regarding the removal of the Jesuits from the entire Veneto region (March 3, 1609) following the papal interdict of 1606 which had been issued against Venice. To the great joy of Pope Alexander VII, the Jesuits were finally permitted to return in 1657, but with certain conditions, among which was a prohibition against the teaching of youth. For his role in the return of the Jesuits, Cornaro earned high praise from the Society of Jesus, which was repeatedly voiced by Father Gian Paolo Oliva (1600–1681), Father General of the Society. In a letter of June 26, 1665, he declared Cornaro "among the top protectors, and among the most singular benefactors which our Society lists in Italy." Later, informed that two Jesuit fathers had devised a plan to obtain Venetian citizenship so as to have the right to teach publicly not as Jesuits but as Venetian citizens, Oliva wrote to Cornaro begging him "not to permit the artificial citizenship which, with little reflection, any of my priests desires or proposes or dreams of. We must venerate the decrees of the Most Serene Republic and not flash them about with self-absorbed appearances" (October 12, 1676). Instead, he begged Cornaro to use all his influence in the senate to eliminate the prohibition against teaching.[58]

The life of Giovanni Battista was not devoted entirely to political and administrative activities or the search for honorary titles. He was also involved in cultural activities, both as a patron and as a connoisseur of the arts. I will address this aspect of Cornaro's life in later chapters. To illuminate the moral character of this man, whose contradictory personality makes it difficult to form a precise judgment, I will quote an anonymous contemporary, expressed in a historical-political review of one hundred people of the Republic of the Veneto region:

> Giovanni Battista Cornaro is the most virtuous man of all the nobility. Woe to him who dares defame him, he will be quickly banished. In his several properties there is wheat, there is oil. He has a fluency in speaking and is frank. . . . He has a proud spirit, with some exceptions, because in service to the doge, which he has rendered at Peschiera and Bergamo, he has succeeded perfectly and splendidly, for which he rightfully deserves esteem . . . he is immune to the temptation of gold . . . he has a rather French inclination, not because of his sense of duty but because of his pleasantness and vivaciousness. He is, however, a good Venetian, not having anything which causes him to deviate from the common good.[59]

In the end, one can reach an opinion from a careful reading of his testament and the other documents in which Giovanni Battista revealed all his personal aspects: religious, civic, familial, social, cultural, and humanitarian.[60]

He died on March 15, 1692, at the age of seventy-nine, and his funeral rites were celebrated with great solemnity. They were held in the basilica of San Marco, where only the doge and the procurators of San Marco were so honored, and he was buried in the family tomb in the church of San Luca.[61]

THE CHILDREN OF GIOVANNI BATTISTA CORNARO

As I have already said, a few months after the death of Giovanni Battista, his widow left her apartment in the Procuratie, to which she no longer had a right, and moved to her palace at San Luca where she attempted to reorganize the administration of its goods. She displayed great practicality and courage in such moments of tragedy, as at the time of the death of her daughter Elena, and when faced with the loss of her husband she personally took care of the funeral arrangements.[62]

Unwell now for some years, Zanetta had to look after herself. Upon suggestions from her doctor and her confessor, and with their written recommendation, she asked for, and received, certain dispensations from the pope.[63] She outlived her husband by five years, dying on September 15, 1697, at the age of eighty-one, and she was buried in the church of San Luca in the family tomb.[64]

We know very little about her first four children. Francesco, the firstborn, married Isabetta Grigis in 1655. Giacomo, on March 1, 1664, was registered, together with his brother Girolamo, in the Golden Book of the Republic and was therefore qualified to hold public positions. In 1670 he (Giacomo) was a commissioner at Peschiera, a position in which his father had preceded him many years before.[65] At Codevigo, where a bailiff administered his property, he performed a gracious deed by standing as godfather for the son of a commoner, the so-called godfathership of San Giovanni.[66] In Venice he made a humanitarian gesture toward a fruit vendor from the Giudecca part of the city whom the noblewoman Adriana Giustinian had imprisoned for falling behind in his payments. Cornaro paid the entire debt and had the prisoner freed.[67] He died in 1690 without leaving descendants.

Of Caterina, born illegitimately in 1636 and recognized in 1641 along with Francesco as the child of Giovanni Battista, we know only that she died at age seventeen. She did not die, as has been written, before the birth of Elena, but when Elena was already seven years old and thus capable of feeling the void that Caterina's death left in the lives of her parents.[68] Baldassare, as I noted above, died at two years of age, and no documentation regarding his sister, the one referred to as the "unnamed nun," has been found.

Caterina Isabetta, the "second Caterina," was born on February 20, 1655. She was not, as others have written, the last-born child.[69] In a sense, she was more privileged than the sisters who preceded her because at her birth she found nine-year-old Elena, who would be not only a childhood companion but a model of sweetness, goodness, and virtue, and a worthy example to follow in her studies. She grew up at Elena's side and displayed a similar love for scholarship, studying history, speaking Greek, Latin, and French well, writing poetry with ease, and attracting the admiration of many learned individuals. Giovanni Mabillon dedicated literary compositions to her and acknowledged her as both a true copy of Elena and another glory for the Cornaro Piscopia family.[70]

Having just turned eighteen, and bearing a rich dowry, Caterina married a nobleman of her own age, Antonio Vendramin, son of Andrea, from the parish of San Fosca, with whom she had two daughters: Isabella, who became a Franciscan nun of the Third Order at Murano, and Elena, who married Lorenzo Contarini of Tommaso.[71] Twenty-five years later,

Vendramin was overcome by a fever in the Cornaro home in Padua, perhaps contracted during his inspection of his wife's properties in Codevigo and Conche (province of Padua). He died shortly thereafter, on November 22, 1697, at the age of forty-two.[72] In memory of her husband and out of her own devotion, Caterina had an artist from Bassano, Orazio Marinali, sculpt a pedestal for one of the large candelabras that decorate the chapel of Saint Anthony to whom the basilica at Padua is dedicated. The work, completed in 1712 after Caterina's death, fits in well with the other pedestal done by Filippo Parodi (Genoa, c. 1630–1708?) because of its fine and precise execution. It carries a brief inscription in memory of its donor and is signed with the sculptor's initials.[73]

Thus freed of family obligations, Caterina dedicated herself mainly to religious works, to the instruction and the moral and material assistance of humble people, always manifesting great humanity, goodness, and peacefulness. But the surest revelation of her noble qualities is to be found in her testament. Since Caterina was repeatedly described as greatly resembling Elena, I believe that in reading these documents, one can grasp the spirit of Elena through Caterina's words (see appendix, document 5).[74]

She died at the beginning of May 1707 and was buried, as was her wish, next to her husband in the Vendramin family tomb in the church of Santa Maria dei Servi in Venice.[75]

Girolamo Baldissera, the last child, was born on March 27, 1657, and was baptized the day after. (Pynsent errs when, in the genealogical tree of the Giovanni Battista Cornaro family, she positions Girolamo as the second child, born in 1637 after Francesca and before Elena.)[76] He was a legitimate son, as I have shown above, and on March 1, 1664, was registered in the Golden Book.[77] He received an education befitting his social status, and his good literary training is briefly documented in a sonnet he composed for the graduation of Angelo Sumachi, a nobleman of Zante.[78] On September 3, 1681, he married Delfina Tiepolo di Giovanni, with whom he had two daughters who bore the names of their famous aunts, Elena and Lucrezia.[79]

In 1685 he spent sixteen months, the length of that office, as governor and captain of Treviso with a monthly salary of thirty ducats, showing himself to be a man endowed with excellent qualities, prudent in government, with a conciliatory disposition. His subjects' admiration is expressed in a pamphlet published on the occasion of his departure from that city: "made tutelary arbitrator of all things, you have come forth as a sweet tyrant of hearts, and mixing love with fear in the hearts of the citizens, you made us adore you with fear and fear you with adoration."[80] True, this is a laudatory pamphlet composed in the triumphant style of the time, but it helps us understand the personal and governing qualities of

Cornaro at Treviso. He revealed the same qualities in 1694–1695 when he was governor of Bergamo.[81]

Wise in governing his subjects, he aparently did not inherit the family's skill in administering his own affairs. His estate dwindled continually, and he was often forced to take actions that reveal to us the weakening of his finances. On November 1, 1705, he rented for five years his beautiful palace on the hill above Este to the nobleman Francesco Farsetti. This was the palace, connected to the mountain and the park, which had access through a very elegant Renaissance arch (a work of Giovanni Maria Falconetto) to the villa built by Alvise Cornaro in the sixteenth century.[82] Later, to eliminate a large debt accumulated due to his delinquent payments to the parish of San Giorgio in Padua, he gave up annually part of the rent of a house he owned in that parish, indicating that he was even disposed to selling it.[83] Subsequently, his economic difficulties forced him to other humiliating renunciations.

In 1708, with a notarized document, he decided to return to the Franciscan Conventual Friars some land that Alvise Cornaro had obtained from them in 1535 for thirty ducats a year and had transformed into a splendid garden. The friars, authorized by their community, accepted restitution of that piece of property. The humiliating position Girolamo had reached, probably because of the difficulty in paying that rent and many outstanding annuities, can further be seen in 1720 when these same friars had to bring suit against him because he continued to defer payment of his debts.[84]

His second renunciation occurred when he allowed the presidency of the Arca del Santo in Padua to demolish the grandiose funeral monument erected in its basilica's central nave between 1684 and 1689 in honor of his sister Elena Lucrezia. It was of such overwhelming proportions that it impeded the view of the main altar. The Conventual Franciscans had already made several attempts to obtain a concession which would put in its place a former funeral monument, as well as remove the other ones already in the nave that were no less cumbersome. To this end they had tactlessly tried to put pressure on Cornaro, who ended up being inflexible in his refusal. Years later the two presidents of the Arca were sent to Venice (Count Pellegrino Ferri and Father Gianpaolo Cesarotti, as the guardian), in part to repeat the notarized request to Cornaro. The two were so diplomatic that he consented with a notarized act (July 4, 1727), granting their request "voluntarily and spontaneously, moved by the pure stimulus of piety and religion." But he also demanded that in place of the monument a marble bust of his sister be erected with the same inscription as the monument, that the statue which was removed be his property, and that the presidency of the Arca would have to do all the work at its own expense "without said gentleman Girolamo Cornaro Piscopia incurring even the slightest inconvenience."[85]

The conditions were accepted, and the demolition work began immediately. A month later, in August 1727, the Venetian sculptor Giovanni Bonazza (active from c. 1695 to 1730)—and not Antonio Verona as claimed by Ronchi and by Checchi-Gaudenzio-Grossato—was commissioned to execute the bust and the memorial tablet. He swiftly completed the work so that on October 17 he received the balance of his fee (400 lire) as shown by the receipt published by G. Bresciani Alvarez.[86]

Girolamo Cornaro, stricken with fever and pulmonary tuberculosis, died on the evening of December 17, 1734, at seventy-seven years of age. With his death, the lineage of the Cornaro Piscopia of San Luca was extinguished after four centuries.[87]

3

CULTURE IN THE CORNARO PISCOPIA HOME

MARCANTONIO AND GIACOMO ALVISE

On Tuesday, June 5, 1646, in the parish of San Luca in Venice, Elena Lucrezia Cornaro was born, the fifth child of Giovanni Battista and his domestic partner, Zanetta Boni. The following day, Elena was baptized and registered as the daughter of Giovanni Battista and the "offspring" of Zanetta, the later term being used to obscure the parents' irregular relationship.[1] (Since they did not find Elena's baptismal record in her parish church, owing to a hurried search of the archive, Pynsent and Dalmazzo concluded with excessive naiveté that the child was baptized in one of her father's country villas.[2]) Her ten-year-old sister, Caterina, took care of her, gradually becoming her inseparable companion and guide in her developing experience of the people and events of daily life. This affectionate bond between the two sisters was broken suddenly by Caterina's death in the flower of her youth. One can only imagine the anguish of Elena's heart, sensitive and intelligent as she was at age seven, when her sister died. This little girl surely understood what she had lost with that death.

Now she was left alone, since her only surviving brother, Francesco, the firstborn, was already a young man of eighteen and near to marrying; his world was far distant from hers. Her parents, though very attached to this only daughter, displayed the reserve typical of Venetian patricians even in the intimacy of the family, where one's spirit has rather the need for expressions of affection. Intimacy and familiarity were not part of Venetian family life. The informal *tu* was never used between parents and children. Fathers and mothers preferred to be respected and feared rather than loved. In the morning before breakfast, with a deep bow or curtsey, the children kissed the hands *a siòr pare e a siòra mare* (of sir father and madam mother), not daring to speak or to be seated without their permission.[3] We do not know to what extent Giovanni Battista Cornaro's family life responded to the influence of Venetian custom and discouraged complete and trustful communication between Elena and her parents. This atmosphere influenced her personality, which was already inclined by nature to be taciturn and solitary; it accented her tendency toward reserve, reflection, and an interior isolation. These lifelong characteristics favored her dedication to scholarship, a propensity she manifested early in life along with a precocious and keen intelligence.

Her first biographers made this flattering assertion which, however, should not be stretched to the point of affirming that Elena, even before her use of reason, gave signs of great piety and talent in every discipline.[4] This would undoubtedly be an exaggeration. How is it possible to have great piety and knowledge prior to the development of reason? This would require claiming that Elena had innate knowledge, an even greater exaggeration. We know, in fact, that innate knowledge surpasses nature since it is communicated directly by divine intervention to privileged souls. But we cannot affirm that such a charisma had been given to Elena if we think of the philosophical axiom *a posse ad esse non valet illatio* (from what is possible to what is is not a valid inference). The child had inherited a passion for study. It was in her blood.

In the Cornaro Piscopia lineage there were always lovers of the arts, sciences, and scholarship. Wherever they governed—as captains, mayors, chancellors, or provincial commissioners—they left a testament to their love of art, commissioning many extant works. The Chapel of San Marco in the church of the (Franciscan) Friars in Venice is one such example. Giovanni Cornaro had it built in 1378 according to the wishes expressed in the will of his father, Federico il Grande (not his grandfather as Berruti writes). This chapel, one of the major works of Venetian Renaissance art, contains his earthly remains as well as those of several of his descendants from the Piscopia branch.[5]

In the sixteenth century, the two brothers, Marcantonio and Giacomo Alvise, were patrons of the sciences and liberal arts and were held in high esteem by learned men of the time. In 1586, Filippo Pigafetta (d. 1604), the famous traveler and explorer, dedicated his translation of the *Trattato dello schierar gli eserciti* (Treatise on the Array of the Troops) by Leone VI, the wise emperor of the Orient (866–911), to the two Cornaro brothers, praising their knowledge of maritime and terrestrial warfare as well as of civil government.

Guglielmo V, duke of Bavaria (1579–1597), referred to them in a letter of 1591 as *clarissimi viri nobis sincere dilecti* ("most honorable men sincerely beloved by us"). He also lamented the gossip spread by them against the capital sentence that he had imposed upon Marco Bragadin, also known as Mamugna, and invited them to explain themselves more frankly. D'Ayala remembers the two Cornaro brothers as patrons of military affairs.[6]

Marcantonio, born in Padua on May 20, 1543, who had acquired a great competency in the military sciences during his career as a captain in the Cypress and Andro war, was an expert in hydraulic engineering. He wrote two works to the Sages of the Waters (the magistracy overseeing the lagoon and the surrounding water) concerning the lagoon and the Venetian rivers, proposing ways to eliminate and prevent the flooding caused especially by those waters coming from the Trevigiano territory. His suggestions are still fundamentally valid today, when various solutions are proposed to the problems of saving Venice and regulating its lagoon.[7]

Giacomo Alvise was the true spiritual heir of his grandfather Alvise of the "sober life." This architect, man of letters, and patron, who had made his palace in the Santo district of Padua a gathering place for artists and men of letters (Falconetto and Ruzante were his close friends), was understandably worried about the fate of the palace after his death. To avoid splitting up the property among his many heirs, he arranged in his will to have it all passed on to his grandson Giacomo Alvise, not only because he was the firstborn, but perhaps also because he perceived him as inheriting his love for the arts and culture.[8]

He had perceived correctly. Giacomo Alvise, born in Venice on September 13, 1539, was reluctant to participate in public life. He established himself in Padua in the famous palace with his wife, Caterina Bragadin, and devoted himself to the education of his children, the administration of his estate, and the cultivation of the liberal arts and sciences. He was especially interested in medicine, and in several contributions to the *Trattato della milizia* (Treatise on the Militia) by Valerio Chiericati, he suggested efficacious remedies for preventing various diseases among the troops, remedies which Chiericati assessed as valuable and of great use.[9] Cultured men, who used to gather for their learned conversations in the home of the scholar Gian Vincenzo Pinelli (1535–1601), after his death continued their meetings at Giacomo Alvise Cornaro's palace until the idea arose of founding an academy that was known as "Concerning the Ricovrati." Around him we find the cardinals Cesare Baronio (1538–1607) and Roberto Bellarmino (1542–1621); Torquato Tasso (1544–1595); Gian Francesco Mussato (1533–1613); Sperone Speroni (1500–1588); Brother Paolo Sarpi (1552–1623); Aldo Manuzio, the Younger (1547–1597); and many others of greater or lesser fame, such as the Germans Martino Hasdale and Nicolò Nonstiz, Giovanni Eutel Zugmesser, and the Benedictine monk Girolamo Spinelli, a disciple of Galileo and later the abbot of Santa Giustina in Padua (the

Pisan scientist familiarly called him Girolamo). But above all of them in importance was Galileo Galilei (1564-1642).[10]

Between the two there existed not only a bond of mutual esteem, but also of trust and affectionate friendship. Cornaro even became the intermediary for those who wished to confer with Galileo or ask him questions—a kind of spokesman for the master on these occasions. The meetings of the two friends, which took place almost always at Cornaro's, were facilitated by the fact that their residences were contiguous.

The proximity of their homes and of their spirits leads me to surmise that Cornaro was among the first, if not precisely the first, to be informed of the discoveries and inventions of the master. Indeed, in the Cornaro home and in Cornaro's very presence, Galileo showed Baldassare Capra his geometric and military compass, explaining how the instrument worked. Later, when Galileo sued Capra in Venice for plagiarizing the compass, Cornaro intervened in lively defense of his friend with a declaration to the Reformers of the Studio of Padua who oversaw the University of Padua (April 6, 1607), and with three letters of encouragement to Galileo, trying to get their mutual friend Girolamo Spinelli to participate as an efficacious witness at the trial, which concluded with Capra's condemnation. Cornaro, after unsuccessful attempts by Galileo, succeeded in getting Zugmesser, who had accused Galileo of having plagiarized his compass, to come to his own home. In the presence of Cornaro and other gentlemen, each gave a practical demonstration of his own compass, which proved that the Fleming had plagiarized from Galileo. Cornaro released an official account of this event to the Venetian senate.

The bond of intimate friendship between Galileo and Cornaro originated not only in these events, but also in the esteem and trust that the Florentine scientist felt for this intelligent Venetian nobleman with a passion for the sciences and the ability to appreciate their painstaking results. Galileo gave Cornaro samples of the instruments he invented and also his notes on mathematical studies and manuscripts regarding the method for the extraction of the square root. Regarding his studies for extracting the cubic root, he explains that they were "here in Padua in particular in the writings that he gave to the illustrious Signor Cornaro six years ago."[11]

Lorenzo Pignoria (1571–1631) mentions Cornaro as a cultivator of letters and the sciences in two letters to Paolo Gualdo (1553–1621), included among the *Lettere d'uomini illustri* (Letters by Illustrious Men). Calvi also mentions a correspondence of a cultural nature between Cornaro and the Venetian explorer Filippo Pigafetta. There are twenty-seven surviving letters written by these two in the thirty-year period from 1574 to 1604 in which Pigafetta furnishes geographical, historical, political, economic, religious, and folkloric information gathered during numerous trips across Europe, Palestine, and Egypt—always eagerly received by Cornaro. Pigafetta writes from Florence and from Pisa, where he was in the court of his friend, Grand Duke Ferdinand I; or from Paris, having been sent there by Pope Sixtus V to induce the king of France to enter into the alliance against the Turks; or from Rome, where he acted secretly as Pope Innocent IX's servant; or during his voyage to Croatia with Gianfrancesco Aldobrandini, a nephew of Clement VIII (ruled 1592-1605). He sends news on the region between France and Belgium, on England, Hungary, Danzig, Stockholm, Budapest, Constantinople, the Baltic Sea and the Black Sea, the Vistula, the Straits of Gallipoli and Gibraltar, on the Holy Land, Egypt, and many other places that he visited. He shows himself to be well informed on the war of Crete, on the siege of Paris, and the sensational victory of Lepanto (1571). Often he adds descriptions of the fortifications of cities, on the strongholds and war tactics he was able to observe. These letters, which have great historical value, were the result of Cornaro's encouragement; Pigafetta might not have provided such interesting descriptions had he not had a lover of culture like Cornaro as his correspondent.[12]

For over twenty years, from November 4, 1581, to April 20, 1604, these two conducted a friendly correspondence with the duke of Modena and Reggio, Alfonso II (October 1559–October 27, 1597), and with his successor, his cousin Cesare d'Este (October 29, 1597–December 1628). There are thirty-one letters, until now unknown and unpublished. Written for the most part from Padua, they clearly display Giacomo Alvise's passion for scientific studies and research, medicine, and travel, and reveal a man of great sensitivity.

Some letters deal with routine matters. He proposes, for example, that the duke appoint Albertino Fabiano, one of his dearest friends, to the office of counselor of justice (Padua, September 28, 1584); or he insists in several letters that the young Castellan nobleman, Filippo De Rossi, be set free from jail in Parma, where his youthful pranks had incurred ducal justice (Padua, September 1596, September 20, October 11, 1596). On another occasion, he requests him to expedite an unending case in the tribunal of the papal Rota on behalf of the Venetian noblewoman Giulia Molin (Padua, February 19, March 9, April 2, 1591), or recommends an aspiring Paduan as assistant to the ducal stable master. These requests are always written with great confidence in the duke and with certainty of being granted, "perché non si può mancare alli amici in certe honeste domande" (because one must not be remiss with friends in certain honest demands) (Padua, June 19, 1587).

It is a friendship in which Cornaro is careful to respect the honor of the duke and for this reason, as soon as he finds out that Giulio Cesare Branaccio (Naples 1515–Venice after 1586) plans to publish a military work in which he would have revealed war secrets of the dukedom in favor of the enemy, Cornaro is quick to warn the duke, in order to prevent its publication (Venice, November 4, 1581). The security and the prosperity of the dukedom find in Cornaro an intelligent understanding and collaboration. From Venice he informs the ruler of having explained to his brother Marcantonio his desire to have the waters of the Po lowered, a project which Marcantonio, an expert in hydraulics, judges to be not only possible but useful, announcing his readiness to meet personally with the duke to illustrate his plan (Venice, March 3, 1582).

His passion for scientific experiment leads him to two important discoveries which he shrouds in secrecy. Regarding the first, he writes that it is an invention "very honest and very useful for your mint" and that he is willing to reveal it only to him, assuring him that it has to do with something serious and not "of alchemy or anything else which is deceptive, so that it will be found convenient and useful to you, Sir, and to your people, both in your state and everywhere outside it." Since the invention requires an accurate explanation, Cornaro makes arrangements to go in person to Modena to describe it to the duke, "to whose trust I would like to commit my secret and not to others" (Padua, November 25, 1584). Illness, however, prevented the trip. He therefore charged his very trustworthy friend Albertino Fabiano, who went there to take up his position as counselor of justice, to disclose to the duke himself the secret of his invention (Padua, December 28, 1584). Three years later, Cornaro told the duke that he had prepared "an easy and sure gun-flint of his invention," which he would like to send him but which instead he preferred to bring personally, "together with a formula for treating all illnesses and which is already miraculous even while I am still testing it" (Padua, December 5, 1587).

A few months previously he had written: "I send to your Serene Highness a Paduan skin for water, which as fate will have it, did not turn out as well as I would have liked" (Padua, May 2, 1587). This may have been an animal skin worked and chemically treated by Cornaro with his own formula to make it waterproof (the first raincoat?). A few days later the duke thanks him for the gift asserting: "I can't believe, albeit, that coming from your hands it is not of excellent quality" (May 6, 1587).

Despite his love of study, Cornaro did not neglect his material interests and, in particular, his attachment to the land, a passion inherited from his grandfather Alvise, who had drained swamps and brought new land into cultivation. In fact, in anticipation of the inevitable death of a certain Pio Enea degli Obizzi, whose landed property would have passed into the control of the duke, Cornaro asked if he could rent the land—but at a modest price, because the Venetian Republic had already taxed him 40,000 ducats for the war against the Turks (Padua, May 19, 1589). A few years later he asks that the duke concede to him "on fair terms, a quantity of your uncultivated lands, since I have a son who is very much inclined to agriculture, and I would like to engage him in such an occupation" (Padua, January 30, 1594).

Such was the peaceful life in Padua of Giacomo Alvise Cornaro, devoted to study, caring for the family interests, and performing humanitarian deeds. He also traveled in Italy and to Germany, where he was "summoned by his serene highness of Bavaria on the spur of the moment" (Padua, March 9, 1591). Perhaps he went there to explain his and Marcantonio's involvement in the events leading to the execution of Mamugna. Years later he writes letters from Prague, sending greetings and best wishes to the duchess (April 13, 1604) and asking the duke if he might undertake some task on his behalf (Prague, April 20, 1604).

With this letter I end my discussion. Even a rapid glance at Cornaro's interesting correspondence illustrates the personality of this noble and learned member of the Cornaro Piscopia family.[13]

Giacomo Alvise Cornaro died in Padua on August 29, 1608. A letter from Prague, written by a person named Hasdale and addressed to Galileo in Padua (Prague, April 15, 1610), shows that he was sincerely mourned, especially by men of culture.[14]

GIROLAMO

His son Girolamo inherited not only his property, but also his love for culture. Although he served the Republic as captain and governor, first in Rovigo and then in Verona, he did not neglect his studies, especially of hydraulics. Taking up the same topic already treated by his uncle Marcantonio, he also wrote some *Discorsi sulla laguna* (Discourses on the lagoon), which were compiled and published by his son Giovanni Battista after his death. The inventory of his private library documents his interest in a variety of other subjects—sacred, profane, literary, philosophical, historical, judicial, geographic, mathematic—giving us an idea of the characteristics at the time of the library of a patrician family that loved culture. Girolamo certainly interacted with men of letters residing in Venice, for we find works noted in his library catalogue that were probably received as gifts from the authors themselves, men who perhaps frequented his home for reasons of friendship or culture.

Girolamo died on January 12, 1625, leaving in his will these precise instructions regarding the library: "the same orders and declares that my library be kept and registered in the way which has always been my intention, and must remain in the house equally accessible to all my children and their legitimate descendants as perpetual caretakers, and especially I wish it to be of use to those who desire or need to serve in the embassies or who would acquire honors by means of the *collegio*."[15] These stipulations reveal the lover of culture and the impassioned bibliophile, concerned that his library, compiled with love and great care, not be dispersed but remain intact as a source of intellectual energy for his decendants.

The executors of his will (his father-in-law, Guglielmo Thilmans, and Matteo Van Losen) had the notary G. Piccini compile (November 20, 1629) a thorough inventory of all the objects present in the Cornaro Piscopia home after the death of Girolamo's widow including, obviously, the books. The notary executed his task with the greatest precision and, regarding the library, attested to having inventoried the books "with exquisite diligence and put them back into two especially prepared, large cupboards."[16]

This inventory, with more than 1800 listings, has fortunately survived. The authors of single works are indicated, as is the title (though often imprecise or incomplete), the shape, the number of volumes, the binding, and all the bibliographical data, thus revealing the competence of the compiler and the scientific value of the library itself.[17]

GIOVANNI BATTISTA

The library became in substance the sole property of Giovanni Battista, the only surviving male heir of the family. It was in good hands. We know that he was not only a politician and businessman, but also a man of letters and the sciences, in which he had received schooling appropriate to his social status. He was known as a respectable, intelligent man with a passion for learning that he imparted to his daughters Elena Lucrezia and Caterina.[18]

He was extremely fond of the library not only because it was a testament to his father, but, above all, because it was an inexhaustible source of intellectual and moral treasures and of serenity. He had a special room in the palace for the library, which he had augmented with valuable Greek and Latin manuscripts, rare editions painted by Manuzio and Gabriele Giolito, historical works (especially Venetian) and other material, in artistic bindings; there was also a display of mathematical, geometrical, and astronomical instruments. In another room, he established a rich art gallery with many works by Titian, Jacopo Bassano, Carlo Loth the Bavarian, and others, and displayed there the military trophies won by the Cornaro Piscopias. In short, he had created in his palace a section which one might call a sanctuary dedicated to art and science, a library known as one of the best among those of private means. Many scholars, even nonresidents of Venice, wanted to visit and consult, such as Carlo Rinaldini, a professor of philosophy at the University of Padua, who later became one of Elena Lucrezia's teachers.[19]

There is nothing to indicate that Giovanni Battista left any scientific or literary compositions, but we know that he had the honor of becoming a zealous collector of the cited *Discorsi sulla laguna*, both of his great uncle, Marcantonio, and of his own father, Girolamo. Tommaso Gar (1808–1871) even describes the manuscripts that contain these works and mentions that they were gathered by Giovanni Battista Cornaro, superintendent of San Marco, son of Girolamo.[20]

Besides his books, Giovanni Battista cultivated learned individuals, whom he frequently befriended and hosted in his house. When in May 1685 Giovanni Mabillon (1632–1707) was in Venice for scientific research, Cornaro siezed the opportunity to meet the learned Benedictine, famous throughout Europe, who certainly was aware of Elena Lucrezia's degree. Mabillon accepted his invitation and visited him on Sunday afternoon, May 27, 1685 (he entered it in the diary of his trip to Italy). We can well imagine that Cornaro, after having spoken to him at length of Elena, had him admire the library and the annexed collections. Mabillon, a refined connoisseur, made it known that he greatly appreciated the library.[21]

Cornaro also had a friendly relationship with the scholarly bibliographer Antonio Magliabechi (Florence, 1633–1714), a librarian at the Palatina Library of Florence, an avid collector of books and manuscripts, friend and correspondent of Mabillon. In a letter from Florence on April 22, 1687, Magliabechi writes of having received as a gift from Giovanni Battista Cornaro, procurator at San Marco, two recently published books: the biography of Elena, with many annotations which Mabillon later included in his diary of his Italian itinerary, and a copy of *Le pompe funebri*, the "funeral ceremonies" celebrated by the Accademia degli Infecondi in Rome in honor of the young woman.[22]

Cornaro's family pride and his love for art spurred him to undertake, as he himself confessed, expensive renovations of his old palace at San Luca, expanding the rooms, enriching it with ornamentation, stucco, and sculptured cornices, and extending the facade up to the Grand Canal. The completion of this plan was precluded by his death, but he left it as his wish to his heirs, exhorting them to mount on the facade the Cornaro Piscopia family crest and that of Lusignano, the Cypriot royal family. In short, he desired that this palace be the equal of the other celebrated palaces facing the Grand Canal, which was and continues to be the most famous Venetian thoroughfare, where many picturesque nautical festivals used to, and still do, take place.[23] The history and art of the palace were well worth Cornaro's attention and financial investment.

The palace was built for the Zane family in the twelfth century, probably by the Lombardian architect Nicolò Barattieri (active in the second half of the twelfth century). Perhaps using material from previously demolished buildings, he created a Veneto-Byzantine structure typical of the period, with capitals and the original columns on the portico and the upper loggia, fortified with a continuous window. Along this loggia runs a fourteenth-century fresco as a crowning embellishment, with allegorical animal-like figures in relief joined by the Lusignano royal crest, a decoration of the knighthood of Cyprus bestowed on Federico Cornaro by Pietro I, king of Cyprus. Four statues adorned the atrium—Apollo, Diana, Geometry, Prudence—sculpted by the Bassanese artist Orazio Marinali, and the internal courtyard contained a *vera da pozzo*, a copy of a tenth-century Byzantine model.[24]

The palace had already undergone some internal and external transformations on the upper floors in the fifteenth and sixteenth centuries, and Giovanni Battista Cornaro wanted to return it to its original state. This was impossible, however, because of its varied uses and frequent changes in ownership.[25]

As a man in love with culture, Giovanni Battista Cornaro was one of the first patrons of the Accademia Veneziana dei Delfici, founded in 1647 and closed in 1690. From Fiorelli we know, furthermore, that he had as a protegé the learned Don Alvise Gradenigo, who emigrated from Crete, doing his best to get him named custodian of the San Marco library in 1669. The cosmographer of the Republic, Father Vincenzo Coronelli, dedicated to Cornaro the engraving depicting the Island of Cyprus in his *Isolario*. According to the custom of the era, various people commended Giovanni Battista's patronage of men of culture. Father Francesco Macedo (1596–1681) dedicated to Cornaro one of the seven poems entitled *Aedes monetaria* in which, describing the Venetian mint, he calls the Cornaro home an admirable mint where the precious coin, Elena Lucrezia, had been made. Muti sends him a scholarly letter; Angelo Sumachi, a noble of Zante, when he received a doctorate in philosophy and medicine in Padua in 1668 dedicated his doctoral thesis to him. Many other names could be added to the list of those who dedicated their compositions to Giovanni

Battista Cornaro Piscopia not so much to flatter him as to recognize him as a learned man who appreciated such gifts. In fact Rinaldini, professor of philosophy at the University of Padua, calls him a "very magnificent patron," and Fiorelli adds that his era had no reason to envy the patrons of past centuries because it had a splendid one in Giovanni Battista Cornaro, "who recognizes no limits to favoring the wise."[26]

4

Elena Lucrezia's Education

Women and Scholarship in the Seventeenth Century

From the preceeding chapters it is clear that Elena Lucrezia's early passion for scholarly studies found a favorable environment in her home; not only was her father a man of understanding and culture, but love of learning was also a venerable tradition in the Cornaro Piscopia family. They noticed Elena's inclination toward reflection, her love of books, and her desire to know and understand, which was much more pronounced in her than in her brothers or peers. At first, they did not consider it important, thinking this a common phenomenon among children, whose spontaneous curiosity about everything soon gives way to other interests and problems. The first to realize that in Elena, this was not the usual annoying and often indiscreet curiosity of children but rather a serious and meditative desire to know, the *curiositas* of the Romans, was Father Giovanni Battista Fabris, the parish priest of San Luca, a friend of the family and, it seems, also Elena's first confessor. He wanted to test her intellectual capabilities, believing that they were well worth cultivating. A doctor of theology, a student of philosophy—particularly of Aristotle, about whom he had written commentaries and published various works (impossible to find notwithstanding my thorough research)—an expert in Latin, and good in Greek, Fabris dedicated himself to these disciplines even after 1630, when he was elected parish priest of San Luca, and 1646, when he also became second vicar general of the Venetian Patriarch Gianfrancesco Morosini (1604–1678). To beautify his parish church, he undertook various initiatives and increased devotion to its patron saint, even writing a brief biography of him, *Vita di S. Luca Evangelista* (Venice, 1643).[1]

Fabris was a scholar, but first and foremost he was a pious priest with wide experience, a conscientious director and counselor, greatly respected throughout Venice for his doctrine and holiness. Many had sought his counsel in order to make decisions in their own lives or to learn the Lord's will in their concerns. In one such episode, the young Gregorio Barbarigo, almost thirty, upon his return to Venice from the Conference of Munster in Westphalia, where he had accompanied the Venetian ambassador, Alvise Contarini, was admitted to the college of the Sages to be introduced into the political life of the Republic. Determined to abandon the world and to enter religious life, yet uncertain as to which order to choose (the Discalced Carmelites, the Camaldolese Fathers, the Somaschan Fathers), he went to consult Fabris, who later became his confessor. After praying briefly, Fabris told Barbarigo, "You will embrace the ecclesiastic state, you will go to Rome, and you will be elected bishop. That is what the Lord has ordained for you." Afterward, Barbarigo went to Milan to question a noted cleric about the matter. He gave him the same answer. Finally, he went to Rome to consult Cardinal Fabio Chigi, whom he had met in Munster and who later became Pope Alexander VII (Siena 1599–Rome 1667). But the opinion of Cardinal Chigi confirmed that of Father Fabris and the cleric in Milan.[2]

Fabris, persuaded of Elena's exceptional intelligence and of her intense love of learning, advised Cornaro to start his daughter out in classical studies, to give her a superior cultural foundation, and offered to be her first Greek teacher, with Giovanni Valier, a canon at San Marco, as instructor in Latin.[3]

Before accepting the proposal, Cornaro certainly had to think carefully, knowing well that public opinion in Venice, as everywhere in Europe, was opposed to women's education. This view resulted not only from prejudice, but also from the abundant adverse literature and rigid pedagogy of the previous two centuries. Although many treatises on the dignity of women were written in the fifteenth century, some even advocating equality in education, the place of women in life remained traditional. According to the treatise *Della famiglia* (On the Family) by Leon Battista Alberti, women must be wholly responsible for domestic chores, toward which their education must be precisely and practically directed. A husband's most precious possessions must be shown to her, except books and ancient writings—which were to be hidden and locked up securely so as to prevent not only her reading them, but also her even seeing them. Household governance, modesty, administrative wisdom, sweetness, meekness, activity, were the traditional qualities of the ideal woman as outlined by Alberti.[4]

In the sixteenth century, after the Renaissance had elevated women to the same cultural dignity as men—Erasmus of Rotterdam and Baldassar Castiglione supported the same education for boys and girls, contrary to the opinion of Juan Luis Vives, who recommended that only men should become teachers.[5] This provision of the Council of Trent, although it sought to strike at the disorder of those cloisters in which during the Renaissance there was dancing and acting among the students and the nuns, was totally condoned by Silvio Antoniano, the most authoritative exponent of the pedagogical ideals of the Counter-Reformation. To the enquiry, "Should young women be taught letters?," Antoniano responded in precise terms. "As for those of humble status, it is not necessary that they even know how to read; for those of middle status it is not unfitting that they should read; for the noblewomen who must later be mothers of families in great households, by all means I would praise the idea that they learn to read and have a modest knowledge of arithmetic." He further opposed women knowing how to "orate or write poetry" or learning languages, not seeing the advantage that would be derived from this for the common good or for the girls themselves. He also feared that instruction would make the female sex haughty and would give it frequent occasion to equate itself with the male sex. In their own interest, knowing how to say the Office of the Virgin and to read the lives of the saints would be enough for girls. As a rigid purist, Antoniano harshly criticized the *Gerusalemme liberata* of Torquato Tasso, wishing to purge it so that it could be read by nuns. The views of Antoniano continued into the seventeenth century, with the warning: "Women, be content with the offices of the female sex and leave to men those of the male sex."[6]

To understand this century's opinion regarding women's studies, reading one author in particular, Antonio Giulio Brignole-Sale, would suffice. He wrote: "Education for a woman? Why? So that she would know? What? How to speak well? No, in fact, how to injure. Think not because she studies good things that she will become a better person. Women are wicked. The better you feed her, the worse she becomes. No one, in fact, who had a brain as big as a goose would ever want as a wife one who has this horrible gift of knowledge, worse in a woman than in a huge humpback, a putrid breath, a rotting oak. A woman of letters for a wife? Mercy! Rather let Lucifer come, we would have more peace."[7]

This is not an isolated exaggeration. It would be easy to gather an entire anthology of similar passages from the Italian writers of the seventeenth century. It is true that in this century there were in Italy, and even in Venice and Padua, women skilled in poetry and literature. But these were rare exceptions, that only confirmed the prevailing reactionary mentality.[8]

Therefore, Giovanni Battista Cornaro had to go against the current if he decided to allow Elena Lucrezia to undertake a course of study. He knew he would be setting himself up for criticism and derision that would involve his daughter and her teachers. Nonetheless, he followed the advice of Father Fabris, to whom he gave authorization to begin Elena's lessons. According to what Deza, her first biographer states, she was then seven years old. The lessons would therefore have begun in 1653 when Fabris was seventy-one years old. He was more than mature in age but still had a very lucid mind and great competence. His calm and penetrating teaching together with his personality as a spiritual man allowed the rapid progress of his student both in Greek and in spirituality.

LITERATURE AND SCIENCE

Elena's schooling with Fabris lasted fifteen years (not a year or so as De Santi affirms), until his sudden death in 1668 at the age of eighty-six (not in an unknown year as Dalmazzo writes).[9] Elena was twenty-four at the time. Under the tutelage, as Deza states, first of Father Giovanni Valier, a canon of San Marco, and then of a certain Bartolotti, who probably had substituted for him, her study of ancient and modern Latin had progressed steadily. Even though we do not know how many years this instruction lasted, the brief Latin compositions that survive demonstrate that she had assimilated the language well. The same can be said of Greek. Her father chose for her the best master of Greek in Venice at the time, the learned Father Alvise Gradenigo, much praised by his contemporaries.[10] Gradenigo, protopriest of the Greek rite, belonged to the large Greek colony that had established itself in Venice in the thirteenth century with its own hierarchy and church, San Giorgio dei Greci (St. George of the Greeks). Born on the island of Crete, he was married to Regina Tzancarolo and had two children: Antonio, the first student in the Greek College of Rome and later a monk in the Abbey of Grottaferrata (Rome), who died in Venice in 1674;[11] and Giovanni, godson of Cornaro, who studied first at the Jesuit Roman College (accompanied by Girolamo Cornaro) and then at the Greek seminary at Sant'Atanasio in Rome. Giovanni obtained two letters of recommendation from Elena Lucrezia to Cardinal Francesco Barberini, and in 1677 he had a philosophical debate with Elena herself in the new Procuratie of Venice.[12]

In 1669, the year following the death of Father Fabris, Alvise Gradenigo replaced him in teaching Elena classical and modern Greek. On January 31 of the same year he was admitted to the Accademia dei Ricovrati of Padua; shortly thereafter, due to the influence of the procurator Cornaro, who had also become his godfather, he was nominated to the sought-after and advantageous position of guardian of the Library of San Marco, succeeding another Greek, Leonardo Villaro of Athens. In her schooling, Elena learned the Greek language so well in both its ancient and modern forms as to become the pride of her teacher. She herself, in a letter to Cardinal Francesco Barberini, expressed her pleasure at having a tutor like Gradenigo. Deza recounts that when Gradenigo, who aspired to the title of honorary abbot of Cardachi on the island of Corfu, was challenged by those who contested his candidacy on the grounds that he didn't know classical Greek but only modern Greek, he brought as his defense some Greek compositions of his student Elena, claiming that if she knew classical Greek that well, the person who had taught her must know it even better. Thus, the teacher brought home a true triumph. Referring to Gradenigo, Rinaldini said that it was truly good fortune for Elena to have had this very qualified man and *omniscium* (omniscient one) who taught her with supreme diligence and competence.[13] We don't know how long the instruction by Gradenigo continued, but we may presume that he helped Elena until she received her degree in philosophy in 1678. Gradenigo died in 1680. Of his literary compositions, the only one that remains is a long epigram composed in 1674 in honor of Elena Lucrezia. Yet we know that he was preparing a complete edition of *Etnica*, a work by the Greek geographer Stefano di Bisanzio (sixth century A.D.). He had also coordinated and collected poetic compositions by various authors in honor of the Greek noble, Angelo Sumachi, published under the title *Epantismatologia* (Padua, 1668).[14]

Besides Latin and Greek, Elena also learned French and Spanish and devoted herself to the study of mathematics and the natural sciences, astronomy and geography, always with great commitment. The benefit of the Spanish language would soon reveal itself in a translation from Spanish of a small religious work by Giovanni Lanspergio, published in Venice in 1669: *Colloquio di Cristo nostro Redentore all'anima devota* (Dialogue between Christ Our Redeemer and a Devoted Soul). She dedicated this work to Father Giampaolo Oliva, Father General of the Society of Jesus, in recognition for having provided her with a tutor from the Jesuits. Her knowledge of Spanish also showed itself in mathematics, a short time later, with an explanation of an intricate Archimedean theorem to Carlo Rinaldini, professor at the University of Padua, during his first visit to the Cornaro home.

The Jesuit tutor mentioned above was almost certainly Father Carlo Maurizio Vota. Born in Turin on February 8, 1629, to a Milanese family, he entered the novitiate at Avignon on November 12, 1645. He taught literature at Macon (1646–1648), was a student of philosophy at Lyons (1649–1651), and then taught literature in Nice (1651–1655), all followed by theological studies at the Roman College (1655–1658). He was ordained a priest in 1659 and after a brief sojourn in Genoa (1660), was sent by Father Oliva to Venice (1661), where he made his solemn profession of vows (February 2, 1663) and remained for the next seventeen years, that is, until 1678, the year of Elena's graduation. A man of profound and encyclopedic culture, an expert in literary and scientific fields such as mathematics, physics, astronomy, and geography, besides being a polyglot, Father Vota soon attracted the admiration and esteem of the learned, participating in the educational life of the city. He was head of the Venetian academy of geography until his departure from Venice.[15]

Clearly there would have been no time for any teaching of Elena, as De Santi would have it, by the Jesuit Father Giovanni Macrini (or Magrini) (1632–1698) who taught only at the University of Ferrara, first philosophy, then theology, and later mathematics. He was also concerned with the embankments of the Reno River, at the request of Cardinal Ferdinando D'Adda (1649–1709). He was then invited to Piacenza by Duke Francesco Farnese (1678–1727) to fortify the banks of the Po River against floods. There is no information about his having lived in Venice.[16]

The scientific direction given to Elena's studies by Father Vota can be deduced from various elements, the first being his own education. After his novitiate and his studies, he taught in France, where at the time the theories of Pierre Gassendi (1592–1655) were widespread. Gassendi was a philosopher and scientist, a great admirer of Galileo and his devoted supporter, from whom he even received a telescope as a gift. Perhaps he did not have the courage to assert publicly a defense of the Copernican system, but it is certain that he had no doubts as to its scientific validity.[17] Father Vota could surely not remain insensitive to this movement of modern science. Furthermore, when he came to Venice he found himself in an environment still strongly influenced by Galileo's eighteen years of teaching at the University of Padua (1592–1610). With his discoveries in astronomy, mechanics, and calculus, he had opened new avenues to modern science. Even after the departure of Galileo from Padua (1610) and the death of the two Venetians who were closest to his spirit and to the new scientific movement—Gianfrancesco Sagredo (1620) and Paolo Sarpi (1623)—fervent Galileans were not lacking, but they were overshadowed by the Italian Baroque literary movement that was spreading in Venice, as in all Italy, which sought to express the unusual in wordplay and far-fetched concepts. However, Vota's student belonged to a family which was traditionally Galilean, a tradition begun, as we have already seen, by the intimate bond of friendship between Giacomo Alvise Cornaro, her great-grandfather, and Galileo and faithfully transmitted within the family. In the private library inherited by Giovanni Battista from his father and used by Elena for her studies, the scientific works were for the most part in the Galilean vein.

The scientific, humanistic, and linguistic schooling imparted to Elena by Father Vota lasted for the length of his stay in Venice. He therefore was able to assist her until the day of her degree in philosophy and had the joy of participating in this rare triumph of his student.[18] During these seventeen years, he had the time to give her a solid and complete educational background, rendering her truly a master of the French and Spanish tongues. This was one of the pillars of Elena's vast culture, making her an object of admiration and providing her with a resource from which she would always draw abundantly for her literary compositions, academic discourses, and familiar correspondence with illustrious persons and scholars.

At this point, Elena, as was required by the normal program of study (the *ratio studiorum* of the Society of Jesus), having completed her literary and scientific instruction, could move on to other subjects. It was decided that she would first study philosophy and then theology.[19] She thus began the philosophical studies that played so great a role in her life, not only because they expanded her cultural knowledge in the speculative field, but also because they led to a university degree, in those times an unheard of accomplishment for a woman. She also had the good fortune of meeting an eminent teacher of philosophy, a professor at the University of Padua, Carlo Rinaldini, who had come from the University of Pisa where he had taught for eighteen years.

Carlo Rinaldini belonged to an old and noble Sienese family that later moved to Ancona, where he was born on December 30, 1615, the son of Scipione and Angela Fanelli. He studied at the University of Bologna, dedicating himself especially to philosophy and mathematics, and offered his services to Popes Urban VIII (1568–1623) and Innocent X (1574–1644). He also became a tutor to the sons of Taddeo Barberini, prince of Palestrina, captain of the pontifical army, and brother of Urban VIII, thus gaining the esteem and benevolence of all the Barberini. In 1649, to increase his own standard of living and to assist his family, he accepted a position teaching philosophy at the University of Pisa where, despite the condemnation of Galileo's theories, he taught his students (privately, if not in his public courses) the doctrines of Galileo and Gassendi. Gassendi later was invited to teach publicly in the Accademia del Cimento, which he had helped to establish in 1657 along with Leopoldo de' Medici, a brother of the grand duke of Tuscany. Rinaldini was admitted to the academy and charged with writing a paper exposing the principal errors of Aristotle and other ancient philosophers on the subject of physical science which could be corrected by means of experience. Rinaldini carried out this task with great competence, emerging as the equal of his illustrious colleagues Giovanni Alfonso

Borelli (1608–1679) and Vincenzo Viviani (1622–1703). Angelo Fabroni, after mentioning various men whose culture had brought recognition to the Accademia del Cimento at Pisa, writes: "among all the teachers whom I have named, the one who stood out in studies, intellect, and doctrine was Carlo Rinaldini."

The president of the academy boasted that, with Rinaldini as their teacher, students had the best possible training in philosophy, and that no other Italian academy could compete in that discipline with the Pisan academy. Fabroni further declared 1667 to have been an unfortunate year for the Pisan academy because of the departure of both Borelli and Rinaldini, who was called to the University of Padua. On August 17, 1668, he was admitted to the Accademia dei Ricovrati in Padua. When Cosimo III, grand duke of Tuscany, later attempted to get him to return to Pisa, the University of Padua increased the favors it bestowed upon Rinaldini. He held a professorship in philosophy with great honor until 1698, when he resigned and retired to his native Ancona and died a few months later at the age of eighty-three, leaving several philosophical and mathematical works.[20]

The encounter between Rinaldini, Giovanni Battista Cornaro, and his daughter Elena Lucrezia was completely accidental. Having gone to Venice on business, Rinaldini heard from a friend of the goodness and kindness of the procurator Cornaro and of his magnificent library. Spurred by the desire to visit it, Rinaldini introduced himself to the procurator, who graciously welcomed him and entertained him in the hall of the library.[21]

PHILOSOPHY AND THEOLOGY

The first encounter between Rinaldini and the woman who would soon become his student and in whose glory he would himself one day come to bask took place right in the library itself. Here is how he describes this encounter:

> While I was leafing through the works of Archimedes, which were on the table, I came across the theorem of the application of a straight line pulled between the circumference and the diameter [of a sphere]. There appeared in the library a young woman with a beautiful face, well proportioned, of delicate complexion, with a majestic head, dignified features—and she began to speak about that theorem. I was in such awe that I couldn't speak. In time, I

summoned my courage and asked the procurator to tell me the name, the family, and country of this beautiful girl, as illustrious in her spiritual qualities as in her body and almost as if she had fallen from heaven. He smiled and said: "As for her name, it's Elena Cornaro." And I: "Is she by chance Your Excellency's daughter?" He nodded. "There is, then, no reason to be surprised."

Rinaldini also mentions this encounter in another work, published in 1668. Their meeting, therefore, should be dated between the end of 1667 and the beginning of 1668, and not much earlier as De Santi maintains. In fact, we should remember that Rinaldini went from Pisa to Padua in 1667 and began his university teaching there on October 1 of the same year.[22]

From that day on Rinaldini became an intimate friend of the Cornaro family, returning frequently to their home to discuss science with Elena, who later became his student until she received her degree in philosophy. He continued to go to Venice to visit his friend the procurator even after Elena had graduated and established her residence in Padua. He was therefore Elena's teacher for about ten years. This amount of time should not seem excessive if we consider that the lessons were given privately in the Cornaro home in Venice, but without regularity either in the day or in the time since Rinaldini was still teaching at the University of Padua. Elena thus studied many things on her own, based on the directives of the professor.[23]

As already noted, Rinaldini, since his teaching days in Pisa, was a convinced follower of Gassendi. In fact, French philosophy had exercised great influence upon Italian thought, and Gassendi was especially admired in Tuscany where Rinaldini, forbidden to teach Gassendi's theories publicly at the University of Pisa, where Aristotelian philosophy predominated, explained the doctrine privately to his young students. Gassendiism, which Galileo supported, had even spread to Padua, thanks to the freedom of thought permitted to the professors there because of the protection provided by the Republic of Venice.[24]

In spite of this, Aristotelian thought remained dominant in Padua. Diverse interpretations of Aristotelian doctrine clashed with one another, often in a bitter, passionate fashion. Close to the followers of Thomism, famous teachers, such as Nicoletto Vernia who taught at Padua from 1465 to 1499 and Alessandro Achillini (until 1508), taught Averroism. Agostino Nifo (1473–1538) and the two schools of thought, though they had conflicts among themselves, agreed to accentuate the dualism between spiritual and material reality. Representatives of Paduan Aristotelianism, more or less in harmony with Christianity in the second half of the sixteenth century and the first half of the seventeenth century, were Giacomo Zabarella (1533–1589), a teacher in Padua from 1564 to 1589, and Cesare Cremonini (1550 or 1553–1631), who had become famous across Europe.[25]

Rinaldini had to keep all this in mind while deciding the direction of Elena's philosophical studies, especially since she was preparing for a degree in theology at Padua where the Aristotelians still prevailed. Furthermore, the chancellor of the university was the bishop, Cardinal Gregorio Barbarigo. Therefore Rinaldini, though dissenting personally from the Aristotelian tradition, attempted to adapt to the environment as he had done in Pisa and oriented Elena toward a more open and new Aristotelianism, one which examines the phenomena directly rather than the texts that treat them theoretically, refusing to consider the great ancient thinkers as absolute repositories of the truth. With her scientific preparation and detailed knowledge of mathematics and astronomy, Elena probably already understood this trend in contemporary science and had no difficulty following the orientation proposed to her by Rinaldini regarding philosophy and the classical philosophers. The Cornaro library contained the works of almost all the greatest philosophers, such as Plato, Plutarch, Porfirio, Cicero, Seneca. The best represented, however, was undoubtedly Aristotle, with his complete works in various editions, in the original text or translated into Latin or in the vernacular, with or without commentary—in other words, a large collection of publications in all or in part of the works of this philosopher. Material for study was therefore abundant, and Elena used it assiduously and intelligently. Rinaldini added some works of his own, authoring a treatise on mathematics and geometry, with questions pertaining to philosophy, which he said he had written expressly for the illustrious young Elena Lucrezia Cornaro Piscopia: *De resolutione et compositione mathematica* (Patavii, 1668).

The professor soon realized the extraordinary progress of his young, 22-year-old pupil, marveling at her knowledge of the various sciences, at the five languages that she knew at the time, at her dedication in the study of philosophy and in her initial studies of theology and Hebrew. Furthermore, he was conquered by her grace and the ease of her scholarly conversations. He felt she was a walking encyclopedia, a true prodigy of letters of that era. He was proud of this and treated her more like a daughter than a pupil, to which she responded with great docility and gratitude. In this atmosphere of mutual esteem, he often called her his Minerva, and she referred to him not as her teacher but as the father of her culture.[26]

Personal growth had always been the sole motivation for all Elena's studies, including those in philosophy. Rinaldini had guided her in the diverse sectors of philosophy, among the various works and authors, so that Elena knew how to approach their ideas; she was capable of criticizing, completing, or adapting them with sureness and competence, more like a teacher than a student. By 1678 she had reached a level of preparation such that she could, had she so desired, have tackled the examination for the doctorate both in philosophy and in theology, subjects which she had studied practically simultaneously. Her calm, reflective personality inclined her primarily toward the speculative studies of philosophy and theology, the latter being the science that best satisfied the demands of her profound religiosity. Rinaldini's assertion that she climbed the summit of theology, penetrating even the most difficult questions, is confirmed by Elena's biographers, who introduce at this point Father Ippolito Marchetti from Camerino, an exemplary man and eminent theologian of the Congregation of St. Philip Neri (the Oratorians), as her theology instructor. They further state that he was a guest in the Cornaro home in Venice for five years, until his death, so as to be better able to teach Elena theology, and that he edified the Cornaro family with his goodness.[27] Upon closer examination, however, we find that such claims are impossible to verify.

First of all, Marchetti died in 1662 when he was seventy-two years of age, after contracting a fatal fever in September 1661. Therefore, he would have had to enter the Cornaro home at age sixty-seven and begun teaching Elena theology in 1657, when she was only eleven.[28] Therefore Elena supposedly studied theology with Marchetti from age eleven to sixteen. With all due respect to her prodigious intelligence, I believe that she could not at that age have been intellectually prepared for the study of theology. This subject requires a preliminary or at least concomitant philosophical preparation, without which the various definitions, principles, and theses—not to mention theological terminology in general—are incomprehensible. Furthermore, the *ratio studiorum* prevalent at the time wisely prescribed the study of philosophy before that of theology. What kind of theology could have been taught to an 11-year-old girl, at the age of catechism study? Elena could have perhaps learned notions of elementary philosophy that were self-taught, gleaned from the numerous works in the family library, but her methodical study of philosophy began with Rinaldini and not before 1668. There is, therefore, no room for Marchetti in the chronological order of Elena's studies, and the claim is perhaps based on the assumption that this famous theologian must have come to the Cornaro home for the purpose of teaching theology to Elena.

Why was Father Marchetti in the Cornaro home? It seems reasonable to surmise that Cornaro engaged him as a chaplain, a very common position in the noble families of the time, even in Venice. Elena mentions the presence of a chaplain in her home in a letter of 1676 to Cardinal Francesco Barberini.[29] His tasks were to celebrate Mass, to deliver some sermons in the private chapel, to teach the rudiments of doctrine and Christian morality to the children and the servants, and to act as a religious consultant to the host family. For such duties there was certainly no need for an illustrious theologian. It seems likely that the family offered Father Marchetti this position in order to provide a home for him in his declining years.

A more likely candidate as Elena's theology instructor is the Franciscan Conventual Friar Felice Rotondi,[30] who had a degree in theology and was a teacher and dean of studies in the friary of his order in Venice (1662), as well as a friend and confidant of Cornaro's. In addition, to plead the case of Elena's father, Rotondi was called to the University of Padua in 1665 as a professor of theology *in via Scoti*, and on September 16, 1678, he was accepted into the local Accademia dei Ricovrati. He had thus become a teaching colleague and friend of Carlo Rinaldini's. These circumstances led Cornaro to choose him as Elena's theology instructor. Later, in a letter to Rinaldini, he wrote that he had seen her more as a master than as a student in theology, recognizing that her intelligence was far superior to that accredited to her or spread about by learned men.[31] Such statements, even if they are somewhat extreme, help us to understand how diligently Elena had dedicated herself to the study of theology. In fact, Father Rotondi, for his personal prestige and especially because he considered the pupil so well trained in theological science—as well he knew—decided, with the approval of Cornaro, to introduce her to the Sacred College of the University of Padua and to request that it grant her a degree, something completely new and unusual in those times for a woman.

Although somewhat taken aback, the Sacred College, showing its open-mindedness and respect for freedom, reacted favorably to the request and even arranged a special ceremony for the occasion. However, due to the indomitable opposition and direct intervention of the chancellor of the university, Cardinal Gregorio Barbarigo, the event did not take place, and Elena had to settle for a degree in philosophy. Nevertheless, Cornaro, Father Rotondi, and Rinaldini remained determined to obtain the degree in theology in the near future.

HEBREW AND MUSIC

Seriously committed to her theological studies, Elena constantly studied the Bible. In order to read the original texts, she decided to learn

Hebrew. It was not difficult to find a teacher in Venice, which had had a flourishing Jewish community since the beginning of the thirteenth century, established by immigrants from Germany, Spain, Poland, and the Aegean Islands. Notwithstanding the victims claimed by the plague in 1630, it is calculated that in 1655 this community numbered more than 4800, the largest population ever of Jews in Venice. As to the conditions under which Jews lived during the seventeenth century and in the first half of the eighteenth century, Venice was one of the few places in Italy where the Jews, though confined to the ghetto at night, did not have to worry about suspicious and inexorable policemen watching their every move. Venice continued to maintain its autonomy with respect to ecclesiastical authority and permitted Jews a certain freedom from the sanctions laid down by the papacy of the Catholic Church. Venice had a ghetto and required the distinctive beret, but, according to a decree by the senate in December 1601, Jews were not required to attend preaching, and individual proselytizing leading to their conversion was forbidden. There is no evidence of forced baptisms; every rumor of ritual homicide was contested; and the Inquisition seldom brought action against the Marranos, i.e., judaizing Christians.[32] Contacts between Christians and Jews were generally cordial. Christians continually visited the ghetto, were present at the major Jewish religious functions, participated in Jewish family feasts, and attended the recitals and concerts given in the ghetto. The Jews did likewise with the Christians. They participated in the splendid feasts organized by the city and were often invited to small family entertainments—a commingling that was agreeable to both sides. Religious prejudice was completely absent in higher intellectual circles, although present in some aristocratic environments; yet it did not affect the peaceful coexistence of the two communities. The Jewish community of Venice, because of its wealth, its international connections (not exclusively commercial), its fondness for pomp and grandeur, and because of the learning of its teachers, enjoyed an existence that was the envy of most of the Jewish communities of the Diaspora during the seventeenth century.[33]

Giovanni Battista Cornaro, having to choose a Hebrew language instructor for Elena, sought the best that Venice had to offer. And the best, from the point of view of culture, honesty, and respectability, was Rabbi Shemuel Aboaf. Born in Hamburg in 1610 to a family of Marrano Spanish immigrants, he was sent at age thirteen to study in Verona where his grandfather Jacob had already moved. There he was the disciple of David Franco, a famous scholar of Spanish origin, whose daughter Mazzaltob he married without requesting any dowry. His fame as a scholar grew rapidly. As a rabbi in Verona, he founded a highly esteemed academy and developed intense charitable activity. In 1650, since he belonged to a rich merchant family famous for its benevolence, he was called to direct the Venetian community. He had no need for even minimal profit from his rabbinical duties for his living expenses.

Few scholars of his time could equal the fame which he enjoyed. Not only did he know Hebrew and Italian, but also Spanish, German, and Latin. He became a renowned rabbinical authority, to whom questions were posed from every part of Italy and from London and Hamburg. He was intensely pious and inclined to asceticism; he fasted, perhaps with excessive regularity, and ate meat only on Saturdays. He hungered for the study of the Torah, day and night. Like other members of his family, he was extraordinarily charitable, maintaining his neediest students at his own expense and personally bringing assistance to the homes of the poor. Neither his riches, his social condition, nor his family tradition had any influence on his ideas. He did not permit public ceremonies to be held in Italian, nor did he approve Hebrew studies being taught to non-Jews, the wearing of masks portraying human faces, or the publication of engravings to illustrate the Bible. He frowned upon the use of tobacco, considering it a vice that made one waste precious time which could otherwise be used for studying. In short, in seventeenth-century Venice, Aboaf represented those Jews who remained committed to orthodox Judaism in their studies as in daily life.

Toward the age of eighty, Aboaf underwent, for some obscure reason, a persecution that forced him to leave Venice for a while (some claim that he went into voluntary exile for a transgression or omission he had committed). Returning to Venice, and feeling himself very near death, he gathered his children together around his bed for his final words of advice: never pronounce the name of the Lord God in vain; be scrupulously honest in every action; never speak ill of anyone nor use disparaging language; be zealous in the education of youth; and attend the synagogue every day with utmost punctuality. He died on August 22, 1694, mourned as a holy rabbi, and was buried in the ancient cemetery of Venice's Lido; later, in accordance with his wishes, his body was exhumed and taken to be reburied "in the sacred ground of Palestine." Regarding his writings, besides various unpublished works, we know of *Debar Shemu'el* (The Word of Samuel), a collection of responses, published in Venice in 1702 by his son Jacob.[34]

Such was the moral and intellectual stature of the man who taught Hebrew to Elena. Their meetings took place in an atmosphere of great mutual esteem, she knowing that she had an incomparable teacher and he, in turn, an exceptional pupil dedicated to deriving the maximum benefit from his lessons. It was more an encounter between two great intellects than between master and pupil, notwithstanding their different stations in life.

There appears to be no factual basis for the story told by biographers (followed later by other researchers) that Elena often could not sleep at night because she was tormented by the thought of her Hebrew teacher's eternal damnation; that in several conversations she spoke of his conversion; and that he, though recognizing the truth of Christianity, nonetheless excused himself in tears for being unable to abjure because he and his family needed the salary he received for his duties as rabbi.[35] This contradicts what is known about the rabbi—his spirituality and moral rectitude, his religious zeal and asceticism, the stable financial position of his family, his generosity, and his deathbed testament to his children. Furthermore, as I mentioned above, a decree by the Venetian Senate prohibited every sort of individual Christian propaganda intended to convert the Jews, which was used by both Catholics and Jews in defense of their own faith. I also said that Aboaf was opposed to the teaching of Hebrew to non-Jews. If he agreed to teach Elena, he truly made an exception out of respect for the procurator; one must believe that Elena would have reciprocated by respecting her teacher's religious views.

The student-teacher relationship between the two continued even after Elena graduated and moved to Padua. On January 1, 1680, the French Cardinal d'Estrées came to visit her and, at his invitation, she presented a paper that included elements revealing her knowledge of Hebrew. The cardinal was amazed and wanted to meet her instructor, the rabbi, who was then immediately introduced to him. Aboaf, in fact, had helped Elena prepare for that important occasion, when she demonstrated her mastery of that very difficult language and its enrichment of her own cultural background. It is worth noting that in a Hebrew bibliography, Elena Cornaro is listed among the Christian Hebrew scholars.[36]

All Elena's biographers agree that she studied music, among the other liberal arts, and that she achieved some expertise. (We know that in 1663, Carlo Grossi, a musician from Vicenza, dedicated some of his compositions to Elena.[37]) They do not agree on the type of instrument she played, and no one mentions the name of her music teacher. It is certain that, for the artistic value of music in itself and for its remarkable influence on Elena's mind and spirit, an important place should be reserved for her music teacher—a certain Maddalena Capelli, an organist. Most likely a Venetian, she was hired around 1663 with a yearly salary of fifty ducats plus food and clothing. She settled permanently into the Cornaro home, even bringing her own furniture, suggesting that she was totally free of family ties.[38] She was an orphan, and possibly she had been educated in one of the pious musical conservatories of Venice.[39]

Her duty was to teach Elena music and accompany her singing on the organ. We may safely suppose that to be able to do this, Capelli had to be at least Elena's age, that is seventeen years old or perhaps a few years older. She was a young teacher gifted in culture, with a gentle spirit kindled by the exercise of her art. She had refined aspirations akin to those of Elena, and was not inclined to marriage, as we know from Cornaro's testament of 1690. At that time she was still unmarried, and it is very possible that she remained so until her death. Given these circumstances, it may be that Capelli was also an affectionate companion and confidante, almost a sister to Elena. She was at Elena's side both in Venice and later during the five years spent in Padua until Elena's death, that is, for a good twenty years.

I think it likely that Elena played a small organ, not a rare item in the refined homes of the era, or perhaps a harpsichord with pedals, which was a more common instrument at that time. Various biographers indulge in the idea that Elena was a virtuoso harpist, violinist, or harpsichordist. It is certain only that she played the organ or the pedal harpsichord, since they require the same technique. Others have written that she used to compose lyrics in various languages, setting them to music and singing them while she played the harpsichord, that she was, to use a modern-day phrase, a sort of singer/song-writer. That she was prepared to sing while she herself played the harpsichord or the organ, accompanied by Capelli, is also possible. But when performing in public, she probably did not sing and play simultaneously, since that does not conform to contemporary performance practice. At any rate, the problem is clearly resolved by Giovanni Battista Cornaro himself who, in his testament, affirms that Capelli had come to his home for his daughter Elena "to play for her while she sang."[40]

Capelli accompanied Elena to Padua for the purpose of music, even though by that time it had become for her more an artistic outlet and a diversion than a subject of study. When Elena was afflicted by the various illnesses that would lead to her death, Capelli became a loving consoler and solicitous care-giver, even in the humblest and most delicate chores, just like a sister. This is perhaps the Maddalena whom various biographers of Elena refer to not as a servant or maid but as "the young Maddalena whom she had in her company, in whom she confided a great deal" and to whom she entrusted the fulfillment of some important tasks soon after her death, as we shall see.[41]

The study of music was very important to Elena's cultural development, and she addressed it with her customary seriousness and intelligence. In her various literary compositions, she frequently reminisces about this aspect of her education, revealing her love of music and her knowledge of its technical language. These qualities, we may believe, were manifested even more through her public musical performances. If she shunned the applause of her admirers, her parents and

Capelli rightly delighted in it, the latter seeing her efforts as a teacher so well fulfilled.

After Elena's death, Capelli returned to Venice to look for a place to settle, but the Cornaros, grateful for her work and fond of her as if she were their daughter, made her stay with them. The procurator remembered her in his testament (August 5, 1690), and Caterina, Elena's sister and widow of Antonio Vendramin, left in the postscript to her will (1707) ten ounces of silver to Capelli, who at the time was sixty-six years old.[42]

Two brief observations emerge from this analysis of Elena Lucrezia Cornaro Piscopia's studies: one regarding the teachers, the other the student. Concerning the first, we must recognize that they were all eminent in their fields. The procurator Cornaro was always concerned about finding the best. In a letter to the University of Padua, after his daughter received her degree, he writes that she has been instructed by the most famous teachers. Caro, in his funeral discourse in honor of Elena Lucrezia, with the exaggeration typical of the era, adds that the sole difficulty encountered in finding her professors was not the lack of scholars, but only their reluctance to teach a student of such elevated intelligence before whom they felt more like pupils than teachers.

As for the student, the observation made by Rinaldini in his speech on the day Elena received her degree is significant: she had always been inclined to study, but had immersed herself "more than enough." Precisely this excessive effort undermined her delicate health and led to her premature death, as her father acknowledges in the letter cited.[43]

5

A Degree

Post-Tridentine Theology

Under the tutelage of Father Rotondi, a Conventual Friar, Elena had seriously devoted herself to the study of theology. But what was the nature of the theology she studied? In what direction had her teacher led her?

We can surmise that she followed the direction given to theology by the Council of Trent (1545–1563), characterized by an elaboration of the new way of seeing the world at that time. If humanism had already made itself heard in demanding a return to original sources, thus turning greater attention to the Bible and the writings of the Church Fathers, the controversy with Protestant doctrine over sacred Scripture and tradition—defined at Trent as the sources of divine revelation—and the defense of contested ecclesiastical institutions sparked the development of an historical theology.

This new kind of theology, begun in the sixteenth century soon after the Council of Trent, developed rapidly in the seventeenth century in response to two great problems of the time: humanism and heresy. The relatively new, positive theology was not born solely of humanism, but also of the necessity to respond to heresy and to test the conformity of Catholic dogma against its origins. While the modern heresies challenged the identity of the Roman Church at its source and proposed its radical reform, the Church itself was engaged in the same task, and Catholics had to mount an enormous effort to respond to Protestantism.[1] The nature of modern Catholicism was conditioned in large part by these reforms. Until then, scholastic theologians, totally undisturbed, had based their discussions on the life of the contemporary Church without worrying about historical criticism. But since the reformers had reduced the authority of the churches to a purely human level and no longer probative, they were now required to follow the innovators into their own territory:

to refer to the primitive Church and the text of the Bible. From this came the creation of positive theology on the part of the Catholic theologians on the one side, and the study of tradition on the other. For this reason, in the seventeenth century innumerable treatises were written with the intent of demonstrating the "perpetuity of the faith." The aim of positive theology was to prove that the current teaching of the Catholic Church conformed to biblical and patristic teaching on the faith of the apostolic or early Church. This is what certain authors call "positive theology of the origins." The Council of Trent and post-Tridentine theology mark, therefore, a real change in the Christian world. It was due to the positive theology of the seventeenth century that the development of Protestant doctrine was successfully halted, containing it within the circle traced by the first reformers.[2]

This was the vast and delicate field of theology that Elena encountered when she began her studies. From day to day its theses, proofs, discussions, obstacles, and errors became ever more familiar to her, and her teacher marveled at the progress she made in a subject so demanding and otherwise unusual at that time for a layman, let alone a woman.

She must have elicited wonder of a different sort in her own day—and perhaps even in us—this young patrician woman who dedicated herself to the study of theology, the sacred science *par excellence*, in seventeenth-century Venice. The city was tormented by a profound and worsening religious crisis caused by the spread of Protestant ideas, especially the schismatic theological concepts and liberties of Father Antonio Rocco, a philosophy assistant in the monastery of San Giorgio Maggiore. He was a notorious unbeliever, warned several times by the Inquisition, and the author of one of the most licentious books of his time, *Alcibiade fanciullo a scuola* (Archibald, a child in school). Atheistic doctrines were further propagated in Padua by Cesare Cremonini who, from his university chair, propounded daring philosophical, religious, and moral theories to the youth, including Venetian nobles. He was able to influence the minds of young students for some forty years (1590–1631) and always with impunity because he was protected, as were all professors at the University of Padua, by the Venetian Republic. Jealous of its "Venetianness" and on the pretext of guaranteeing freedom in teaching, the Republic was not answerable to the Apostolic See. The result was a great decadence in the practice of the faith, a growing ignorance of religion, a disinterest in serious study, and an all-out race toward vice, a phenomenon which manifested itself more among the nobles than among the poor, simple, working-class people.[3]

Since conditions in Venice were similar, it is natural to wonder whether the study of theology in general, and by a young patrician woman in particular, still made any sense; specifically, whether in addition to the desire for sacred erudition and personal spiritual enrichment, Elena and Father Rotondi had in mind an authoritative return to the noble Christian values and morals from which an entire social class had been diverted. This could be. In any case, despite the agreements and disagreements that her study of theology created around her, Elena continued diligently in this field, at a pace equal to her study of philosophy. By 1677, she reached a level of accomplishment such that Father Rotondi, having consulted Rinaldini, his intimate friend and Elena's philosophy professor, decided to introduce her at the University of Padua, requesting that she be granted a degree in theology.

THE UNIVERSITY OF PADUA IN THE SEVENTEENTH CENTURY

There could have been no other choice for Elena than the University of Padua, primarily because the Venetian Republic had prohibited its subjects from studying at any other university since the fifteenth century. Its decree was made even stricter in the seventeenth century by including banishment for life for transgressors, a fine of 500 ducats for their fathers, and the promise of a reward for informers. The purpose was to halt the flight of subjects to other universities (especially to Bologna, Pavia, and Parma), thus diminishing the age-old prestige of Padua, which was already encountering difficulties with the emerging repercussions of renewal in the realm of education.[4]

In the seventeenth century, the University of Padua, the first descendant of the University of Bologna, had the honor (until 1610) of counting among its professors Galileo Galilei, whose name is associated with scientific renewal, owing to the method he himself introduced. The mention of his name alone suggests the importance that this university had attained, as well as its fame throughout Europe. In the seventeenth century, professors of great worth taught there, among whom were the previously mentioned philosopher Cremonini, Ercole Sassonia, Albanio Albanese, Giorgio della Torre, Domenico and Antonio Marchetti, Alessandro Vigonza, Girolamo Capivaccio, and still others.[5] Such professors attracted students from every part of Europe, who were welcomed and protected. With their carefree lifestyle, they brought great activity to the city. Padua relied so heavily on the university that whenever the number of students diminished, there was an immediate search for the cause—and its remedy. However, the students' unchecked liveliness and the guarantee of protection on the part of the authorities at times led them to commit acts of violence, threaten the safety of the people, and disturb the peace of the city.[6]

It is worth quoting a report by Angelo Marcello, the capitano of Padua in 1658, sent to Doge Domenico Contarini regarding student life at the University of Padua in the seventeenth century.

> In centuries past, this university produced such eminent men in all disciplines that it meritoriously earned seniority in glory above all others. Perhaps at present there may be many doctorates: but they do not flourish, as before, producing illustrious graduates who, being a majority among the learned, make the name of this university resound throughout the world. I don't know if the Lord God permits this because we have tolerated too much freedom in the past of notorious nonbelievers or if this is the result of changing the manner of lecturing, with the students losing the benefits of methodical lessons which, when they wrote them themselves, instructed them perfectly in all subjects; indeed for some time this was the case with respect in particular to foreigners, who made disparaging remarks about the ancient fame of this institution, and thus caused a lack of enrollment. This remains certainly very prejudiced by the excess of freedom permitted to the students because scholastic conceit has notably increased, one which seeks to satisfy every whim. I know that in one's youth some lively activity is natural; but extremes are vices which public prudence must consider to be very harmful to the entire state of Your Supreme Highness. These pernicious acts allow these students to come to Padua where they learn to respect neither princes nor laws as usually occurs in the insolent interference with lessons, in the use of those recently of age, in the abuse of freshmen, in the increase of long and short firearms, and in the diabolical practice of the "halt who goes there." These excesses are forbidden by Your Serene Highness, yet are nonetheless scandalously practiced, compromising not only public decorum, but also the peace of the city, and all too often resulting in the homicide of those very students in the neighborhoods in which this behavior occurs where police don't patrol and, therefore, these areas are attractive havens for hoodlums, who to unsuspecting youth demonstrate terrible behavior, all to the disturbance and mortification of good folk. There is an ever increasing dissoluteness which requires a good purge and reform as regards the honor of our Lord God and

reminds the students of the most fruitful tested forms. With the observance of the law, obedience is revived and modesty is preserved.[7]

Marcello, who as captain was responsible for public order in Padua and thus was well acquainted with both people and events, provides an authoritative description of the university environment that Elena would have encountered in obtaining her degree, one she had never previously experienced. Some authors wrote that Giovanni Battista set up a residence for his daughter in Padua several years before her degree was awarded so that she might better prepare herself in the necessary studies.[8] Until today it has seemed plausible that Elena stayed in Padua for a few years before 1678, if not to take courses at the university, at least to familiarize herself with the programs of study and all that could have a direct or indirect bearing on the doctorate in theology to which she aspired. This opinion must be abandoned, however, considering certain facts and documents that prove that Elena did not live in Padua before obtaining her degree on June 25, 1678, that she went there only a few days before and established herself there during the following year, 1679. Until then, she lived with her family in Venice.

On May 30, 1677, for example, she was involved in a philosophy thesis defense with the young Giovanni Gradenigo, son of Alvise, custodian of the Marciana Library, and her Greek teacher, in the rooms of the Procuratie inhabited by her family.[9] On November 18, 1677, the Reformers of the University of Padua wrote from Venice to the rectors of Padua (governor and captain) to request the use of the public library or another site suitable for the graduation ceremony of Elena Cornaro, which would be held in Padua. This letter leads us to understand that she was still living in Venice on that date.[10] Also during the winter of 1677, Carlo Cato de Court, a French gentleman and man of letters, and the Abbot Ludovico Espinay de Saint-Luc, a French nobleman and professor at the Sorbonne in Paris, came to pay Elena a visit. Another rather persuasive argument supporting Elena's residing in Venice throughout 1677 rests upon thirteen signed and unpublished letters she wrote from Venice between April 18, 1671, and December 18, 1677, to Cardinal Francesco Barberini in Rome, in which she speaks of people and events in Venice where her day-to-day life was evolving.[11] Another document, in which it appears that Elena was residing in Venice until nine days before her examination, is a letter of June 16, 1678, written in Venice by the reformers of the university to the authorities in Padua: "Being that the noblewoman Elena Lucretia Cornaro, daughter of Mr. Giovanni Battista, procurator, must come here to be recognized for her degree, a doctorate in philosophy . . . the aforementioned noblewoman is to be afforded every courtesy and honor of one who has rendered herself deserving of such in every regard." Finally, we have Caro's statement in his eulogy at Elena's funeral: "Cum se Venetiis evectam contulit Patavium, factura eius doctrinae periculum" (She left Venice to come to Padua to take her examination in her discipline).[12] In fact, she appears to be in Padua on June 22, only three days before the ceremony, to conclude some formalities mandated by the procedures for the doctorate.

On Sunday, May 30, 1677, when Elena brilliantly defended her thesis in philosophy with Gradenigo in front of a rather large crowd of nobles, women, and scholars who had come to Venice from various parts of Italy and from abroad for the traditional Festa della Sensa, she amazed everyone with her knowledge. A rumor had begun among those present that the following November, Elena would go to Padua to receive the degree and many had decided then and there to attend the exceptional event.[13]

THE OPPOSITION OF CARDINAL BARBARIGO

News of the upcoming conferral of a degree on Elena could have been spread only by her family, her teachers, and particularly by Father Rotondi, for whom the thesis defense proved anew the excellent philosophical and theological preparation of his pupil. He felt that it was time for her to obtain the long-desired degree in theology—desired not by Elena, but by Rotondi, by Rinaldini, and, above all, by her father. Because of Elena's love for her father, she reluctantly agreed to prepare for the degree; she had no desire ever to teach theology, but knew that the honor would make her father happy.[14]

Therefore, steps were immediately taken according to the required procedure. Elena filled out the application for the degree in theology and presented it to the Reformers of the University of Padua (at the time Angelo Correr, Battista Nani, and Leonardo Pesaro), the three magistrates assigned by the Republic to supervise the university. Their duties included coordinating the examinations and the degrees.[15]

Faced with this unusual request, even though taken by surprise and conscious of the prevailing attitude toward the education of women, they judged it to be legitimate. Elena was, after all, a Venetian from a patrician family and had completed long and serious studies with teachers such as Rinaldini and Rotondi, renowned and esteemed professors of the University of Padua. Therefore, they approved the request without difficulty, and even took care to write immediately (November 18, 1677) to the authorities in Padua so that they could begin to notify the professors of the school of theology to make themselves available for Miss Cornaro's examination. This extraordinary notice aroused great surprise among the theologians of the university, although they probably had already heard about it from Father Rotondi, their colleague. Everyone knew that a doctorate in theology could not be conferred without the consent and signature of Cardinal Gregorio Barbarigo, who as bishop of Padua was also the thirty-ninth chancellor of the university. He had been in Rome since September 21, 1676, and was detained there by Innocent XI until the end of February 1680. Alessandro Mantovani, who as vicar-general substituted for the bishop in governing the diocese when he was absent and also represented him in the position of chancellor, wished to avoid any personal responsibility in such an unusual case, full of embarrassing consequences. He therefore informed the cardinal and put the entire matter in his hands.

Three documents reveal that in the meantime Padua was preparing to confer the degree. The theologians hastened to present the case in detail to their Venetian colleagues and certain illustrious individuals of the University of Paris who were passing through Venice at that time. They posed two questions: first, whether a woman, having been educated, could receive a degree in theology in a public university and wear the insignia of that degree and, second, whether to obtain that degree the graduate had to receive the minor ecclesiastical orders or at least the first tonsure. They responded affirmatively to the first question, that a woman could wear the ermine cowl (the sign of doctors of theology); regarding the second enquiry, they made note that Elena, even without the minor order of acolyte, would have been like "a golden candelabra in the Church of God." Even the theologians of the University of Louvain, when asked, proffered the same view. While waiting for the response of the bishop, which would presumably be a favorable one, they prepared a special ceremony for this extraordinary situation, adapting the one usually used for ecclesiastical candidates, bringing to it variations suggested by the circumstances. Elena would be declared a maestra laureata in sacred theology with the right to all the honors and privileges of doctors in theology and reconcilable with her sex. She would be crowned with laurel, have the ring slipped on her finger, and receive the book—but closed, with the express prohibition of publicly teaching the truths of the faith, which she was instead to meditate upon. In place of the chancellor's embrace, it was to be imagined that she received an embrace from Christ, her divine spouse. Finally, she would have the blessing imparted to her in the name of the Holy Trinity. After this document, another more advanced one was immediately prepared so as to have a complete record of the conferral of the degree in theology, as if it were already the eve of the event.[16]

Giovanni Battista Cornaro took advantage of Cardinal Barbarigo's presence in Rome right from the beginning, recommending that he take charge of various paperwork in the Roman Curia for him. The procurator found that the cardinal was generous in his availability to him, and in his written correspondence with the noble Giulio Giustianian he states that he was ready to "satisfy the wishes of the Procurator Cornaro, which are singularly pressing to me" (Rome, September 26, 1676). In another letter he wrote: "To the Procurator Cornaro I render infinite thanks for the kind memory he has of me" (Rome, October 9, 1676).[17]

As we can see, there was an excellent relationship between Cardinal Barbarigo and Procurator Cornaro who, writing to him for business reasons, referred to a degree he wished for his daughter Elena. Granting a doctorate in a subject formally and traditionally conferred the right to teach the subject anywhere in Christendom. The cardinal thought he meant a degree in philosophy, and although the idea of granting it to a woman was completely new, he was willing, given Elena's vast education and virtue, to begin discussions, even when he was told that it concerned a theological dissertation. But when Alessandro Mantovani informed him that Cornaro was asking him to award a degree in theology to his daughter, the cardinal responded with a total refusal; he had not known that Elena aspired to such a degree and could not imagine that a woman would want to teach theology. Faced with this refusal, the relationship between Cornaro and Barbarigo, which until then had been calm, became stormy. A very active correspondence began among these two, the vicar-general of Padua, the Reformers of the university, and others, with the goal of smoothing out the difficulties and finding a way to save the honor of the Reformers of the university, of the Cornaro family, and of Elena herself, now compromised by the cardinal's unexpected denial. It was suggested that Elena undergo a pure and simple theological defense without going any further. Barbarigo hoped that Cornaro would be satisfied. Instead he was offended.

Barbarigo was informed of this, probably by his vicar-general and by Father Rotondi, who had modified the ceremony used to confer the degree in theology on ecclesiastics and adapted it to Elena's case.[18] He hoped that the cardinal, seeing the limitations placed on the ceremony, would grant his permission. Instead, the cardinal said it was ridiculous to call Elena a teacher without giving her permission to teach, going so far as to forbid her to do so; that to give a degree to a woman in theology was to make all the universities laugh just as some pitiless foreign prelate friend of his to whom he had explained the situation was already laughing; and that this affair was contributing to discrediting the University of Padua. The Reformers, therefore, had to persuade Cornaro that Cardinal Barbarigo would never consent to confer a degree in theology on a woman. To satisfy Cornaro and his daughter, Barbarigo proposed that she hold a public theology debate in Padua, following which he was said to be willing to declare her worthy of any degree. In this case, her sex—the only thing that kept her from assuming the university professorship—was no impediment; in his view it was a positive solution because it exalted the intellectual merits of the young woman.

But in reality, it was a formula deprived of any content. Both the Reformers of the University of Padua and the procurator of San Marco, Giulio Giustinian, a friend of Barbarigo's and also of Cornaro's, attempted to persuade Cornaro. Cornaro, anything but unprepared, understood that they wanted him to capitulate. Feeling personally offended, he immediately sent Barbarigo the text of the famous modified ceremonial along with a not very respectful letter, hoping to induce him to commit himself to awarding Elena's degree. A short time later (March 12, 1678), Barbarigo wrote to his friend Giustinian, complaining about Cornaro,

> who sends me two documents, but I didn't have time to read them; and it seems to me that he confirms that it would be a mistake [to grant] what is requested. It is definitely true that the Lord Procurator Cornaro writes to me in such a form in which, if he continues, I will not respond to him: because in the end, politeness is welcome in every circumstance and in every person.... And I am evermore convinced that making a woman a doctor is a mistake. And responding to everything would be easy. But it is not worth it.... I don't see any way to retreat from that which is established, if we don't want to make ourselves look ridiculous to all the world. Time will fix the soul of His Excellency, the Procurator.

The task of appeasing Cornaro he left to the tact and prudence of Giustinian, saying he would agree to any other proposal he and the Reformers of the university might suggest to escape this ugly embarrassment, as long as no one ever mentioned the degree in theology again.[19]

Therefore, it was a definite no. Giustinian pushed himself to find a way to quell this storm, aroused by letters with insults and reprisals, proposals and counterproposals, requests and refusals, kindness and rudeness—all of which had destroyed the serenity of many souls and eroded friendships. In the meantime, Elena, the involuntary cause of this agitation, was composed and ready to step aside, as long as this huge tempest could be calmed for all.

In a letter to the vicar-general on January 22, 1678, Barbarigo said he had not understood that Cornaro was requesting a degree in theology, believing it was in philosophy. Giustinian saw that this could perhaps be the long-awaited point of agreement.[20] He advised Cornaro to refuse the prestigious degree in theology for his daughter and to request instead one in philosophy, equally prestigious; it would be the only one in the memory of man, of supreme glory not only for Elena and the family, but also for the university, for the Venetian Republic, and for the world of scholars. Faced with this proposal—which saved his honor, put an end to the thorny, interminable dispute, and calmed Elena—the procurator acquiesced. Giustinian also obtained the consent of Barbarigo, who wrote a letter of gratitude to him from Rome on March 26, 1678: "I am glad to thank you heartily for your very prudent behavior, with which you released me from a great difficulty in which I found myself and from which I would not have escaped without the kind assistance of Your Excellency, completely patient with the Procurator and with such kindness toward me."[21]

The road to a degree in philosophy was therefore open to Elena, and a wave of serenity finally entered the Cornaro home.

Before proceeding, it seems opportune to investigate further the reason why Cardinal Gregorio Barbarigo, in his position as chancellor of the University of Padua, refused Elena permission to graduate in theology.

Several explanations have been given. First of all, to bestow a degree on a woman and especially in theology, was unheard of, not only for Padua but for every other university. It is said that the cardinal made his decision so as not to compromise the prestige of this Venetian atheneum and to avoid the disdain of the various universities that believed women to be incapable of teaching at the university level. But the statement of Barbarigo, that Elena could be declared "worthy of every degree when her gender does not hinder it, it is the only thing that precludes her rising to the chair," suggests that the real reason was not St. Paul's prohibition against women teaching (1 Tm. 2:12), but a church practice in force at the time, immediately after the Council of Trent. To avoid further erosion toward Protestantism, the church was rigorous in the teaching of doctrine. Teachers of dogma had to be very capable and well prepared.

Since the Church believed women to be inferior in cultural and social affairs, holding that they were incapable of difficult reasoning (particularly on the truths of the faith) and feared that in assuming a role in Church teachings women would be inclined to formulate personal interpretations, slipping toward the "liberal examination" of the Protestants, any teaching at a higher level by women was prohibited. Elena was permitted to teach by memorization, avoiding any explanation or interpretation of the Bible or the catechism. This meant that she was given the task of monotonous repetition of questions and answers to children. The Church's attitude deprived it of the valid educational contribution that women would have certainly made. How many intelligent females were there who, in fact, surpassed men even then or could have at least competed with them with considerable results? Cardinal Barbarigo, an intelligent man, was certainly persuaded of their capabilities and their right to teach but, as a man of the Church, he had to follow the common practices of his time, and since he put them before his personal convictions, we can consider him worthy of respect, even of admiration.

Besides, one may surmise, without exaggerating, that in the three years he spent in Rome at the side of Pope Innocent XI as a trusted advisor, Barbarigo had explored this issue. In fact, he deals with the question from Rome and, if he proves to be intransigent in his refusal, this is a sign that he was conscious of being in line with the directives of the Church and of the hierarchy.[22]

ELENA CORNARO PISCOPIA'S DEGREE IN PHILOSOPHY

The attempt to obtain a degree in theology having failed, Father Rotondi, her theology teacher, leaves the scene, and Rinaldini, the philosophy teacher, enters. Knowing how well his pupil was prepared, and in full agreement with Cornaro, Rinaldini convinced the still reluctant Elena to request the Reformers of the University of Padua to admit her to a degree in philosophy. In deference to the *Patavina libertas* (Paduan freedom) maintained by the University of Padua, they looked favorably upon the request, and on June 16, 1678, wrote to the Paduan authorities, begging them to be accommodating in every way so that the ceremony could take place with all the decorum which the young patrician woman's knowledge and virtue deserved and which the honor of the country demanded.[23] Some authors believe that Elena, to reduce as much as possible the confusion that might occur around the day she received her degree, had her father agree not to have it conferred during the fair or on St. Anthony's feast day (June 13) when Padua always had great crowds of worshippers and sightseers. For this reason, June 25 was chosen.[24]

On Wednesday, June 22, introduced by Professor Carlo Rinaldini, sponsor of the degree, Elena asked the Sacred College of Philosophers and Physicians, represented by four *collegians*, to be admitted to the philosophy examination, *more nobilium* (by the custom of the nobles), on Saturday, June 25, at 9 a.m.. The request was accepted, and on the same day the circular of convocation was sent to all the members of the Sacred College asking them to be in attendance by nine o'clock.[25] Also on June 22, in the presence of her two witnesses, Elena pronounced the profession of faith prescribed before the degree, swearing *se esse catholicam et bonam christifidelem* ("herself to be Catholic and a good faithful Christian").[26]

Two days later (Friday, June 24, 1678), the puncta were chosen, i.e., the passages which Elena would have to discuss during the doctorate of philosophy examination.

Ex P.° Posterior. Tex. 9°
si igitur scire ut poscimus etc.
Ex P.° Physicor. Tex. 42
quod igitur contraria quodammodum...

She was given the information so that she could prepare appropriately.[27]

The eve of the long-awaited day had finally arrived, and tension mounted in the Cornaro home. Even Elena, notwithstanding her excellent preparation, was preoccupied. We can imagine that she spent the evening with Rinaldini compiling supporting information on the two Aristotelian passages she would have to discuss, thus giving a final touch to her preparation for the next day. For some days now, relatives, friends, and admirers of Elena had lived in an atmosphere of joyous expectation while the news of the event was spreading, and the presence of many people was anticipated. And attend they did. The crowd exceeded all predictions, since from the earliest hours of the morning, nobles, knights, ladies, educated men, and ecclesiastics had filled the hall of the Sacred College reserved for those awarded the doctorate (not the great lecture hall of the university as Dalmazzo writes).[28]

When at the appointed hour the College of Philosophers and Physicians gathered to attend the examination, the hall was packed as never before, with even more people wishing to enter. The decision was made to move to a larger place, and the assembly was reconvened immediately in the chapel of the Blessed Virgin in the nearby cathedral. When the city authorities, the College of Philosophers and Physicians, and the vicar-general (representing Cardinal Barbarigo as university chancellor) had taken their respective places, the four professors sponsoring the degree, Girolamo Frigimelica, Carlo Rinaldini, Angelo Montagnana, and Ermengildo Pera, moved forward and introduced Elena Lucrezia Cornaro Piscopia to the Sacred College. She *more nobilium* or *alla nobilista*, that is, with the privilege of the nobility, spoke extensively on the topics assigned, but was exempted from the discussion with those who would argue against her, as in a formal debate; she defended the two passages and spoke so ably that she astonished the entire examining committee. When she finished her defense, two small ballot boxes were brought in as usual. The professors, however, held unanimously that there was no need for a vote on such an excellent defense, so evident was the favorable result. But Elena asked that even for her, they follow the normal procedure of a secret vote. Then Domenico Tessari, vice prior of the college, rose to speak, saying that although the university statutes required a secret vote, he would propose that the assembly approve the candidate by acclamation, due to her extraordinary and brilliant philosophical discussion. All accepted the proposal and *communi consensu acclamatione et vivae vocis oraculo philosophiae magistra et doctrix acclamata fuit coram universo doctorum coetu* ("by common consent and vocal acclamation to the oracle of philosophy, she was acclaimed teacher and doctor before the whole gathering of learned people").[29]

At this point, Elena, who according to custom had left the chapel before the vote, was introduced to make the petition for the degree from her teacher, Rinaldini. Before crowning her, he gave a laudatory discourse in which he first praised the civil and military deeds of the Cornaro Piscopia family—rendered still more famous by Elena. He then called attention to her great intellect, her nobility, and the persuasive strength of her eloquence; her elegance of style, her knowledge of various languages, her musical talents; and surpassing all other qualities, her ensemble of virtues, particularly of chastity, a royal virtue and the dignity of life. He concluded by affirming that if the Greeks had been proud of their Helen, so admired in the ancient world for her beauty, on that day the Italians were to be even more proud of their own Elena, a noble prodigy of nature.

It was a touching and exciting moment for all when Rinaldini approached the blushing graduate to give her the doctoral symbols: the book for a teacher, the ring for a victorious combatant in the philosophical competition, the ermine cape for a doctor, and, finally, the laurel crown, symbol of triumph. The professor concluded the historic ceremony with words that certainly expressed the modest thoughts which must have been running through Elena's mind. "Do not revel too much either in the very ancient crown given you by your lineage or in the one which on this radiant day I place on your head by Apollo's wish, woven by the muses and dampened by your hard work. In fact, another extraordinary and much more sublime one is reserved for you in heaven."[30]

And so on June 25, 1678, the first woman graduate received her degree[31] by means of a regular act of the Sacred College. This was a proud moment for the University of Padua, which adapted to the times and courageously crossed the secular barriers that excluded women from higher education. This degree, which, according to Cardinal Barbarigo and various universities, should have dishonored Padua, became instead an event to boast about, one that earned it praise from foreign scholars.

The document conferring the degree, compiled on that same day by the ecclesiastical authorities, informs us that Elena Lucrezia Cornaro Piscopia was acclaimed concordantly *magistra et doctrix in philosophia tantum* ("teacher and doctor in philosophy as well").[32]

It was a day of triumph and of joy for the family, friends, and admirers of Elena and especially for her father, who finally witnessed the achievement of the goal for which he had fought and suffered so long, and which augmented the glory of his family. We don't know if this event restored the friendship between Giovanni Battista and Barbarigo that had been damaged by the cardinal's opposition to the degree in theology for Elena. Even if the disagreement lasted longer, it must have ceased completely when the two met during the cardinal's pastoral visit on November 4–5, 1683, to the parish of Codevigo, in which Cornaro had the jurispatronage. The cardinal and his entourage were his guests on the night of November 4, perhaps because canonical narrowmindedness had been won over by the insistence of Cornaro.[33]

After the ceremony, Elena was taken back to her palace by carriage amid the acclamations of the crowd.

Amid so much admiration, it is astonishing to read a private document that describes the solemn ceremony of Elena Lucrezia Cornaro Piscopia's doctorate in sarcastic terms.[34] It was written by a doctor of the Sacred College of Philosophers and Physicians, Gaspare Ottaviani Cantu, who nonetheless does not appear among those who signed the register recording the defense of her degree.[35] The reason is not known for this biting irony:

> She made her defense in the Blessed Mother chapel in the cathedral with confusion and disorder as never before heard, with little satisfaction to all; she lost her train of thought in her discussion of the points regarding both functions, in other words, she got the doctorate on her own,[36] nor have I ever been able to find in the Thomaso Garzoni Hospital the right place for such madness.[37] On July 9, 1678, she made her entrance into the college as is the custom. There is also the custom that those who receive the doctorate in the fashion of nobles deposit a sum of money, as others do, and in addition, a pair of gloves is given to each one of the doctors. The monetary deposit was refused by the illustrious gentleman of the banks [of the college], and Mr. Cornaro, her father, with swiftness accepted the offer and gave only the gloves, in very bad taste, with a price tag of 24 farthings

a pair. To the promoter, who was Rinaldini, the dolt,[38] a miserable ten-ounce silver fruit bowl was given. She was graduated with a crown of flowers and the ermine stole was placed on her shoulders; and thus in a carriage she was taken to her palace to the triumphant saint of her madness. The doctors of the college all received her with robe and stole.

The exceptional event provoked innumerable literary compositions exalting the knowledge and virtue of Elena, as well as the increased celebrity of the University of Padua. Everyone seemed enthusiastic upon hearing that a woman had finally succeeded in obtaining the doctorate forbidden to women for centuries, and they felt obliged to express themselves in writings of every kind.[39] Many portrait engravings and paintings of Elena were done at the time and circulated with inscriptions, emblems, allegories, Greek and Latin couplets, and some reproductions to illustrate her biography. Among the portraits, the one engraved by Sister Isabella Piccini (a nun in Venice from 1665 to 1692) stands out and was considered until the last century as very rare and highly prized.[40] In addition, we know from a letter of July 9, 1678, from Carlo Airoldi, papal nuncio in Venice, to the Vatican secretary of state, that in those days Cornaro was going around Venice handing out poetic compositions in praise of his daughter for the doctorate she had just earned.[41]

Elena spent two weeks waiting to participate in another ceremony in her honor at the university necessary to complete her degree: her induction into the College of Philosophers and Physicians. Since July 5, the prior of the college had been sending out invitations to the various members to participate in the ceremony on Saturday, July 9, presided over by the four sponsors of Elena's degree and including 43 members (seventeen philosophers and 26 physicians). While Elena waited outside the hall, according to custom, the prior of the college announced the reason for the convocation and proposed that the admission of the new graduate to the college take place by acclamation, as was done for the degree. The decision was unanimous. Elena was immediately led into the hall and, in the presence of the committee, took the oath of fidelity to the statutes of the college and received the first place among her fellow members (Giorgio della Torre moving to the second place). Then, together with the physician Antonio Maria Orsato, she was selected by lot as an examiner for the degree in philosophy of a young man named Daniele Magnavini from Montagnana. Many objections had been raised against him, but they were easily surmounted and he obtained an excellent vote (39 for, 5 against).[42]

This was the only official act completed by Elena as a member of the College of Philosophers and Physicians. Dalmazzo, however, states that

Elena undoubtedly exercised the duties of *magistra* (teacher), even if we know nothing of the time or manner of this teaching.[43] First of all, we must remember that the Venetian patricians, although possessing degrees, never, by law, could ascend to a university chair to teach. Elena, conscious of and jealous of her noble state, always avoided anything that might tarnish it even in the slightest way, nor did she need a stipend from the school. Furthermore, she had agreed to accept the degree without the possibility of teaching. If she had wished to teach, she would have encountered a difficulty even greater than the one posed by the degree. But she requested the doctorate only to make her father happy; this ratification of his daughter's education was very important to him. We should also remember that Giovanni Battista Cornaro never had any intention of exploiting Elena's degree for financial interests or for other material advantages. With his daughter's achievement he presumably only desired to recover for himself and his family that honor which he had compromised by his youthful deeds and his marriage to Zanetta. One should also keep in mind that Elena became ill even before receiving her degree. Already in a precarious state of health, she could certainly never have withstood the strain of teaching.

One could compare the behavior of Elena Cornaro with that of another young noblewoman, her contemporary correspondent, the Countess Veronica Malaguzzi Valeri from Reggio Emilia. Her father, Count Valerio, had her study several subjects privately and, seeing her rapid progress and remembering nonetheless that *carmina non dant panem* (songs do not give bread), immediately thought to put his daughter's talents to work for the family. He used all his energies to find her some splendid patron from whom he could seek help for his family of eleven children, which was in financial difficulty.[44] His supplications to the courts of France, Austria, and Tuscany resulted only in letters of praise and nothing more. The girl did not see her genius recognized by the world and, pious as she was, she became a nun, together with her twin sister, in the Convent of the Visitation in Modena, where she died in 1690.[45]

We might also compare the motivations of Cornaro and Malaguzzi: the former encouraged Elena to study solely to obtain the maximum prestige for himself and for the name of Cornaro Piscopia; Malaguzzi wanted primarily an advantageous economic position from the education of his daughter.

As for the two women, we should note that Veronica Malaguzzi's taking of the veil seemed to result from her disappointment at not being valued for her education. Elena Cornaro, on the other hand, though seeing herself officially recognized for her education, preferred to stay apart from others even to conceal herself in a convent.

After the ceremony of her admission into the College of Philosophers and Physicians, Elena could not excuse herself from attending, on July 15, the solemn assembly organized by the Accademia dei Ricovrati, to which she had belonged since 1669, to celebrate her doctorate. The authorities of the city were present and, after an instrumental and vocal concert, Ottone Bronckhorst, count of Gransfeldt, in a lofty discourse praised the knowledge and virtue of that eminent female member who so honored the academy. He used this as an opportunity to propose to the participants a debate on an academic theme that was very pertinent to the occasion: supposing one had to entrust the governing of a kingdom to a woman, which would be preferable, a woman dedicated to arms or one dedicated to letters? The nobles Gianantonio Dottori and Roberto Papafava debated the question. Many Italian and Latin literary compositions were invoked in honor of Elena who, at the end, thanked the academy with a scholarly discourse.[46]

In the meantime, the chorus of applause surrounding her was heard even outside Italy. In Lyons, Paris, Amsterdam, Leipzig, Altenburg, and Utrecht they wrote about her education, her degree, and the admirable example of respect for freedom demonstrated by the University of Padua, whose glory from this event was envied.[47]

Numerous, also, were those who personally expressed their admiration. Two such letters, dated August 20, 1678, and composed in elegant Latin, were sent separately to her by two French individuals who had met her in Venice a short time before her degree was awarded: Carlo Cato de Court, a gentleman and scholar, and the Abbot Ludovico Espinay de Saint-Luc, a professor at the Sorbonne. The abbot's letter merits a partial quotation:

> By letters of a friend I heard what recently occurred in Padua, that is to say that the principal university of Italy has granted a degree to you for your superior knowledge and wanted to register you among its members. I couldn't let the occasion escape me to congratulate you on your accomplishment, an honor that you have deserved for some time, and to express my full approval regarding this decision of the famous university which, not held back by the opinions of common men, overlooking your gender, awarded you the insignia of men, wisely considering that your particular merit should be decorated with extraordinary honors and that in such a circumstance one need not seek a precedent, you yourself being without equal, having arrived at the apex of erudition and at the glory of knowledge. It seems to me, too, that in this event the university has given more to itself than to you,

preceding the other universities of the world which, no doubt, will approve and follow the judgment of the flourishing University of Padua, notwithstanding that they envy her glory for having given this example first. I salute you, oh glory of our century.[48]

After so many emotional days, Elena could finally return to her family in Venice. It would be a brief visit, since toward the end of 1679, Elena moved permanently to Padua. On January 1, 1680, she received at her beautiful palace a visit from Cardinal d'Estrées, who had come purposely to see her and listen to her.

6

ELENA CORNARO PISCOPIA: SCHOLARLY WOMAN

REPERCUSSIONS OF ELENA LUCREZIA'S DEGREE

By obtaining a doctoral degree, not only did Elena Lucrezia begin a new period in her life, she also established a precedent for the aspirations of every woman who sought official acknowledgement of her educational accomplishments. In fact, a few months after that great event, a professor of the University of Padua, Carlo Patin, began explorative paperwork to have his eldest daughter, Carla Gabriella, obtain her degree.[1] Probably since the day of Elena's graduation, Patin, who attended the ceremony, had envisioned having his daughter obtain a doctorate and had received from some colleagues a promise to support his initiative. Indeed, it seems that he intended to avail himself even of the assistance of Rinaldini, Elena's sponsor, who, for the most part, appeared disposed to cooperate.

From the time of Elena Cornaro's degree, the opposition of Cardinal Gregorio Barbarigo to any sort of degree for women had aroused in the university community the fear that other young women would aspire to high academic honors without fully deserving them. A few months after Elena Lucrezia's exceptional recognition, that very fear was expressed officially. On February 7, 1679, the Reformers of the University sent an admonition to the rectors, i.e., the two Venetian governors, of Padua directing them to rebuff any young women who aspired to some sort of degree, and they severely rebuked the professors of the university who had undertaken to support them: "they must not admit females under any circumstance to the doctoral degree, nor take steps which lead toward this end without previous notice and agreement by our magistracy."[2]

I think this provision sought to preclude Carla Patin's doctorate, which Procurator Cornaro opposed; he may have been the principal inspiration or quasi-instigator of the Reformers of the University of Padua. Cornaro saw in Carla Patin an unworthy rival to his daughter Elena and thought that her doctorate would diminish both Elena's glory and the prestige of his entire family. Furthermore, he considered the suspected participation of Rinaldini in the project a personal offense. He therefore blocked its realization by shrewdly provoking the admonition sent by the Reformers of the Paduan University. A few days after that official document, Cornaro, in a long letter of February 27, 1679, arrogantly explained to a professor of Padua that Rinaldini was the reason for his opposition.[3] Cornaro's letter captures well his singular personality. In presenting the entire event, he offers interesting particulars on Elena Lucrezia and also reveals, with questionable objectivity, unpublished aspects of Patin's life and certain of his ideas about the University of Padua where he taught. Cornaro recognizes Patin's undeniable erudition as a collector of coins and recalls the assistance given to him in establishing himself in Padua after his flight from Paris; yet he is amazed that Patin, after stating that he had never encountered, in his numerous trips throughout Europe, a woman as learned as Elena Lucrezia, and having never spoken of either his wife or his daughters as learned individuals, should now request that one of his daughters receive a degree.[4] He continues:

> and yet, as is known, [Patin] is a great bragger about himself and his things while diminishing the virtues of others, which he is convinced he possesses to the highest perfection: things which are well known to all the world and not unknown to that city, nor to that University and to the lecturers of the same institution of whom he has always spoken disrespectfully, and particularly so of the Grand Treasurer of Poland, who, wishing to have a consultation with the professors of medicine of that University concerning the illness of his daughter, Signor Patin stated that he was extremely knowledgeable, while the others were truly ignorant, something of which Your Excellency is better informed than anyone; while being a very worthy lecturer at such a famous University, even at the present time, to obtain his own end, he flatters everyone. I know not what possessed him and why he has resolved to send his daughters to Padua, removing them from a far-off monastery in Paris several leagues atop a mountain where they had been for some time; they arrived in Padua last October, as is known, and thus suddenly Signor Patin spread the word of the virtues he supposed his eldest daughter Carla Gabriela to possess, so that he has taken a fancy to having his daughter receive

a doctorate in that University, bypassing his very famous Sorbonne, but desiring first to have her reach intermediate goals in philosophy as a preparation for the doctorate: a thought instigated by those, who for their indirect end would enjoy such an action; for which he invited several gentlemen lecturers of the University, among whom, as he said (and there are witnesses) that Your Excellency had not only to argue with him, but then bestow the degree, saying that you gave her your word.

Remembering the opposition to Elena's degree from the Paduan university community (Cardinal Barbarigo?), which feared discrediting itself by conferring the degree on a woman, Cornaro proceeds, saying that those who are encouraging Patin are wrong to do so. He expresses amazement at the ease with which Carla Patin's candidacy was accepted: no one had ever heard of her; she was poorly educated in a monastery outside of Paris; now she comes to Padua as a scholar for a degree. He adds sarcastically:

> But reflect upon this: that in Paris and in all of France, the country of his birth, the qualities and abilities of that young girl were well known and only a little time had passed since she left the monastery, whence reflecting on the amount of time which passed when our Lord Jesus Christ, having instructed His Apostles for a few years, after His death, infused knowledge and tongues into them by means of the Holy Spirit, of whom Patin was the monkey; so that you might laugh and joke that this girl, without teachers, by virtue of her father, miraculously came to possess knowledge; from which would issue the question of which virtues are possessed by those who receive a doctoral degree from such a university.

Cornaro asserts that if Carla Patin were to obtain a doctorate, the fame of his Elena Lucrezia would be compromised, that she would be judged to be at the same cultural level as the French woman, something unthinkable after so many testimonies written by illustrious persons and cardinals, like Bouillon, Delfino,[5] and Cardinal d'Estrées, who had come purposely to see and speak with Elena Lucrezia and later spread her fame throughout Europe. And he continues, with malice:

> This monkey business of Signor Patin should not surprise us, since his means of proceeding even against his own Lord and King has brought him disgrace and exposed him to the mockery

of being burned in effigy and having his goods confiscated; whereby he is exiled from his homeland, and while he should be showing respect to those who deserve it, and proceeding with the necessary reserve, he despises everyone; and even more willingly he does and will do this, while such actions he sees as being to his benefit rather than to his harm.

Excuse me, as I have said above, for this long, but necessary explanation for precise information, since otherwise I don't care about his procedures and similar attempts.

The letter concludes by expressing renewed sentiments of gratitude to the recipient, for the many kind gestures shown to himself and to his Elena Lucrezia, expressions which make us think almost certainly that this letter is addressed to Rinaldini.[6]

In the meantime, an anonymous letter was received by one of the Reformers of the University of Padua, but attributable to an authoritative member of the university, expressing amazement that this magistracy, worried about Patin's business, had attempted to pressure him in a letter of February 6, 1679, to support the request of Patin: "it is something I don't care much about, except the extent that it could be detrimental to the University and its reputation before the whole world, and not for the increased honor of those who are concerned." He further observed that Patin could spend his money in public service instead of wasting it on his daughter, and he should show himself to be a little more respectful toward the city of Padua which had welcomed him as a fugitive from his homeland, extending him kindness. Therefore, the anonymous writer advised against awarding a doctorate to Carla Patin, who if she were as deserving as her supporters claimed, could have obtained the degree in France.[7]

For his part, the enterprising Patin, without delay, had arranged everything for his daughter's doctorate. The preliminary discussions for the examination would take place at home or in the public library, or better still, in the government palace, "the conclusions being dedicated to the officials of the city. The participants are of three kinds in this city; either lecturers or friars or students. One finds many of the first who promise my daughter this honor, and it would be more dignified."[8]

But the governor of Padua, according to the instructions received from the Reformers of the Paduan University,[9] denied the authorization, declaring himself willing to grant it only if the instructions were revoked by the same Reformers.

Next, on February 29, 1679, Patin implored an influential person of Venice to have the decision of February 7 annulled.[10] But the revocation was not granted and therefore was not followed upon because the university held scrupulously to the established norms.

In order to establish scholastic studies and instruction appropriate for women, obstacles had to be removed and many confused ideas of a socio-religious nature had to be clarified. This was a pedagogical and moral polemic which took place over several decades around the middle of the eighteenth century after Antonio Vallisnieri had ignited it in the Accademia dei Ricovrati of Padua, proposing the thesis: "Whether women had to be admitted to the study of the sciences and the noble arts."[11]

When in 1740 Giovanni Nicolò Bandiera (1695–1761) published an anonymous book[12] in which he argued that the most difficult and demanding studies of philosophy, physics, and theology were worthwhile not only for men but also for women, he ignited many debates regarding the originality and broadmindedness of its theses, so much so that Rome attempted to place the work on the Index. For this acknowledgement of the capabilities of women, Bandiera was generally defined only as "a beautiful spirit," while L. A. Muratori, who had himself coined the phrase, judged the work negatively.[13]

THE ACADEMIC ELENA

Hostility toward women's studies was slow to subside. Half a century passed after Elena's degree before Laura Bassi became the first graduate of the University of Bologna, May 12, 1732, and a century later Pavia had its first woman graduate in the person of Maria Amoretti, June 25, 1777.[14] These examples emphasize the distinction of the University of Padua for having first given women access to studies and for recognizing women's intellectual capabilities by awarding the degree to Elena Lucrezia Cornaro Piscopia.

A decade earlier, though, she had already received an important acknowledgement with her induction into the Accademia dei Ricovrati of Padua, which was proposed in the private session of February 11, 1669: "This was harmoniously acclaimed verbally by all, without supplication of the Ricovrati Academy and thus was unanimously accepted."

The prince of the academy, Count Girolamo Frigimelica, gave the news to Elena on the very same day. In a letter from Venice, March 29, 1669, she responded with gratitude for the great honor of belonging to the illustrious society.[15] She assumed the academic name of "l'Umile" (the Humble One). The session was opened in Padua on November 25, 1599, by Father Federico Cornaro, a Venetian patrician who housed the academy for a while in his palace and called it "Cornara."[16] After various periods of prosperity and decline, in 1668 it was brought back to life by Vincenzo Contarini, captain of Padua, located first in the Sala dei Giganti (Hall of the Giants), and later in the Sala verde (Green Hall) of the Captain's Palace.[17]

At only twenty-three years of age, Elena was thus a member of the scholarly association to which her teachers, Alvise Gradenigo and Carlo Rinaldini, several university professors, and many other learned men belonged. Finding herself among such noble minds at such a young age caused her no discomfort, and the academy members recognized her as a woman with a keen intelligence, a vast educational background, and a dedication to intense study. She considered her membership in the academy a duty requiring the best of her own intellectual capacities in cooperation with the prestigious noble association. The Paduan Accademia dei Ricovrati, as respectable as it was, was not immune to the shortcomings of the numerous academies that had mushroomed in Italy. The decadence of nationhood was accompanied by frivolity in the literary field. If the academies of sciences and of music reached a high degree of development, the literary academies were reduced, for the most part, to gathering places for do-nothings, joined together in strange groupings, courting each other in turn with pompous verses and bizarre metaphors. By their names alone one can comprehend the vacuous nature of these associations.[18] Nonetheless, the academy was, at its best, a vehicle of education. The seventeenth century was a period of glorious scientific research, indicating a new direction and new goals to the academies. The Ricovrati in Padua, along with a few others, knew immediately how to make them their own.

Elena, though young, was nonetheless accustomed to evaluating things for herself. She was therefore very cautious in accepting the offers of membership directed to her by several other academies. She chose intelligently to accept membership in the Accademia degli Infecondi of Rome, started at the beginning of the seventeenth century, with the name of "Inalterabile"; the Accademia degli Intronati in Siena, founded in the middle of the thirteenth century or later;[19] the Accademia degli Erranti in Brescia, founded in 1619; and two Venetian academies, Dodonea and Pacifici. She presented three scholarly discourses at the Pacifici and became its president in 1670.[20]

Elena displayed her educational accomplishments at other venues as well. For example, the important philosophical debate which she held on May 30, 1677, in the hall of the Procuratie of San Marco with the young Greek Giovanni Gradenigo and two valiant philosophers, Father Fiorelli, an Augustinian, and Cano, a Somaschan, is comparable to an academic session. Elena conducted her discussion in either Latin or Greek, both of which she used so proficiently that the crowd in attendance—the complete senate, nobles, scholars, and foreigners who had come to Venice for the traditional Festa della Sensa—was amazed.[21] Elena also held debates and scholarly conversations in response to her father's wishes. Important people passing through Venice sought to visit her, while others came from afar just to experience personally her exceptional cultural attainments. In 1670 she was visited by Cardinal Langravio of Assia, with whom she discussed with great ease the geometric-astronomical properties of the sphere.[22] In 1677, Cardinal Bouillon, almoner and counselor to the king of France, came, according to the wishes of his sovereign, to Venice from Rome, where he had participated in the conclave of the preceding year. Two scholars from the University of Paris accompanied him, Carlo Cato de Court and Lodovico Espinée, with whom he was to test Elena's knowledge so that he could convey his impressions to the king. The cardinal, well versed in the sacred and profane sciences, was amazed by his conversation with Elena, and in a gesture of esteem, gave her his portrait as a gift. From then on he spoke everywhere of the great erudition and virtues he perceived in the young, noble Venetian woman, and he continued to correspond with her. Elena later had recourse to him on behalf of Professor Carlo Rinaldini.[23]

The marvelous things about Elena Cornaro recounted by Bouillon in France occasioned, a few years later, another important visit, this time by the French cardinal, César d'Estrées.[24] This able diplomat, sent to Rome by King Louis XIV to negotiate with the pope on the question of the *regalìe*,[25] went to Padua to verify whether all the great things said of Elena Lucrezia Cornaro Piscopia were true. The cardinal arrived in Padua with his entourage on the first day of 1681 (1680 by the Roman calendar). According to a description written by a family member of the Cornaro household, the reception, in keeping with the custom of the times and the prestige of the procurator Cornaro, was worthy of the cardinal. These two men, after a private encounter with Elena, introduced the people of the cardinal's retinue to her, including two doctors of the Sorbonne. The conversation immediately took on a scholarly tone. Elena Lucrezia read and commented on the passages from Socrates presented to her in their Greek texts, as she did also with readings in Hebrew, and she continued by speaking in French, Spanish, and Latin. She also gave a musical display on the organ and pedal harpsichord.

To dispel any suspicion of exaggeration in a description made by a member of the family, we do well to read the description of Father Tommaso Maria Peyre, a Dominican who was accompanying Cardinal d'Estrées. In a letter written to a Somaschan friend, Father Giovanni Maria Foresti, the day after the visit, Peyre reports very soberly the impressions of the cardinal and his retinue:

Dearest Master,

My illness caused by a bit of fever forbade me yesterday to be at a conference which I truly hoped to attend. The Cardinal d'Estrées, after paying his devotion to the Saint and respect to Cardinal Barbarigo, had no other desire in this city than to admire the virtue of the most illustrious Elena Cornara Piscopia, whose reputation carried her praises to him. And so, having put his thought into action, he went to visit this lady, and from what His Eminence told me, he recognized that her virtues surpass her fame, not only in the skill of so many languages, but in the depth of many speculative, moral, and historical disciplines; and he told me that this was someone capable of attracting any great person from the most remote parts of the world, and that he was leaving enraptured, to sing her praises everywhere. The same evening in an Academy the most learned lady gave a very elegant eulogy lauding his Eminence, which he thoroughly delighted in, and he was applauded by all. In these particulars I have had consolation, as you might imagine, since I have always held in homage such great virtue. I felt it was a good idea to communicate this to you briefly because I am ready to depart, weakened as I am by the recent fever.

With affection, and a heartfelt embrace, I remain

Your ever obsequious and obliging servant
F. Tomaso Maria Peyre.[26]
Padua January 2, 1681

The academy session mentioned in the letter took place in the Accademia dei Ricovrati and was an extraordinary one, held in honor of the cardinal and organized by the association and not by Procurator Cornaro, as was erroneously written and repeated.[27] Elena Lucrezia participated in an academic capacity and not because the session was organized by her father. After discourses by three academy members on the subject of the comet which had recently appeared, a musical concert was held and many Latin and "Tuscan" poetic compositions were recited. Elena read a eulogy in honor of the cardinal, who then wanted it as a keepsake. A ball followed which Elena did not attend. D'Estrées spent the night as a guest of Cardinal Barbarigo in the episcopal residence, and the next day he departed for Rome.[28]

Even aside from her academic activities, Elena Lucrezia's dedication to scholarship continued. After her degree, it became her sole occupation, almost a vocation. Her only impediment was her fragile physical condition, which had grown worse under the strain of preparing for her doctorate. Padua appeared to be the most appropriate place to both satisfy her cultural desires and deal with her unstable health. Her father decided toward the end of 1679 to have her reside in his palace in Padua in the Santo district, currently via Cesarotti. The famous Alvise had beautified it and lived there. He then left it as an inheritance to his grandson Giacomo Alvise, who in turn left it to his son Girolamo. The building then passed on to his only surviving son, Giovanni Battista, Elena Lucrezia's father.

ELENA'S RESIDENCY IN PADUA AND HER STUDIOUS LIFE

The Cornaro residential complex comprised four buildings forming a quadrangle. Facing the street was what Alvise called the *casàsa vechia* (old house); behind it is a building with a balcony; on the right side, the *odeon* or lodge; on the left, the *casa nuova* (domus nova or new house); and in the middle, a wide courtyard or *cortile*. The *casàsa vechia* was made up of what Alvise had inherited from his maternal uncle, Don Alvise Angelieri, which he had planned to enlarge with the acquisition of a few smaller, adjoining houses, incorporating them into the main house so as to obtain "the most beautiful house in all the cities of Italy."[29] It was a spacious house with numerous rooms, also called *casa dipinta* (painted house) because the facade was covered with frescoes by Girolamo del Santo, and a small chapel annexed to it was painted by Falconetto.[30]

This house, however, was not destined to remain the permanent residence of Alvise Cornaro. When a new building was built on the left side of the courtyard that was incompatible with the other two (the one with the balcony and the lodge, which were comfortable and appropriate for such a gentleman), Cornaro withdrew to the silent interior of the courtyard of the *domus nova* to live alone with his bride Veronica Spilimbergo (or Agugia).[31] The spacious *casàsa vechia* he reserved for famous guests and as a barrier against the noise of the street. This was a peaceful and comfortable environment enlivened by the gardens, lungs of greenery, which Cornaro called *la anima di essa casa* ("the soul of this house").[32] To enlarge them he obtained, on August 20, 1535, from the Conventual friars, as a perpetual claim, a wide strip of land situated behind the apse of the basilica, bordered on one side by the road (via Cesarotti) and on the other by the river, up to Pontecorvo.[33] Cornaro, a fervent reclaimer of land, transformed this property, not very fruitful in the hands of the friars, into a huge garden to which one had access from the lodge by means of an underground passageway (about 50 meters long). In the southern part of the garden, a staircase to the river enabled Cornaro and his guests to come and go through the huge garden, boarding and disembarking in absolute privacy.[34]

The famous Alvise Cornaro lived and died in this little castle, as did his grandson and heir, Giacomo Alvise; his great grandson Girolamo; and for almost five years, until her death, Elena Lucrezia. It is not surprising that she preferred the interior courtyard section of the house, that is, the *casa nuova*. This location was ideal for a studious woman who loved the quiet life and was, moreover, a Benedictine oblate, which put her in a spiritual state of consecration to God, although she continued to live in the world.[35] The new house in the courtyard, protected by the old house against the noise and distractions of the street and the surrounding district, looked like an immense cloister, and because the other buildings in the quadrangle were not used, the area maintained a quiet, almost monastic calm, broken only rarely when the noblewoman had to receive distinguished persons and scholars. This house, therefore, was not only appropriate but ideal for Elena.[36]

In this environment she consecrated herself—this is the right word—to her studies, neglecting neither the means nor the people to expand her knowledge. At the same time, she would temper her intellectual efforts with works of piety and charity. This was the program of her life. In Padua it was known that the Cornaro palace was not serving as a literary salon, but as a refuge for a young noblewoman immersed in her studies. Immersed to what degree? No one can tell us better than the man who directed her philosophical studies for years and had prepared her for the doctorate.

Professor Carlo Rinaldini attests that Elena dedicated herself to studying "more than necessary."[37] The teacher-student relationship which had bound Elena to Rinaldini in preparing for her degree now transformed itself into the pursuit of common cultural interests, favored by her residence in Padua. In a letter to Cardinal Bouillon from Padua, September 5, 1681, Elena writes of having entrusted all her studies to the guidance of Rinaldini, "a rare man, truly complete, one among the most illustrious in the sciences."[38] In their frequent meetings Elena, anxious to deepen her own philosophical and mathematical knowledge, sought to learn more and more from him. She even urged him to continue his scientific research. In fact, Professor Rinaldini needed this stimulation. Often when one is skilled in the speculative realm, one is inept, more or less, in practical things. Rinaldini was timid and awkward in character, often disoriented if faced with difficulty. When, for example, he had to go to Venice for a hearing concerning a servant who had robbed him, he seemed almost desperate, unable to think of anything else; he could not believe that a servant, whom he assumed to be loyal, could have betrayed his master. Naiveté. They both speculated—he upon philosophy, the servant on the purse of his philosophical master.

Elena was worried that Rinaldini, distracted by this theft, would lose interest in their intellectual pursuits. She therefore wrote to him at the home of her father in Venice, December 13, 1681, to reprimand him gently for not having yet completed certain scientific works. She then insisted that he return to Padua to fulfill the promise he made to her of publishing those works, and she pointed out that scientific speculations do not exempt us from facing the reality, at times bitter, of daily life. The professor responded, acknowledging that he was remiss about finishing the second part of the philosophical work, and he apologized, observing that, due to the theft, he had for a long time been unable to immerse himself calmly and profitably in studying. He concludes by promising to complete his work soon so as to dedicate it to her as his Minerva, his inspiration and stimulus.[39] Rinaldini's esteem for Elena as a studious and learned woman was longstanding. Since 1668 he had been composing a scientific treatise primarily for her, writing that among the innumerable disciples he had had during his long teaching career, no one surpassed Elena Lucrezia, whose intelligence he compared, in the style of Virgil, to a cypress fanning out above scant shrubs.[40]

Eager for Rinaldini to publish his scientific studies, Elena had written to Cardinal Bouillon in Paris on her own initiative at the beginning of May 1681, asking him to obtain permission for Rinaldini to dedicate a new philosophical work to King Louis XIV, which was granted on May 14, 1681.[41] The following September, she again wrote to the cardinal to advise him that upon its printing, the king would be sent the first volume of Rinaldini's work. She assured him that the book dealt with profound thought, where didactics, rhetoric, and poetry were developed by a man skilled in the subjects. She also promised to send him, when it was printed, the second volume, containing Aristotle's *De Natura* with a competent commentary by Rinaldini and not a poor one, as was the case with so many other facile commentators.[42] Cardinal Bouillon, returning to Paris after having accompanied the king on his military campaign against Strasbourg, replied on November 14, 1681, that he awaited the volume with avid curiosity and he would present it to the king. He assured her that Rinaldini was so well-known in Europe that he needed no special praise and that the king would surely appreciate the gift because it was sent by her: "You, in the meantime continue, as you have done thus far, to love and protect learned men, among whom you yourself, with your elevated genius and indefatigable studies, have earned an honor and a name unique in all the literary world."[43]

Finally, after a delay in the Parisian customs offices, the volume reached the cardinal, who hurried to present it to the king and to write to Elena from Paris, on April 5, 1682, expressing the full gratitude of the sovereign, who announced that he was sending, by means of the new French ambassador to Venice, a gift for Rinaldini.[44] On December 22 he wrote from Versailles that the king, instead of entrusting the promised gift to his ambassador, preferred to send it to her so that she could give it to the author personally. The gift consisted of a gold necklace with a medallion weighing a pound and a half, a sign of gratitude from the king of France to Rinaldini for having dedicated his work to him.[45] In those days, Rinaldini was still in Venice for the suit against his servant thief. Elena therefore informed him of the cardinal's letter and congratulated him for having earned the favor of the cardinal by his personal merit, but also "by my recommendation: in fact I did not neglect to say everything I had to on your account." She assures him that the cardinal would not be remiss in presenting to the king

> the volume of the philosophical work, produced by your fertile muse Minerva in which you spoke in such an erudite and knowledgeable fashion that I seem to be in Aristotle's school in Athens when I read those pages so dense with thought. Come now, have courage! Finish the second part. Your treatise on physics is especially awaited by all. It is awaited because we have realized that when in nature a disturbing phenomenon occurs, you with your experiments on nature are capable of explaining it, something which we didn't learn from other teachers. Nonetheless, I willingly await the delay of this work because I know you are engaged in the publication of the third and last part of your *Analysis*.[46]

In the same letter she insists that he try to conclude the trial against the servant quickly so he can put the finishing touches on that philosophical work, which she hopes is written in a clear style and is as free of trivial ornament as were the previous ones. Once again she repeats: "I am overcome by a great desire for this work, as I was with the others."

Even during Rinaldini's absence, Elena does not relent in her tireless pursuit of learning, which for her, already suffering physically, becomes a burden, almost a harsh labor, sweetened by brief intervals of music, as much as was necessary to relieve her cultured soul.[47] It is work that fills all her days; she is sustained by the knowledge that she is walking her chosen path, from which she does not intend to waiver for any reason. To this end, in a confidential outburst, almost a confession, she writes to Rinaldini: "As you and almost everyone knows, I have reached and will never abandon my literary Sparta, and as Cicero says, even if I should be abandoned by it, I nonetheless will stand firm in my first decision, as the right thing and proper to my occupation and especially to my way of life."

Then, to motivate the teacher to a swift return to his intellectual labors, she writes that if his courtesies regarding her were truly sincere, there is no need for her to insist any further. She expects only that he prove it to her. To the clear reasoning of his student, Rinaldini could only answer by returning to Padua and his studies, realizing that he was never better off than when he could enjoy conversation with this young woman, a true honor to the female sex.[48]

At this point we may ask, did her tenacious application derive from a natural and spontaneous inclination, or rather from the continuous stimulus of her proud father, obsessed by the desire to increase the honor of the family through his daughter's intellectual accomplishments? Both motivations are valid. As I noted above, on the day she received the doctorate, Rinaldini publicly acknowledged Elena's natural inclination to scholarship. But certainly her father's ambitions were also a factor. Nonetheless, an excessively severe judgment of Cornaro would be unfair. Elena herself treated these paternal sentiments with indulgence and showed that she understood them and wanted to comply with them as far as her weakened condition would allow. As she recovered from her exhausting work in preparation for her examination, she wrote to her father from Padua, July 6, 1680, saying that due to the kind care of her physicians, she felt strong enough to be able to resume her studies soon so as "to redeem from the destruction of time the name of our house."[49]

ELENA'S WRITINGS

Elena never had the slightest intention of making any specific contributions to the development of letters or the sciences by virtue of her studies. She was too modest to entertain such ambitions. Her only goal was to satisfy an innate desire for knowledge and to comply with the ambitious yet understandable aspirations of her father. She had no desire to establish herself in the world through her erudition, nor did she wish to be known to posterity as a woman of letters. She wrote literary compositions, but only for her own personal enjoyment or to please her parents, her family, and her friends, and always with the intent that they remain strictly private. During her last illness, in fact, she entrusted Maddalena with the task of destroying, immediately upon her death, all her writings and instruments of penance. Unfortunately, the order was carried out punctually.[50] The few writings that survived were saved due to her father's love or the foresight of the people who had received them. Her four academic discourses were preserved because they were stored in the archives of individual academies.

These observations may help to dispel the disappointment of some and the harsh judgments of others: disappointment in those who expected of Elena a quantity of writing proportionate to her long and varied studies; harsh judgments on the part of those who expected a rigorous and severe criticism of her to decide whether she merits a place among the learned.

Elena completed her first literary work in 1669, when she was twenty-three: an Italian version of the first Spanish translation[51] of the ascetic work, *Alloquium Jesu Christi ad animam fidelem* (Exhortation of Jesus Christ to a Devout Soul) written by a Carthusian monk, Giovanni Lanspergio (1489–1539). It is a beautiful and pious letter of Jesus Christ to a soul desirous of serving him faithfully and perfectly, worthy of comparison to the best compendium of ascetic theology and to the illustrious pages of the *Imitation of Christ*. Considered the principle work of Lanspergio, it spread quickly in the vernacular of all the European nations. Elena's translation is one of three Italian versions known to date.[52] Elena dedicated it on the feast of St. Ignatius Loyola (July 31), founder of the Society of Jesus, to Father Giampaolo Oliva, Father General of the order, as an acknowledgment for having provided her two Jesuit fathers, one as a spiritual director, the other as a teacher for her literary and scientific studies. In the preface, she warns the reader to pay close attention to the text, which offers a literal translation as the best way of expressing the thoughts of the author, giving special care to the phrasing and placement of periods. She then apologizes for the inevitable typographical errors, since, at this time, typographers possessed only technical abilities. Printers of the quality of Manuzio and the Giolito, who were not only technicians, but also educated men capable of correcting the author's work and therefore of producing very accurate typography, had disappeared.

What led Elena to translate this work? Certainly it was not the desire to show off her knowledge of Spanish. She wished rather to reveal, albeit indirectly, the program of her spiritual life as a Benedictine oblate and her intention of leading a cloistered life within her family when circumstances made it impossible for her to enter the seclusion of a convent. This little book seems to have been translated precisely to sustain and direct her in achieving this goal.[53] It was favorably received by the public and enjoyed the success of five editions.[54]

Since chronological order is not always possible, I have grouped Elena's other surviving writings according to their genre:

Translation of a small work from Spanish (1)
Academic discourses in Italian (4)
Letters in Latin and Italian (30)
Petitions to the pope (2)
Eulogies in various languages (11)
Epigrams in Latin and Greek (5)
Acrostic, in French (1)
Sonnets in various languages (6)
Odes (1)

In the four academic discourses, three published and one unpublished, delivered probably between 1670 and 1672, frequent historical, literary, and philosophical quotations and constant scientific and artistic references form a sort of loom upon which Elena, with an expert hand, weaves her compositional pattern and offers the wisdom of her vast erudition.

The first discourse, *In lode della serenissima Repubblica e città di Venezia* (In praise of the most serene republic and city of Venice), she delivered on the occasion of her acceptance into the Accademia dei Pacifici in Venice, as was the custom.[55] The question posed to her was: "Se sia di maggior danno ad un regno il troppo lusso o la crapula?" (Whether too much luxury or heavy drinking be of greater harm to a kingdom?). After recalling that love of country is a sentiment capable of inspiring even the sacrifice of one's own life, she moves on to historical references, affirming that in Venice, luxury and drinking never had a firm foundation, even if at times they manifested themselves in notable measure. Noble Venetians never sought refuge, she affirms, from the sacrifices war imposed upon them by indulging in sensual pleasures, or gluttony or drunkenness. The country was justifiably proud of the wisdom of its senators and the valor of its military commanders. These two categories of citizens always consulted together to the point that, in time of need, the senator could transform himself into a valiant leader and the captain into an expert state's counsel. Wisdom and valor grew in the hearts of Venetians like twins. Tiny Venice became a great republic thanks to this collaboration between military valor and political wisdom, while Rome, capital of the world that it was, for lack of such collaboration, was reduced to an accumulation of ruins trampled on by curious visitors.

Her second academic discourse, on the proposition that "Chi aspira ad un posto di comando deve pensare agli obblighi che ne derivano per non esporsi al pericolo di esserne travolto" (He who aspires to a position of command must consider the obligations which derive from it so as not to expose himself to the danger of being overwhelmed), was presented by Elena in 1670 when she was installed as president of the Accademia dei Pacifici.[56] She asserts that even in her time, as always, men will sacrifice their own honor for the ambition of achieving power, the exercise of which seems to be a simple thing, but which in reality contains such difficulty as to render continually unhappy he who holds it. Just as every piece of wood is not suitable for making a statue, so not every man, even though he desires it, is qualified to govern. Governing is a difficult art but also a noble one, as long as the prince does not have recourse to methods drawn from Machiavelli's school, here justly condemned, but adheres rather to the advice of Seneca, who suggests a certain compliance with the aspirations of the populace (*De clementia* [On Clemency], I, 5). The days are long gone when kings and princes exchanged their scepters and crowns for a religious habit and traded their kingdoms for a monk's cell. Today, there is the race for power which only few know how to exercise in praiseworthy fashion, while the majority are incapable and, as Juvenal said, deserve censure.[57]

In conclusion, Elena proposes to the members of the academy the problem: "Whether the praise owed to a superior derives from his ability to govern or rather from the poor ability of some of his successors." After a few philosophical and historical arguments, she takes up a discussion of the true crux of this question, which she had proposed with a certain shrewdness yet without suggesting her motives to her colleagues. She felt obligated to highlight the enormous difference between her presidency and that of her predecessor, the Marquis Francesco Maria Santinelli, whose great moral figure shines even more brightly when compared to the imperfections of a miserable creature such as herself. She exalts the merits of Santinelli at length and diminishes her own, according to the philosophical maxim *opposita iuxta se posita magis elucescunt* ("they shine brighter who have placed themselves next to their opposites").[58] Those who know the profound modesty of Elena Lucrezia understand that these expressions are not the usual self-serving rhetorical phrases, but are the sincere convictions of her noble soul.

A third academic discourse, given by Elena during her presidency of the Accademia dei Pacifici, was political in nature: *Esistenza di una concordia discordante nelle cose sensibili e nelle insensibili dalla quale ha origine armonica consonanza* (The existence of a discordant agreement in sentient and insentient things from which harmonic consonance has its origin).[59] She omits the consideration of the true substances from different elements, among which are the flowers, herbs, fruit, metals, and animals, and prefers to use as an example the human body. She proceeds, therefore, to a minute description of the separate anatomical parts which, although very diverse among themselves, come together to form a harmonic and almost perfect unit. She shuns the theory of chemists according to which all matter is composed of sulfur, salt, spirit, earth, and water and holds as more valid the Aristotelian theory of fire, water, earth, and air. Elena suggests three subjects in demonstration of discordant concordance: music, astronomy, and theology, themes which are particularly dear to her and which she speaks of almost with lyricism. She then subjects the academy members to a discussion of the enquiry: "Whether a captain of the army, to calm a rebellion by his soldiers, must use pacifist or penal means against the guilty?" Pointing out various solutions, Elena quotes Aristotle, according to whom the task of judge is only as difficult as is necessary, since the human soul, which should be free from every stain, often is, unfortunately, an imprisoned flame in this body of mud, precluding it from shining and acting as a spirit, dragging it to excesses. She recognizes being still in the world of the Costantinis, of humane and pacifist governors, but she points out that "present day Neros are not lacking."

As for herself, Elena declares that she wants to remain loyal to the noble Venetian traditions in which she was educated, tested for centuries by the experience of illustrious geniuses: she intends to judge with that clarity and justice to which she has always felt inclined. In her opinion, the captain must know how to use, toward his own undisciplined soldiers, at times a simple threat, at other times, prudence. To this end she introduces the example of two animals, the porcupine and the elephant, the first of which, according to the beautiful description of Claudiano, defends itself from tormentors by raising the quills on its back, while the elephant, as wittily observed by Lucano, with a phlegmatic shake removes the arrows that cover its back.[60]

The fourth academic discourse, on Our Lady of the Snows, still unpublished, was composed by Elena in 1672 on the occasion of her induction into the Accademia degli Infecondi in Rome.[61] This academy, offspring of the Confraternity of Our Lady of the Snows, is located in the College of the Barnabites in the Church of San Carlo at Catinari and used to celebrate its patron's feast on August 5. Elena was charged with composing the inaugural discourse of the academic year which, according to custom, was to be presented upon her entrance as a member. In fact, she sent it from Venice and had it recited in Rome by another person for the solemn gathering on the evening of August 4, 1672.[62]

Her introduction is entirely full of humility, even if the rhetorical figure she chose to display it is affected by the style of the times. Elena expresses, namely, the hope that the luminosity of the snow will give some light to her eloquence, though she fears that the saying of Anassagora will come true—that the snow may not be white, as it seems to the eye, but black and overshadowed by the clouds, "since, mistreated by my words, the prodigious snow of the Esquiline Hill naturally appears blackened to your eyes."

After developing these concepts in prose which, if not immune to the defects of the century, at least tempers them with an innate sense of meter, Elena extolls the admirable works of God in creation, from which emerges the mystical snow, "that is the Virgin herself." She concludes the discourse with a eulogy to the illustrious Roman academy.

A literary production of a totally different nature left to us by Elena consists of thirty letters, sixteen published and fourteen unpublished. Thirteen of the unpublished ones, all in Italian, are addressed from Venice (April 18, 1671–December 18, 1677) to Cardinal Francesco Barberini in Rome. They primarily concern her family or the ecclesiastics and laymen under her protection; in only one, on October 12, 1674, does she request some bibliographical information about the publication of the Greco-Latin works of a Father of the Church.[63] Another unpublished letter, without a date, is addressed to Antonio Grimani, procurator of San Marco, requesting a private conversation with him about a delicate matter which she did not wish to present to him by means of a third party.[64]

Also among these letters are two brief petitions or supplications addressed to Pope Clement X in 1670 and in 1674 seeking permission to visit a few of the convents in Venice several times a year, as well as the one in San Matteo on the Island of Murano where one of her sisters and some close relatives lived as nuns. Permission was granted with a few conditions and limitations.[65]

Among the published letters are the three written in Padua to her father in Venice between July 6 and August 23, 1680. Couched in elegant Latin—an easy task for her—they tell us that her father was also proficient in this language, since he was able to read them. They are all intimate and familial in nature. Elena informs him of her health, her studies, the sultry season, or she expresses joy over the pregnancy of her sister Caterina (married to Antonio Vendramin); she speaks of her concern about the aches and pains of her parents or the serenity of having her mother's company.[66] Four other letters of literary interest are addressed to Christopher Ivanovich, a canon at San Marco in Venice.[67]

She writes to Cardinal Bouillon, as described previously, to praise Rinaldini's soon-to-be-published books, and she writes to Rinaldini to solicit his return to Padua from Venice so that he may complete his scientific studies. Another letter is addressed to the Accademia dei Ricovrati in gratitude for having admitted her as a member.[68] Her correspondence with Giovanni Battista Becci, a Benedictine abbot, and the noble Frenchman, Antonio Erst, is purely a kindness.

The letters sent to Pope Innocent XI are congratulatory; those to Emperor Leopold I, Jan Sobieski (king of Poland), and to Carlo V (Duke of Lorena), transmit eulogies composed in their honor when Vienna was liberated from the Turkish siege (1683). Elena, moved by a sincere enthusiasm for the Christian victory, spontaneously translated the event into poetry, writing Latin *elogi* (eulogies) in epigraphic form, according to the custom of the time, and dedicating them to the aforementioned persons. These compositions, written purely to give vent to her emotions, fell into the hands of her father, who wanted them at all cost to be sent to their rightful owners and subsequently published. Elena obediently sent them with many other letters of homage, and received letters of praise from the pontiff and the other individuals.[69] There are, in addition, three other eulogies composed in honor of Cardinal d'Estrées; Silvestro Valier, a procurator at San Marco; and Angelo Sumachi, a Greek noble.

The occasion for which she wrote the eulogy for the cardinal has already been described. Its text contains references to the cardinal's piety, knowledge, nobility of birth, and merit for services rendered to church and country. As for Silvestro Valier, Elena recalls the dignity of his procuracy, his paternal zeal on behalf of her studies and the University of Padua, and his defense given to the Accademia dei Ricovrati.[70] Angelo Sumachi is honored on the occasion of his degree in medicine; she congratulates him on bringing great luster to his nobility through assiduous study and his doctorate, mentioning also the excellent qualities of his soul.[71]

A book in praise of Father Giacomo Lubrani, a Jesuit from Naples (1619–1693) and a famous preacher in Venice in 1675, contains about 50 poetic compositions, almost all about noble Venetians, as well as a preface by Elena and a group of poems (eulogies and sonnets) in all the languages known by her. She promoted this collection and took care of its publication.[72]

She wrote five brief essays of an epigrammatic nature: two (one in Greek and one in Latin) in praise of Giovanni Cornaro, lieutenant of Friuli, famous for having protected that region from the danger of the plague;[73] one for Sumachi's degree, on whose name and emblem Elena wittily writes verse;[74] and two others, respectively in Greek and in Latin, also called *octastici* and composed for the birth on July 26, 1678, of Prince Joseph James Ignatius, archduke of Austria, son of Emperor Leopold I, whom he succeeded as Joseph I.[75] A congratulatory acrostic must also be mentioned, written in 1679 on the name of Louis XIV, king of France and "peacemaker of Europe." Patin sent it to Claudio Caro Guyonnet de Vertron, historiographer of the king and member of the Accademia dei

Ricovrati in Padua, who published it in a literary collection on famous women of the century.[76]

The final surviving piece of Elena's writing is her *Ode to the Crucifix* written in 1680:

If the earth is shadowed, the sun is darkened
And from its original course its movement inverted;
Vacant is its seat,
Where previously it would cross the sky.
Nor for this I gaze with wonder;
That if suspended on a cross is a God who dies,
Better that the god of time die too.

The infinite made human now expires,
And thus is felt that which is ended;
And if the greater wounded
Fall, it is right, that also the lesser perish,
And within gray evening
The world should be in dark corruption steeped,
Having forged for itself eternal night.

Weep, all you people;
For the one who created you,
His son, amid torments,
Bore death for you.
Yet, ungrateful is man to his Redeemer,
Offending him with endless sin!
O iniquitous fate of the human race:
Which abandons life and chases after death![77]

In spite of its slight play on words and concepts, the ode is easily read even today. It seems to come from the heart, on a Good Friday, more out of pious sentiment and private devotion than the desire for publication. The manuscript was found by her brother Girolamo among Elena's papers after her death and given to Luisa Bergalli, who published it in a collection.[78]

We know of no other works by Elena that escaped destruction at the hand of the ever faithful Maddalena. Certainly there were more, but we cannot ascertain the exact number of those lost. It is true that Elena herself, in the dedication of her first literary work, the *Alloquium*, clearly expresses to Father Oliva her hope of being able to dedicate in the future an "even greater volume,"[79] and in the preface she says to the reader, "I beg you to bear with me to give me the will power for more copious labors."[80] Nevertheless, we do not know to what extent she may have realized this intention.

Mabillon states that during his visit to the Cornaro home in Venice, on May 27, 1685, he had occasion to see a great many (*permulta*) works written by Elena, and Lorenz specifies that a good part of them remained in manuscript form in the family library.[81]

There no longer exists even one letter of her correspondence with Father Oliva, Father General of the Society of Jesus, between 1600 and 1681, but only a rough copy of ten of Oliva's responses, from which we can infer the content of Elena's letters. These are about private matters, greeting cards, requests for a few books on piety and on sacred relics, appeals to ecclesiastics, information on Lenten preaching by Father Lubrani in Venice, and so forth.[82] These letters suffered the same fate as all private correspondence addressed to priests of the Society of Jesus. Until 1550, all correspondence was preserved in the archives of the Society, but from that time on, whenever a private letter was answered, the original was destroyed and there remained only a copy of the rough draft of the reply. Only the letters of cardinals, bishops, princes, sovereigns, and other important people continued to be preserved. Correspondence with private individuals was eliminated for two practical reasons: first, it had nothing to do with the central government of the Society and was therefore unimportant to the central archive; and second, because they wanted to eliminate from the ever increasing shower of letters those which did not directly concern the Society.

Father Oliva, in a reply to Giovanni Battista Cornaro on October 12, 1676, mentioned that he valued the letters when he refers to "your wise papers which you wrote to me and are kept by me as oracles of supreme prudence."[83] This may, however, have been merely an example of his diplomatic art. We know that Father Oliva was a master of the epistolary style, and that he knew how to express a "no" almost as if it were a "yes."[84]

THE VALUE OF ELENA'S WRITING

Detailed research does not show that any other compositions by Elena Cornaro have survived. Bacchini, in dedicating his collection of Elena's work to Vittoria Della Rovere-Medici, grand duchess of Tuscany, defines them as "fragments and remnants of a sudden shipwreck."[85] From Parma, on May 3, 1688, he sent a free copy of the book to Cardinal Francesco de' Medici (1660–1711), son of the grand duchess, politely begging him to be so kind as to read "pages which attest to the ability and erudition of a virgin, very well known to men of letters."[86] Armellini, though acknowledging Elena's limited output, nevertheless considers it sufficient to reveal her talent, erudition, and love for letters, by which he judged her worthy of being numbered among the writers belonging to the Benedictine Order.[87]

Other scholars, who have catalogued the life and works of major Benedictine writers, have considered only a few nuns worthy of mention. Yet they remember Elena Lucrezia Cornaro, to whom they devote a large space for biographical information and, although in an incomplete fashion, they list her writings, praising both their form and content.[88]

Even in the seventeenth century, many persons famous in the literary world were expressing their own judgment on Elena's writings and cultural attainments.[89] True, we are dealing with authors from an age known for its manner of praising, yet the judgments of Elena as a writer remain fundamentally acceptable. In fact, her writings reveal an expressive force, praiseworthy linguistic skill, great formal elegance, and an honesty of intention. Nevertheless, some critics, while admiring her as a woman of knowledge, confess that they cannot find the greatness that writers of the time (even exaggerating, as does Becci)[90] discerned in her.[91] In the opinion of Girolamo Tiraboschi (1731–1794), the hasty decision of her admirers and especially of her tenderhearted father to publish everything Elena had written dimmed her glory.[92]

I think that a careful sampling of the Greek or Latin essays would have better exhibited the elegance and robustness of Elena's literary style. She had assimilated these two languages so well that with the passing of the centuries, the essays have been considered almost constantly as of a classic level. Elena wrote and expressed herself with great polish in Greek and in Latin.

Even her Italian essays, especially her poetry and academic discourses, are generally well done both in language and content, though reflecting to a certain extent the defects of the seventeenth century—the "baroque" century, judged, perhaps too rigorously, as an era of bad taste and decadence. What first was an exception then became the fashion. Writing demanded far-fetched ideas and complicated metaphors.[93] Elena Lucrezia, raised and educated in that century, was its daughter even in this. It was impossible for her writing to be completely free of those stylistic defects. What is surprising is that she was affected only to a certain point, not out of place culturally or literarily in her century.[94]

This is the way she is perceived by A. Belloni, an authority on Italian literature of the seventeenth century. Against accusations that it was a barbaric period, he argues that one cannot call barbaric a century which can boast martyrs of scientific investigation such as Giordano Bruno, Tommaso Campanella, Friar Paolo Sarpi, and Galileo Galilei; a century which can take pride in promoting fertile currents of philosophy; in creating, with Alberigo Gentili (1552–1608), the theory of the rights of the people; in founding, thanks to its scientists, the experimental method; and in elevating, in the person of Elena Cornaro Piscopia, true miracle of universal knowledge, the intellectual and moral prestige of women.[95]

Another authoritative testimony on behalf of Elena as a woman of letters is furnished by Benedetto Croce (1866–1952) in an essay on the blossoming of Italian literature in monasteries and convents during the seventeenth century. Together with a few literary nuns, he mentions two "quasi nuns outside the monastery": Marta Marchina of Naples (1610–1646) and the "scholarly" Elena Lucrezia Cornaro Piscopia.[96]

It is true, however, that none of the seventeenth-century women writers can equal Vittoria Colonna (1490–1547), Veronica Gambara (1485–1550), or Gaspara Stampa (1523–1554) of the preceding century. Nevertheless, among the women of the seventeenth century, none enjoys more fame than Elena Cornaro, whose writings have real literary value.[97]

Contemporary eulogies deal not only with her literary works but also with her formidable erudition. Even to this day, the people of Venice continue to have a boundless admiration for their young compatriot. Whenever someone wants to comment on a woman's extraordinary knowledge, he exclaims, "La xe na Piscopi!" (She is a Piscopia!). Even when uttered with irony, it renders homage to a figure who honors Venice and Italy.[98]

7

Elena Lucrezia and the Demands of the Spirit

The Vow of Chastity

In the preceding chapter, I mentioned that Elena became a Benedictine oblate, totally consecrating herself to God. Before discussing this important act, we must take several steps back in her life in order to examine her alleged vow of perpetual chastity at the age of eleven.

According to Deza, who was the first to write of it,[1] the decision matured in Elena Cornaro when she read the biography of the Blessed Aloysius Gonzaga (1568-1591), in which she seemed to find significant analogies to her own spirituality. Elena was greatly moved when she read of the vow of chastity which he took at the age of nine on the feast of the Annunciation of Mary (March 25) and, in a burst of religious fervor, she decided to imitate him. Consequently, on March 25, 1657, she consecrated her virginity to the Lord, secretly in her heart, making what she considered to be a vow of perpetual chastity. She kept this decision strictly hidden even from those closest to her. Only a few years later, when her father was ready to contract her marriage to a German prince, did Elena herself reveal, amid tears, the existence of this "vow." Procurator Cornaro did not give up and, in order to achieve his goal, asked Pope Alexander VII to release his daughter from this bond.[2]

Deza's story of Elena's "vow" influenced everyone who wrote about Elena; although they might disagree on other points, they unanimously accepted the truth of this passage.[3] If, however, one takes even a cursory look at the theological principles and canonical legislation dealing with vows as spiritual obligations, many of Deza's statements seem questionable, if not untenable. I assume that such principles were in force during Elena's time; they are valid even today after the reform of the Code of Canon Law, except for some secondary regulations from the most famous theologian and canonist of the seventeenth century, the Jesuit Father Laymann, whose line of thinking could be considered as the official doctrine of the post-Tridentine church.[4]

A vow, a promise to God of a greater good which is pleasing to him, may be made by any human being who has reached the age of reason; its validity depends, however, on certain conditions established both by natural and ecclesiastical law. First, the person must have reached the age of puberty (fourteen for men, twelve for women) and must be of sound mind, not coerced by someone in a position of authority, for example, a child who is a dependent of a father or a guardian. According to principles of theology and also of current canonical legislation, the father, grandfather, or guardian can directly annul any vow made by a prepubescent child subject to their authority.[5] If there are no male relatives, the mother may do this.[6]

This digression is necessary in order to explain that Elena was incapable of taking a vow first, because she was not yet twelve, and second, she was a child under the authority of her father, without whose permission she could not assume any commitment. Even supposing that she had made a spiritual contract, her father had full authority to give her a dispensation from it. Therefore, this act must not be called a vow; it was, rather, a burst of fervor in a young heart, an irresistible longing for spiritual elevation.

The many events reported as consequences of Elena's supposed vow are thus to be considered without foundation: her father's request for a papal dispensation, the pontifical concession of such exemption, Elena's tears at the sight of that document, the attempts of an expert theologian purposely called by Cornaro to get the child to withdraw her intention, and even Elena's reprimands to the priest who tempted her rather than helping her as would have been his duty.[7]

To this series we must add Elena's persistent requests to her father to permit her to enter a religious order and the consequent embarrassment of the choice of the convent among those proposed by her parents. Elena supposedly resorted, according to Deza, to the naive means of a lottery, which produced the name of a particular convent that was at the time troubled with internal discord. Deza continues to affirm that Elena entered this convent, but after a few days she returned disillusioned to her family, dressed in her own clothes.[8]

The story sounds too much like a fairy tale to merit consideration. One may nonetheless observe that, if Elena knew of the discord in that convent, she would not have gone there. Furthermore, we cannot imagine what sort of experience of convent life she could have had in just a few days. If this were true, it would demonstrate that the child lacked discernment. Furthermore, Elena had no need to entrust her choice to a lottery since she could have easily entered the Benedictine convent of San Lorenzo where, among numerous young patrician nuns, was her cousin, Cecilia Cornaro, who later became the abbess.[9] That convent and its church, according to ancient tradition dating back to the sixth century,[10] besides being among the religious sites preferred by the nobility, enjoyed preeminence in Lenten preaching in Venice—it was customary to invite the most famous preachers, even at great expense, through the mediation of influential persons.[11]

Let us now consider the true nature of Elena's decision to remain a virgin. The only real motive for this decision was her desire to consecrate herself to God. However, the reasoning of some authors—that Elena, knowing the miseries of conjugal life, supposedly chose not to contract a marriage, but to take the habit and the vow of chastity—seems all too human to me.[12] One must remember how, in that era, the social evil of forced entrance to monastic life was rampant, done to protect the privileges of the firstborn son, or to avoid the unbearable condition of having an unwed daughter in the family. I don't think that Elena, by her choice of a monastic life, would have complied with the latter motive, which would have been contrary to her education, to her profound religious convictions, and to the esteem she showed for the cloistered state. Nor does another motive seem acceptable to me, which other authors consider of primary importance. Elena supposedly was forced to take the vow of chastity because of her inferior condition with respect to the Venetian aristocracy, being born of an "ignoble mother"; she was, therefore, excluded from the list of patricians.[13] True, Elena bore in her veins the blood of her father, an ambitious man who had intrigued (and paid) to obtain the noble title for his children. But she, being of a totally different nature, shied away from any desire for rank or fame.

Some writers have held that Elena took the vow of virginity very early on so she could focus on her studies without the problems and preoccupations of married life.[14] Perhaps it is more accurate to say that her choice was not taken in opposition to the value of marriage, but was a courageous decision undertaken to consecrate herself totally to the love of God. In addition, I think that reasons of health, although secondary, were also influential. Elena knew that convent life, if taken seriously, as it must be, demanded physical and moral sacrifices. She knew that she did not possess robust health, but was almost chronically ill and at times so disabled, as she herself confessed, that even writing a letter became impossible.[15] Her physical constitution would not have withstood the hardships of cloistered life, notwithstanding the generosity of her spirit. Supposedly her own parents persistently pointed out these difficulties to her. Therefore, Elena was increasingly convinced that she would be unable to undertake that particular way of life.

THE BENEDICTINE OBLATE

Anxious to find a solution to her problem, Elena must have discussed her situation with the venerable Benedictine Father Cornelio Codanini, abbot of San Giorgio Maggiore Monastery, a friend and frequently consulted confidant of the Cornaro family.[16] After mature reflection, he decided that becoming a Benedictine oblate would be the most appropriate means for Elena to reconcile her spiritual condition with the continuation of family life. He pointed out to her the many aspects of this Benedictine institution, but always with great respect and gentleness, in order to leave all decisions to Elena.[17]

The oblates are a large family which emerged simultaneously with the Benedictine Order. Although we cannot say that it was instituted by St. Benedict himself (the term "oblate" was initially reserved for the children offered to the monastery and destined to become monks [*Regula monasteriorum*, LIX]), the oblate's identity has been well defined since the seventh century.[18] At that time, besides the *famuli* (servants), a number of lay people, men and women, were admitted to the monasteries as permanent guests and under certain conditions; they were supervised by the abbot, who entrusted them with special tasks to be performed outside the monastery. Being an oblate had two distinct objectives: the offering of oneself through the promise of obedience or other vows and obligations, and the donation of all earthly goods and money, in addition to performing one's own job or craft. There were those who offered much, those who offered little, and those who, not having anything, offered only their own labor.[19] In exchange for the total or partial renunciation of their possessions, the oblates received lodging, food, and clothing from the monastery and were guaranteed assistance for the rest of their lives. They wore habits similar to that of the monks, they lived in seclusion in the monastery, and were called "resident oblates" or "religious."[20]

In all ages there have been examples of generous souls who, although they could not enter a monastery to lead a holy life, felt the need to offer themselves to God and to a monastic community with one or even all three religious vows. These were the "non-residential oblates" or the "seculars," who bound themselves to observe their vows as strictly as if they lived within the walls of the monastery, that is, just as their confreres or religious oblates observed them.[21] Princes, noblewomen, bishops, knights, and commoners listed in the registry of each monastery, were united by a religious tie to the monks, who considered them "brothers" and "sisters" living outside the monastery. At times, their profession of faith was made solemnly in the chapter room of the monastery, and in certain cases they received a religious habit to wear under their street clothes or on special occasions.[22]

The obligations and vows of the secular oblates varied according to their social condition and the limits imposed by their daily occupations. For example, widows and spinsters could commit themselves in ways which differed from a married person or a father of a family.[23] The oblates lived as much as possible under the direction of the monks, and some preferred to settle near the abbey so as to be able to participate in the psalmody of the monastic community. When near to death, the oblate was usually dressed in a religious habit, and he or she was buried in the cloister of the monastery. Masses were offered for the oblate as for the members of the community.[24]

The oblates were closely tied to the Benedictine Order, although the institution experienced periods of spiritual prosperity and of blight throughout its history.[25] One authoritative commentator writes that if the religious oblates who live the same life as monks under the Benedictine rule can be called part of the monastic fabric, the secular oblates or externals are to be considered as the fringe of this garment and belong, as the monks do, to the monastery where they became oblates.[26]

Elena understood that Codanini's proposal was just what she was looking for. She embraced it immediately, considering herself already an oblate while still awaiting the day when she could officially take her vows. With the enthusiasm of a nineteen-year-old, she thus pursued her spiritual projects, while her father wanted a splendid marriage for her. Every time he spoke to her about this, however, he perceived her revulsion and manifest disinterest. Later, when a German prince, as her first biographers write, asked Cornaro for his daughter's hand in marriage, he was greeted with enthusiasm. Motivated by his ambition, Cornaro welcomed the possibility of marrying his daughter to this famous individual. One day he confronted Elena to obtain her consent.

The young woman understood that the moment had arrived to perform the public act of becoming an oblate which, besides satisfying her spiritual needs, would also create an impediment to the nuptials. On the pretext of asking for advice, she went to San Giorgio Maggiore Monastery to see Abbot Codanini. She explained her grave anguish and requested permission to wear the black habit of the Benedictine sisters under her patrician garb and to take at his hand the vows of an oblate according to the rule of St. Benedict, while continuing to live at home. The man of

God, a connoisseur of souls, gave his consent. On that occasion, Elena took Scolastica for her name as an oblate, and from that time on she signed her letters, especially those directed to Benedictines, with the name Elena Lucrezia Scolastica.[27]

Thus Elena began her participation in Benedictine life. With reason, some authors call her "a religious of the congregation of Monte Cassino" and include her among the writers belonging to the Benedictine Order.[28]

Calling her "a religious" may seem a bit exaggerated, given that she continued to live at home and did not wear a religious habit. If this type of life appeared unusual, it was, nevertheless, accepted by the Church. Even the learned Benedictine Mabillon has no difficulty in considering Elena as a religious of his order. He says that during his visit to the Cornaro home in Venice, May 27, 1685, he saw the authentic document of her profession, which took place in 1665, and experienced great joy in learning that Elena had become his sister through that action.[29]

It is likely that she took her vows in the church of San Giorgio Maggiore, *ad aram maximam*[30] rather than at home, as her first biographers claim. They write that when Elena received what amounted to an ultimatum from her father concerning the engagement to the German prince she became very upset, and Cornaro supposedly asked Abbot Codanini to come to the house to advise her; she then took advantage of these circumstances to make her profession.[31] But this version seems highly improbable. This was neither the moment nor the appropriate place to perform such an important act. I don't think that with a troubled heart—and under the gaze of her father—it would have been possible for her to contract a sacred bond that demanded freedom and tranquility of soul. I believe, rather, that Codanini probably just reassured Elena with the promise of persuading her father to give her time to reflect. When she was ready to make her profession as an oblate, he would be waiting for her at San Giorgio Maggiore. It was written, in fact, that Elena ran to the monastery of San Giorgio to become an oblate.[32] From the information attested to by Mabillon it appears that Elena was accepted as an oblate *a patribus nostris*, that is, by the Benedictine community of San Giorgio, and that an official document was drawn up. True, this act took place privately, but with a certain dignity and not in the precipitous, clandestine way described by some authors. Elena preserved the document as a testament to her consecration to God. Inexplicably, it remained among her papers and thus it could be shown to Mabillon in 1685, a year after her death.

When her parents found out what she had done, they knew they had lost the battle and understood how inappropriate it had been to insist upon the marriage proposal. They resigned themselves to the knowledge that their daughter would never abandon them since she had chosen to live the consecrated life at home.

SPIRITUALITY

Although she was aware of the difficulties of reconciling freedom and comfort with the demands of monastic asceticism, Elena learned how to conduct her life with her family as if she were in a monastery. A true spiritual daughter of St. Benedict, she was always faithful to the obligations she assumed as an oblate.[33] If she left the house, her destination was almost always the San Giorgio Maggiore Abbey where she found spiritual renewal in the liturgy of the Benedictine religious community and the guidance of Abbot Codanini. According to some authors, these visits were frequent,[34] and Elena continued to consult the abbot even when in 1673 he was transferred to the monastery of Santa Giustina in Padua.[35]

When Elena settled in Padua, Codanini had become the abbot at San Faustino in Brescia; nevertheless, she found support for her spiritual life at Santa Giustina. She considered it to be her home, in a certain sense, and the monks were like her brothers.

Both monastic and intellectual life flourished at Santa Giustina, a result of the efforts of various abbots to maintain an excellent level of education.[36] A group of monks, some who belonged to Santa Giustina[37] and some who had come to Padua from other Benedictine monasteries to teach religious studies at the university,[38] honored that monastery and the Benedictine order with their virtue and culture. This was a notable attainment in Padua where, as in Venice and in many parts of Italy, the lifestyle of the clergy and religious did not always correspond with, but more often contrasted with, its ecclesiastical nature. Commoners and nobles alike, even if they went to church in great numbers and signed up for membership in various confraternities, left much to be desired regarding religious observance, since many were Christian more in name than in practice.[39]

Elena, a cultured and profoundly Christian woman, was able to reconcile her extraordinary application to her studies with an intense spiritual life. The testimony of her earlier biographers, although it should be used with caution, provides some descriptive details. They attribute to Elena interminable prayers, long fasts, the mortification of her body with hair shirts and other instruments of penance, expiatory vigils, alms without limit, tattered clothing, excessive leniency with her servants, decisions entrusted to lotteries as to the hand of Providence, and so on.

What explanation can there be for these statements? They would indicate that Elena's mind was searching for a mixture of religion and superstition. We might ask why her education did not succeed in freeing her from such a mentality but rather moved her to inflict wounds mercilessly on her own body. How does one reconcile true philosophy, with which she was imbued, with this superstition, or the cult of letters and sciences with such baffling behavior? Where was the exceptional intelligence universally attributed to Elena? We would have to conclude that all the laudatory things said and written about her were nothing more than blind enthusiasm.

I believe, instead, that Elena's soul, permeated with living faith, and her intelligence, nourished by her vast learning, made her consider things from a very elevated, spiritual point of view. The *naiveté* attributed to her may have been a pious attempt by her first biographers to elevate her image, while in reality they depreciated it. The most reasonable assessment of this aspect of Elena's life seems to be that of her first two biographers, Deza and Bacchini. Deza writes:

> But what this demonstrates above all is the flame of charity of that blessed soul, the very normal life which she led in her century, with the observance of the three vows of poverty, chastity, and obedience... her withdrawal was precisely that of a nun: she never went out for recreation and did so for visits only when obedience forced her to. She always wore next to her skin the Benedictine habit of heavy wool, and as far as possible, she observed all the order's rules, always persevering meticulously in the three vows.[40]

Bacchini added a few particulars. He writes that Elena faithfully observed the vow of poverty as an aspect of her life of consecration to God, imposing privations upon herself in order to be better able to help the poor and the infirm. Regarding her devotional practices, he mentions that there had been attempts to attract Elena toward quietism, a mystical practice which had developed in that century.[41] Elena defended herself saying that she was too weak for such elevated flights, preferring to walk on the ancient path of humble and trusting prayer. To this end some biographers state that she often recited the Divine Office, and when she could, she also went every day to the basilica of Santa Giustina to participate in the liturgy of the monks. Elena alternated meditation with various prayers approved by the Church. Her favorite devotions were to the crucifix, the Eucharist, the Blessed Mother, her guardian angel, St. Benedict, and the relics of the saints.[42]

Thus we may deduce that Elena's spiritual life rested upon two principles of Benedictine spirituality, that is, on the *opus Dei* (the divine office) and the *lectio divina* (spiritual reading). According to St. Benedict, all of the *opus Dei*, the preeminent work of God, is of paramount importance (*Regula monasteriorum*, L).[43] Spiritual reading is entirely oriented toward prayer (*Regula monasteriorum*, XLVIII). The monk's book is primarily the Bible, where he finds God's thoughts and the answer to his prayers. Furthermore, he discovers in it strength and security which no book of philosophy would ever provide.[44]

Elena's particular devotions follow the Benedictine tradition: the crucifix; the Eucharist; the Blessed Mother, whose cult is considered to be inseparable from that of her Divine Son; the angels in whose presence, according to St. Benedict, the monk recites the Divine Office (*Regula monasteriorum*, XIX) informing God of all his actions (*Regula monasteriorum*, VII).[45] The relics of the saints, which are the earthly remains of God's dearest friends—potent intercessors in paradise—are kept in the treasury, so-called because it contains what is, after the Eucharist, the major spiritual wealth of the monastery.[46] Obvious, too, is the Benedictine devotion to the members of its own religious family, in particular, to St. Benedict and the patron saints of the abbey.[47]

The Benedictine environments frequented by Elena in Venice and in Padua were monasteries that practiced the methods handed down by the reformer Abbot Ludovico Barbo in his classic treatise on prayer and meditation according to the spiritual current of the *devotio moderna*.[48] This work was certainly not unknown to Elena. Since 1669, in fact, she had worked on the translation of the *Alloquium Jesu Christi* (see chap. 6, sec. 4 above), a work that resembled *The Imitation of Christ*, the masterpiece of the *devotio moderna* throughout the centuries. One confirmation of the orientation of Elena's private piety toward the *devotio moderna* is the presence in her library of works by many writers of this spiritual current, among them Jean Gerson (1363–1429), Antonio de Guevara (1480–1545), and especially the Benedictines Johann Trithemius (1462–1516) and Francesco Ludovico Blosio (1506–1566). In fact, Elena possessed the complete works of the latter.[49]

In her prayer life, there was, however, no affectation or hypocrisy. She acted with great spontaneity and balance. Elena, as one author writes, wanted to be a religious, but in silence and with delicacy, without drawing attention to herself.[50] She was, in short, an ordinary girl, even though she lived spiritually in a manner that was not ordinary and in constant union with God.[51] She tried to get by unobserved, but instead the history of the Benedictine oblates recognizes her as the most renowned oblate of the seventeenth century, though in her era, France counts among its oblates such famous persons as the Countess of Chateauvieux and Cardinal Etienne Le Camus, bishop of Grenoble.[52]

THE QUESTION OF OTHER CONSECRATIONS

According to some authors, after her brief and unsuccessful experience of the cloistered life in Venice, Elena supposedly made three other attempts to enter a convent after having become a Benedictine oblate. The first time, she is said to have decided to enter the Collegio delle vergini di Gesù (The College of the Virgins of Jesus) at Castiglione delle Stiviere in the territory of Mantua, which was founded by three sisters—Cinzia, Olimpia, and Gridonia Gonzaga, nieces of St. Aloysius—and professed the spirituality of the Society of Jesus.[53] She was apparently dissuaded because she was not free to leave her parents and because she would have violated the state's very strict laws regarding religious institutions.

Because of its religious policies, the Venetian Republic had issued several ducal proclamations that intervened in the internal affairs of the monasteries. It regulated monastic recruitment, giving preference to "nationals," that is, Venetian subjects, who were to be accepted before foreigners; it demanded a census of all persons living in the monasteries; it prescribed that superiors were to be elected only from Venetian subjects; and it forbade the transporting of the earthly remains of the deceased religious out of the state requiring, rather, that they be buried in their monasteries.[54]

Elena would supposedly have resigned herself in the face of these difficulties. Nonetheless, after a while—still according to what some writers say—she apparently insisted on obtaining from her confessor, Father Francesco Boselli, a Jesuit, permission to enter a convent at least after the death of her parents. This time her preferences were to have been for the Istituto delle Modeste o Dimesse (Institute of the Modest and Humble) which had their only convents in Vicenza and Padua.[55] This religious family, which followed the rule of St. Francis, was founded around 1572 in Vicenza by Dianira Valmarana, the widow of Pristrato (or Priorato),[56] under the tutelage of the friar minor Marcantonio Pagani. Its members were young widows who, after a trial period of three years, dedicated themselves to catechetical instruction and to caring for women who were ill, remaining free to abandon the community and to marry since they were not bound by vows.[57] This project, which supposedly seemed more feasible to Elena than the preceding one, did not come to fruition because she died before her parents.

Her third attempt, still according to what some authors have written, occurred only two years before her death. Elena developed a great friendship with the Hermit Mothers of Padua, who lived according to the rule of St. Francis, and in particular, with the abbess, Anna Maria Zanolli, whom Elena often visited and aided with food and medicine because she was very ill.[58] During Lent 1682, when the abbess visited the construction site of a new convent being built on via Vanzo, she permitted Elena, as a sign of kindness, to accompany her along with the noble widows Caterina Figimelica and Cassandra Lazara.[59] Her visits to Abbess Zanolli continued in the new convent, and at one of these spiritual meetings she is said to have asked to be accepted as a nun. The abbess apparently responded negatively because she believed it was God's will for Elena to remain in the world.[60]

What should we think of these stories? If they are true, they reveal a great fickleness in Elena and a lack of seriousness in choosing religious life, a bond meant to last for eternity. How do we reconcile this instability in making decisions with the great maturity of judgment attributed to her even as a child, almost as if in her, nature had taken not small steps but great leaps?[61]

I consider it more plausible that Elena, always conscious of the commitment assumed by her as an oblate, remained content with this form of consecration to God. She already had a rule to follow and a well-defined spirituality to practice. Therefore, it was unnecessary to inform herself about other orders. She knew that her vows constituted a commitment of honor, indeed of justice, and that having given her word once, it was to be maintained, especially with God. Thus, far from the thought of other choices, Elena continued on the road she had begun "with an open heart and with inexpressible sweetness of love," as St. Benedict demands of his disciples (*Regula monasteriorum*, Prologus). Solid Benedictine spirituality gave her security in the face of the new forms of piety proposed to her.

Furthermore, evidence is not lacking of her faithfulness as an oblate. Father Oliva, Father General of the Society of Jesus, in a letter written to her at Christmas, congratulated her for having recently assumed the oblate habit and having made herself available to spend the new year

> in withdrawal from life, with a sublimeness of mind, with that habit, that is itself so holy, which by her is eclipsed and clothes her with the array of a lady. In this manner are made most holy both the weekdays and the holy days of this short time, which for us is passing in this present life, by one who disdains the world, and reveals to the eyes of its deceived inhabitants the falsity of

earthly citizenship, while opening to Christ a true sanctuary of celestial life. Thus she lives, because she wants to live forever in the kingdom of the just with that diadem, which is solely shaped by whoever, among the abundant prosperities of the home, cultivates Gospel humility.[62]

Another time, again at Christmas, Oliva wrote of having received a portrait of her. He confessed, though, that he did not find it to be as good a likeness as Father Bossio (who had brought it to him) had said:

And yet I found it inexpressibly false, and not looking like you very much: while representing you in noble garments as a lady of a great family, it concealed beneath a figure so vain, the hidden treasures of Christ, emulated in the harshness of the inner habit and in life conformed to the hairshirt. These joys, which my illustrious Lady hides from the eyes of men, are the truest holy feasts, on which you, my Lady, pray to the Holy Infant: making me blush for not living myself in the house of the Crucifix, in which you, my Lady, live in such splendor.[63]

Similar testimony occurs in other letters from Father Oliva to Elena. From them we learn of the existence of a private chapel in the Cornaro home for which Father Oliva sends a relic—the skull of Saint Faustina, virgin and martyr, taken from the catacombs of Rome—and he takes care to obtain the favor of the "privileged altar."[64] In another letter, he assures her that he has not forgotten this oratory, for which he hopes to send other relics. In return, Oliva asks for prayers for his leadership of the Society which, it seems, must not have been exactly rosy: "Beseech for me from the great martyr [St. Faustina], with your prayers, tolerance among the thorns of leadership, which the Saint achieved at the time of her martyrdom, and a holy death, to end well this life which for me is ebbing."[65]

Elena's faithfulness to the Benedictine Order is made quite clear in the instructions given by her, long before her death, to the ever faithful Maddalena. Elena wishes to be attended in her final moments by a Benedictine father, to be dressed after her death in the complete monastic habit, and to be buried next to the monks, her brothers of the order.[66] How then to explain the claims that she attempted to join very different religious orders after having made her profession as a Benedictine oblate?

Elena, a pious young woman, had a great esteem for all religious orders. The Franciscans and the Jesuits, however, had a special relationship with the Cornaro family and enjoyed its benevolence and friendship.

Perhaps this bond led them to think that Elena had a vocation for the religious institutions marked by their type of spirituality. The claims may stem from their desire to increase the prestige of their own orders by saying that they were preferred by such a famous and virtuous young woman. But what was coveted was really Elena herself!

8

The End of a Life

RESUMING AN INCOMPLETE PROJECT

As recounted above, at the beginning of 1678, Giovanni Battista Cornaro, following the mediation of Procurator Giulio Giustinian, relinquished the idea of having his daughter Elena receive a degree in theology and consented, instead, to a degree in philosophy. This concluded a long and unpleasant controversy between Cornaro and Cardinal Gregorio Barbarigo. From that moment, Elena considered the cause of her theological doctorate finished once and for all, and her father and her professors, Rotondi and Rinaldini, seemed to concur. But the acquiescence of these three was only a tactical move. In the face of the intransigence of Barbarigo, they preferred not to persist in the matter since they hoped that time would change the cardinal's opinion and an opportune moment would come when they could reopen the subject. This was a fire smoldering in the ashes and was kept alive by Rinaldini, backed by Cornaro. To further their cause, they sought the opinion of scholars and universities regarding the legitimacy of a degree in theology for a woman. In 1683, Rinaldini decided that the time had come to act more openly. He prevailed upon his friend and colleague, Father Felice Rotondi, to give him in writing his documented opinion on the matter.[1]

The priest answered him from Venice on July 31, 1683, sending an exhaustive dissertation based on historical, juridical, and theological reasoning. He stated, first of all, that the inquiry proposed to him—whether Elena Cornaro Piscopia, having in recent years received a degree in philosophy, could also obtain a doctorate in theology—was a very controversial subject, since theologians and jurists had not yet determined whether a woman could be awarded a theological degree and therefore assume the title and position of teacher of theology. Notwithstanding the uncertain opinion of some scholars, Rotondi declared himself in agreement with those erudite persons and academy members who considered it possible and, therefore, he was in favor of awarding the doctorate in theology to Elena, limiting the insignia and privileges to those suitable to her status as a woman. He argued that if women were permitted to study theology, and numerous examples existed, there was no reason to deny them the degree in recognition of and reward for their knowledge. In any case, the conditions requested by the jurists for the teaching certificate were reduced to these five: training in teaching, fluency of speech, acumen in interpretation, a facility with words, and authorization to undertake teaching. The first four one could easily find in a woman, and the fifth could be conferred by the competent authority.[2] Furthermore, if women possessed as much capacity as men for the study of theology and gave proof of optimal preparation, they could not be denied the right and honor of access to the corresponding degree. No law until now had prohibited this for women; only their gender prevented it. St. Paul's prohibition against women "speaking" in the assembly (1 Cor 14:34-35; 1 Tm 2:12) was explained exegetically in the sense that the apostle was not opposed to the right of women to prophesy in the assembly (1 Cor 11:5), a right which he acknowledged as theirs; he excluded them only from the official function of teaching within the Christian assembly, not elsewhere.

In his conclusion, Father Rotondi asserted that the degree in theology should not be denied to Elena Cornaro, the glory and ornament of the Venetian nobility, as long as she requested it with the conviction of doing the right thing and something useful for others.[3]

The dissertation, supported by numerous biblical, patristic, and theological quotations, was welcomed by Rinaldini. On August 3, 1683, he expressed his pleasure to Rotondi and sent him, as requested, a detailed report on Elena's doctoral ceremony five years earlier.[4] In fact, Rotondi, having returned to Venice from the general chapter of the Franciscan Order held in Rome that year, had written to Rinaldini to send him the report promptly

> so that I may respond to the requests of the fathers of my Seraphic Order, eminent men due to their dignity and virtue, having recently convened in Rome from all over the world for the general chapter, anxiously awaiting you so that they may together exalt... [Elena's] name and... knowledge which is greater than the fame which has been spread. In their journey, they have been informed of... [Elena's] eminent qualities and virtues and are strongly attracted by them. They would have all flown to Padua to see such an oracle, if the commitments of the provinces had not called them with urgency to their seats.[5]

When Rinaldini sent him the report, Father Rotondi sent copies to his chapter confreres' offices throughout the world.

Although in his scholarly dissertation Father Rotondi had recognized Elena's right to obtain the degree in theology, she herself did not request it, nor did she even care about it. For her, the issue had been resolved five years earlier, since she did not want to renew disagreements with the ecclesiastical authorities. Furthermore, her health, which had been strongly shaken for some time, continually worsened. Her task—*primum vivere deinde philosophari* (first to live, then to be a philosopher)—was much more urgent than a degree in theology. Her father, although anxious for Elena to pursue a new degree, did not press her on this issue. Elena's health was so poor that no other moves were taken, and the following year the project was cut short by her death. Therefore, Rotondi's dissertation remained only a proposed solution to this question of rights without any practical application.

ELENA'S ILLNESSES

Elena's first biographers wrote that she was stricken, several years before her death, by so many and such prolonged illnesses[6] that describing them would have been *Illiadem morborum recensere* (to recount an Illiad of diseases.)[7] We may deduce that from the time of her degree she was tormented by illness. We know that her physical condition, frail by nature, was severely shaken by her strenuous preparation for the degree. Her father, as noted above, in 1679 admitted that his daughter had compromised her health with her studies: "She has lost her health due to exertion and her studies, as is obvious."[8] In May 1678, a month before she received her doctorate, and again in September, 1678, Elena coughed up blood. She never regained her strength completely, but remained more or less in ill health until her death.[9]

Her series of illnesses began with scurvy, which covered her body with vesicles (cysts) and black pustules, tormenting her for two months. After this came a bilious attack with abdominal inflammation and atrocious pain lasting one week. Elena was left so weak that she had to be fed every two hours. A short time later, having regained some of her strength, she was stricken with the so-called "red fever" or *purpura*, which for an entire month covered her whole body with blisters. This gave way to nephritis lasting several months, which even the prompt treatment of her physicians was unable to overcome. She found relief by drinking mineral water from Monteortone near Padua, enabling her to expel three large kidney stones.[10]

Throughout 1683, the last year of her life, Elena suffered from violent pains in her groin. She was stricken by tremors and contractions of nerves all over her body so that at times she appeared to have reached the end of her life. By this time she could hardly stand the drastic treatments administered by the physicians.[11] Predicting the total collapse of her poor body, worn out by so many illnesses, was easy. Elena herself could feel it coming.

Her parents no longer deceived themselves. Since the end of July 1680, her mother had been making prolonged stays in Padua to care for her, while her father made quick visits. The presence of her parents was a great comfort to her, as we see from a letter of July 19, 1680, to her father: "Mama is fine and sends her greetings through me. In the meantime, be aware that I'm dying to see you. I have nothing more to ask of you other than to insist that you come to see us soon."[12] When her illnesses grew worse and the danger of death seemed imminent, her mother stayed with her constantly to comfort her and serve her lovingly.[13]

The last blow to Elena's life was inflicted by a contagious blotch of pox on her shoulder blades which, having burst, became incurably gangrenous. The best scientific remedies were lavished on her with great care and affection by the skillful physicians Domenico Marchetti and Giorgio Calafatti of the University of Padua.[14]

While the illness and pain increased, Elena withstood everything without complaining, but rather with an air of serenity which amazed those around her.[15] A few months before her death she even attended a party for Francesco and Susanna Palladin, friends of the family, acting as godmother for the baptism of their daughter, who was named Elena.[16] Testimony to the ill woman's fortitude is furnished by Father Oliva. In a letter of response to Christmas greetings, he writes to Elena admiring her inner strength during her long and painful sufferings and adds that instead of comforting her, he must learn from her how to suffer. In another letter, after thanking her for her words of praise for the Society of Jesus, he returns to the topic of suffering: "The comments, then, which you made regarding the fearlessness of your spirit, so resigned in God amongst the assaults on your body, stir up in my mind the tenderness of that *Colloquio*, which so piously, you, my Lady translated from Spanish into Italian."[17]

Her quiet acceptance of pain was illustrated one day when the surgeon Domenico Marchetti was lancing the gangrenous pustule to preserve the healthy flesh, making it bleed. Elena did not show the least sign of pain. "But don't you feel pain?" her mother asked. The daughter responded yes. "So why don't you complain?" Elena replied that when one suffers for God one must not complain.[18] Persuaded that she would never get better, Elena tolerated the care of the untiring doctors only to please them and her parents.[19]

In the last week of her life, a high fever caused alternating periods of delirium and calm, unconsciousness and lucidity, reducing Elena to a state of agony. It is not possible that in this condition she could have accomplished all the activities that some biographers attribute to the last three days of her life. According to them, Elena supposedly dictated and signed with her own hand a letter to a cardinal of the Holy Office to recommend to his care some paperwork on behalf of the Capuchin Sisters of Venice.[20] Another day, she is said to have called the chaplain of the house to dictate to him some letters to send to famous people, but she abandoned the idea so as not to commit an act of vanity.[21] The infirm woman then supposedly insisted on being taken out of bed and placed on the floor on some straw to die.[22] It is claimed that on Sunday, July 23, she had an apparition of the Blessed Elena, then of the Blessed Mother of Czestochowa, who had come to comfort her in her pain.[23] On her last day, the dying woman is said to have spent many hours in prayer[24] and a few days before, had summoned her confessor from Venice. The first biographers are not in agreement about his identity, the possibilities being Father Carlo Francesco Boselli, a Jesuit,[25] or Father Michelangelo da Borgo San Sepolcro (Province of Arezzo), a Conventual friar.[26]

As Elena's death approached, the faithful Maddalena undoubtedly fulfilled Elena's request made to her a few years before: "I beg you to have me taken care of by many good religious in the inevitable hour, but particularly that a Benedictine priest be present." As recounted by Bacchini, who obtained the information from the Benedictine himself, Elena had the strength to remind Maddalena about this matter at the opportune moment:

> When she felt the time of death to be near, she had a priest called so that he could care for her soul, and after he had arrived, Elena, having aroused herself to a certain extent from her lethargy, demonstrated great contentment and in a show of respect and acknowledgement, kissed his hand. He then took care of the funeral preparations of the deceased woman, dressing her body in a black habit, as she had prescribed, and completing all the various tasks which were customary in such circumstances among the monks. We feel it is important to mention the name of this man, famous in the Benedictine Order. He was Father Pier Paolo Calderoni da Ravenna, eminent for his piety and erudition, a professor of letters for many years, currently co-procurator of the entire Order and theologian of the monastery in Parma. He helped Elena many times in matters of the spirit; he was the only one to assist her in her death. I have written about all this here to

his recognition since he had spoken to me of this beforehand, and afterward he confirmed it. To him, therefore, belong praise and acknowledgement.[27]

THE END

Thus, on Wednesday, July 26, 1684, at the age of thirty-eight, having awakened from a brief drowsiness, Elena expired, with the people dearest to her at her side, as she had requested.[28] (Some give the date of her death, erroneously, as July 16 rather than July 26,[29] and the year as 1688[30] or even 1689.[31]) Someone later wrote that Codanini was not present, though he received the news in Brescia, where he was abbot of San Faustino Monastery.[32] This is actually impossible since Codanini died in 1680. The death certificate filled out by her physicians declares that she died of a cachectic tumor, since she had been stricken by cachexia, or to be more precise, for some time had lived in a cachectic state.[33]

The pastor of San Lorenzo, after having noted in the death register that Elena had received all the sacraments of the dying, added a eulogy to his extraordinary parishioner:

> The aforementioned lady was a formal doctor in philosophy in the College of Padua and besides her extraordinary goodness in life, she was even more adorned with various virtues, that is, she knew several languages, was experienced in Sacred Scripture, versed in sacred theology, and, furthermore, knew music well, being able to play and compose: in sum, she was the splendor not so much of the state as of all of Italy, the greatest of women in our times.[34]

Though foreseen for some time, Elena's death brought great grief to all those who held her in high esteem — the Cornaros' friends and even the general public. In the family, Giovanni Battista seemed to suffer the most. Not only was he robbed of his daughter forever, but the world of glory that she had procured for him with her extraordinary achievements had collapsed. Lost in grief, he did not have the strength to take care of the urgent matters required by the circumstances. His wife, however, a practical woman who had power of attorney, had already undertaken to make the funeral arrangements. In fact, shortly before Elena's death, in her own and in her husband's name, she had charged Antonio Biasini with presenting a request to the College of Philosophers and Physicians of the university to participate in the funeral of their daughter Elena *brevi moritura*.[35]

The members of the college, who had convened that same day, July 26, in a special session, were consulted about accepting the Cornaros' request.[36] After reading the letter to them, the prior of the association, Alverio Zacco, spoke of the worthiness of rendering pious homage to their sister and heroine (*huic sorori nostrae ac tantae heroinae*) who even after receiving her degree had labored day and night at her studies and had become "the glory and honor not only of their College but of all the *literati* of the Republic." He further requested that they approve attendance at her funeral by acclamation as they had in the past approved her graduation ceremony. This proposal was accepted. The participants were to gather the following Friday, July 28, at ten in the morning in the basilica near the Cornaro home, wearing the black mantle and the ermine stole.[37]

The physicians embalmed her body, which was then clothed in the Benedictine habit—the tunic and the black woolen cowl. They placed on her shoulders the ermine stole, the doctoral garment, and on her head two crowns, one of lilies to signify her virginal state, and the other of laurel as a sign of her degree. At her side lay several open books representing the fields of study in which she had so distinguished herself.

On the two days preceding her funeral the location of her burial was discussed, and although her mother wanted to bury her in the family tomb in the church of San Luca in Venice,[38] it was decided to respect the wishes of the deceased woman and bury her in the funeral chapel of the Benedictine fathers at Santa Giustina. It was also appropriate that Elena's remains stay in Padua, the city that had become her home, where she crowned her studies with a doctorate, and near the Benedictines she had joined as an oblate. The Benedictine fathers quickly accepted her mortal remains.

On July 28, at ten o'clock, according to the orders they had received, the thirty-seven members of the College of Philosophers and Physicians of the university gathered in the basilica, where they were received by the Cornaro family; they accompanied the body to the church of Santa Giustina, each one carrying a candle. Four professors, Count Alessandro Borromeo and Giorgio Calafatti, physicians, and the philosophers Giacomo Bonzanino and Giovanni Cigala, walked beside the coffin[39] for the entire procession. They did not carry it on their shoulders as some authors write.[40] Preceding them were the members of various religious orders and of the confraternities of the cities, dressed in black and with a lighted candle in their hands. A great crowd, which had even come from Venice and other cities, was in attendance. Stores and offices remained closed as if it were a Sunday or public holiday or, better still, a day of citywide mourning. The funeral procession first reached the university, then went along the main street, arriving at Prato della Valle and Santa Giustina. Here the coffin was taken in by the abbot and the monks[41] and placed on a rich catafalque surrounded by several lit candles. After the solemn funeral rites, the noble Paduan Campolongo Campolongo delivered the official eulogy for the University.[42]

Both Deza and Dalmazzo contradict themselves in affirming, first, that the eulogy was given by Father Francesco Caro, a Somaschan father, then by Campolongo.[43] In reality, the speech was written by Caro, a charge given to him by the College of Philosophers and Physicians, and was delivered by the lively Campolongo, then twenty-seven.[44] This discourse was printed in two different editions, Latin and Italian, in Padua and bears the date of July 28, the day of the funeral. It was composed in less than one night, as confirmed by the author, in Latin and simultaneously in Italian; Campolongo probably used the latter so that he might be understood by the great crowd present at the funeral.[45]

When the ceremony was concluded, the coffin remained on the catafalque until night, as the pastor of San Lorenzo, an eyewitness, diligently informs us.[46] Then it was moved into the funeral chapel of the Benedictine monks, but it was buried only toward the evening of the following day, July 29, because the single tomb which they were preparing specially for Elena was not yet ready.[47] Thus, her desire was fulfilled to be buried in the earth and in the same chapel with the tombs of the monks.[48]

This chapel, now next to the corridor that leads from the basilica to the *coro vecchio*, the old choir, was the ancient Chapel of St. Luke the Evangelist, later called the *capitolo vecchio*, the old chapter, built at the beginning of the fourteenth century, decorated with frescoes (1436–1441) by a Venetian, Giovanni Storlato di Filippo. In 1590 it was made a cemetery for the Benedictine monks by raising the pavement to enable construction of thirteen tombs underneath. In the small rectory was the sepulcher of the abbots, to the right of which Elena's tomb was prepared.[49]

The inscription carved on the gravestone recalled the deceased's intelligence, her great virtues, her degree, her Benedictine profession— which had taken place in San Giorgio Maggiore Monastery in Venice at the hands of Abbot Codanini—and her desire, now fulfilled, of being buried in that location.[50] Giangirolamo Testoris, a Benedictine resident of the abbey of Santa Giustina and a professor of sacred scripture at the University of Padua, dictated it.[51]

(Some writers have erroneously stated that Elena was buried in the sacristy of the church of Santa Giustina with great honors because she belonged to the Accademia dei Ricovrati of Padua and other academies; others assert that she was entombed in the basilica of St. Anthony in a superb mausoleum.[52])

The funeral, unfortunately, had a prosaic aftermath in the person of

Father Giuseppe Pisani, pastor of San Lorenzo, who demanded an honorarium from the monks of Santa Giustina amounting to half of the so-called "stola fee." This was an old custom, in fact, whereby a pastor received this sum when the funeral of one of his parishioners took place outside the parish.[53] Pisani notes this claim under the registration of Elena's death certificate. He even applied to Elena's mother, and though at this time she had other worries, she sent him, on July 30, four candlesticks weighing four pounds each. The next day Father Abbot Barbieri had a monk deliver to him two *cechini ruspii* valued at forty lire.[54] Pisani, fully satisfied, then wrote to the abbot expressing his appreciation and asking for his good will.[55]

AN INDELIBLE MEMORY

Politicians and governmental dignitaries, the learned and unlearned, shared the mourning of the Cornaro family. For example, the apostolic nuncio to Venice, Luigi Giacobelli in his *rapporto diplomatico* of August 5, 1684, to Andrea Borghi, secretary of the nunciature of the Venetian Republic in care of the Holy See, informed him of the premature death of Elena who "became famous in the world for her excellence in literature, for the knowledge which she possessed, and for the various languages she knew, all of which adorned her."[56]

The various academies that Elena had belonged to considered it their duty to commemorate her. The Accademia dei Ricovrati of Padua was preeminent. The solemn session of September 1, 1684, which was attended by the city's authorities in addition to numerous members, was opened by Count Alessandro de' Lazzara, president of the academy, with a tribute to Elena's great gifts. A speech by the Theatine father, Filippo Setaiolo, a patrician from Palermo, followed, and "many Tuscan, Latin, and Greek compositions were recited as well as the epigrams of Gabriella and Carla Patin, daughters of Professor Carlo."[57]

Procurator Cornaro, moved by this evidence of their respect for his daughter, on September 5, 1684, wrote a letter of gratitude to the president and to the members of the academy, assuring his future patronage for the association to which he felt indebted. The Count de' Lazzara, in a letter the following day, September 6, 1684, renewed his condolences to Cornaro and added expressions of regard for the whole family.[58]

In a private academic session on September 14, 1684, the count expressed his desire to have printed, at his expense, the literary compositions delivered on September 1, including those of members who had not attended. The academy members immediately accepted the generous proposal of their president, and the collection was published that same year.[59]

In the meantime, from Padua, Carlotta Patin informed Claude Charles Guyonnet de Vertron in Paris of Elena's death. De Vertron responded, saying that with the loss of the incomparable Elena Cornaro Piscopia, the scholarly Accademia dei Ricovrati of Venice (sic) had lost its Minerva, its ornament, its gentle sex, its model, and a wonder of the century.[60]

Even the Accademia degli Infecondi of Rome organized a session in Elena's memory which, for unexpected reasons, took place the following year on the eve of the first anniversary of her death, July 25, 1685. For this solemn commemoration the hall was decorated with five paintings by the Roman artist Tommaso Cardano.[61] The commemorative speech was given by Michele Brugueres. Those present were Cardinal Felice Rospigliosi, Protector of the Academy; the Venetian Cardinal Pietro Ottoboni; the bishop of Acquapendente, Giovanni Battista Febei; and many prelates of the Roman Curial.[62] Poetic compositions by various members were read, and the secretary of the academy, Giuseppe Berneri, spoke the closing words.[63] The speech and the twenty-four literary compositions were published in Padua at the expense of Giovanni Battista Cornaro.[64] Cardinal Rospiglioni sent Marc'Antonio Giustinian, doge of Venice, a copy of this publication, together with a respectful letter, as a gift.[65]

About fifteen days after the funeral of his daughter, Cornaro began the paperwork for an ambitious project thought up perhaps as soon as Elena expired. He intended to erect a grandiose funeral monument, worthy of establishing her fame for posterity. The first tentative approaches to the Conventual Friars were not made directly by him, but by the physician Giorgio Calafatti, a man who enjoyed his complete trust, merited not only by his professional competence, but also by the kind care and patience he accorded Elena. From then on, he became the Cornaro family's physician. At that time, and until the advent of specialists in our century, the family doctor was a person who, besides attending to the physical needs of his patients, often was capable of diagnosing their spiritual conditions. Over the course of one's life he became a counselor, a confidant, a moral supporter of an entire family, who knew they could have recourse, in good times and bad, to this man who exercised his profession as a mission.

Calafatti was such a physician for the Cornaro Piscopia family. He attended Elena until the last, drawing up the notice of her death and later escorting her coffin during the funeral.[66] Later on, he served as a witness to two notary acts of Giovanni Battista Cornaro, for regulating a debt toward his daughter-in-law Isabetta Grigis and for drawing up his will, in which the procurator tangibly remembered him.[67] In 1692, during Cornaro's mortal illness, the first of his physicians is Calafatti, and after the procurator's death, Calafatti became the physician of the families of Girolamo and Caterina Cornaro, his children.[68] He was also one of the witnesses to the notary act of 1708 by which Girolamo Cornaro returned to the Conventual Friars the portion of their garden that Alvise Cornaro had rented in 1535.[69] Calafatti, therefore, the trusted confidant of Procurator Cornaro, was best able to help him in the steps necessary to erect a monument to his Elena in the basilica of Sant' Antonio.

From Bacchini we learn that Cornaro had thought initially of erecting this monument in the grandiose church of Santa Giustina a few meters from his daughter's sepulcher. Those monks, however, had always been determined not to allow burial or funeral monuments in their new basilica so as to avoid turning it into a pantheon, as had happened in their other church.[70]

On August 12, 1684, fourteen friars gathered in the chapter room to listen to a plea presented by Dr. Calafatti in the name of Giovanni Battista Cornaro, requesting permission to remove from the fourth pilaster on the left in the central nave of the basilica a painting depicting the growth of the Franciscan Order, and to erect in that spot a funeral monument to his daughter Elena. The chapter fathers all expressed their favorable opinion.[71]

Cornaro turned immediately to the Bassanese sculptor and architect Bernardo Tabacco, educated in Rome in the style and taste of Francesco Borromini (1599–1667).[72] He must have been one of the artists in the Veneto region with the greatest reputation at the time, if Cornaro, who was accustomed to choosing always the best, decided to entrust the work to him. In planning the monument, Tabacco utilized all his artistic talent not solely because of the importance of the person being honored but because the monument would join the many others already in the basilica and would have to justify the trust that the procurator had placed in him with the commission.

In all probability, the sculptor prepared a design of the entire work for the approval of Cornaro and the friars, a drawing presumably preserved in the archive of the Veneranda Arca del Santo. Since consultation of that archive was denied me, I cannot reproduce the original design. I present, instead, an ideal reconstruction executed faithfully according to the careful description made by Deza, who was personally able to see the monument.[73] From this sketch we can get an idea of the imposing nature of the work, which incorporated a great number of statues, busts, emblems, allegories, and so on, and required many years to complete. When Mabillon visited Cornaro in Venice, May 27, 1685, the monument was already being prepared.[74] It was not yet finished in 1687, according to a letter of

Magliabechi's of April 22, nor in 1688, but only in 1689, that is, five years later.[75]

From the hand of the Bassanese sculptor came a grandiose, solemn monument, for which, as one author states, Cornaro had undergone "an expense worthy of a prince where, sparing no cost, he has depicted all the memorable events of his illustrious family."[76] Although it displayed some of the artistic defects typical of that century, it did not deserve the disparaging verdict of some later artists which, judging by the only surviving statue from the monument, condemns all the others with Virgil's *crimine ab uno disce omnes* ("if one is bad, then all are bad").[77] The accusation made by another Bassanese sculptor, Giovanni Miazzi (1699–1797), denigrates the work of Tabacco in order to promote the Greco-Roman style.[78] If Tabacco had not been a competent artist, he would not have received the commission; Cornaro could have chosen from among several notable sculptors working at the time in Venice and in other Venetian cities.[79] Orazio Marinali, for example, had already created some statues for Cornaro's palace in Venice. The events surrounding the demolition of the grandiose and cumbersome monument in 1727 are described above (see chap. 2, sec. 3).

In addition to the monument, the procurator and his wife wanted to preserve Elena's memory with memorial stones in their houses in Venice and in Padua. In the upper hall of their Venetian palace, above a portrait of their daughter, they placed a tablet with a laudatory inscription dictated by Father Felice Rotondi.[80] They did the same in the beautiful palace in Padua, where they placed two stone tablets; both have disappeared, but the texts survived.[81]

Even the University of Padua wanted to remember its famous alumna in a tangible way. On January 11, 1685, the College of Philosophers and Physicians unanimously decided to have a commemorative medallion minted.[82] A few months later, on March 23, 1685, a letter from Giovanni Battista Cornaro was read at a session of the same college, accompanied by a gold medal which he had commissioned. We do not know if it was to commemorate Elena's degree or her death. By a unanimous agreement among those present, the gift was placed in the custody of the procurator of the college as a memorial of the woman who had so honored the University of Padua with her prodigious culture and whose continued presence was felt in spirit.[83]

Those who had met her and had come to know her could not easily forget her demeanor and personality. Bacchini described her thus: "She was of medium stature and well proportioned, high of forehead and full of majesty with dark, penetrating eyes, a pale complexion and full of dignity and grace. Whoever spoke with her admired her and was filled with respect. She had many talents, a quickness in learning and a tenacious memory. Calm, moderate, and kindly of temperament, she dedicated herself to all that conformed with honesty, justice, and decorum, without ever even thinking in the slightest of anything other than what was dignifying and noble for a young woman."[84]

At a distance of three centuries, this description of Elena's physical and moral features may appear idealized and acceptable only with some hesitation. The noble and cultured Venetian Tommaso Giuseppe Farsetti, who knew Elena personally, anticipated this reaction. In Elena's own time she already appeared to be a prodigious young woman. He wrote that posterity would therefore with difficulty believe that there existed a young woman whose splendid qualities surpassed those of any man, whose excellence could not be equaled. He added that in future centuries there would be doubt that she could have achieved such glory in so short a period of time while others labored longer and achieved less. He concluded: "And we, then, to whom has been given the fate of admiring all of this, almost cannot believe our eyes, uncertain whether what we have seen is really true or if, perhaps, we saw it in a dream."[85]

9

EPILOGUE: SURVIVAL

A LONG SILENCE

In the funeral eulogy delivered before an immense crowd, Campolongo recalled the renowned intelligence and the great virtues of the deceased. He expressed his regrets that death, with a single blow, had taken away a young woman of great hope, the glory of the university, the honor of Padua and of Venice, and concluded by stating that the grave would forever guard Elena's fame.[1]

Prior to the funeral there had already been expressions of homage and respect for the deceased, of whom everyone wished to oobtain some remembrance. People believed and declared that a saintly young woman had died. Deza, Elena's first biographer, observed that if the voice of the people was enough to proclaim a person a saint, Elena would have been canonized in those days by more than 30,000 people.[2] In addition, according to her first biographers, steps were taken by the diocesan ecclesiastical authorities toward an official recognition of the noble woman's sanctity. According to these authors, the bishop's curia of Padua held a hearing at which they recorded, in writing, what famous individuals, teachers, confessors, friends, and people who lived in continual contact with the young lady said under oath about Elena.[3]

A brief "note" much later, and very vague, seems to confirm that such a hearing took place, without producing, however, any proof.[4] According to the repeated testimony of the archivist, Father Claudio Bellinati, no document exists in the archive of the bishop's curia, which could verify it. Even supposing that this hearing had gathered testimony and proof, all would have had to pass into the hands of the bishop, Cardinal Gregorio Barbarigo, who would decide whether to send the paperwork to the competent Roman congregation and request an official initiation of the cause for beatification. In the archive of the Congregation for the Causes of Saints in Rome, no such file exists. Notwithstanding detailed research at the place where all individuals proposed for beatification are registered with the utmost precision, the name of Elena Cornaro never appears. Cardinal Barbarigo, having received the dossier of testimony, probably allowed time to pass and then wisely put the paperwork in his drawer. It then died with him in 1697 or perhaps even before, with the death of Giovanni Battista Cornaro in 1692; he, at least indirectly, would have favored these preparations. It is true that on one Benedictine calendar on the date of July 26, the anniversary of her death, Elena Lucrezia Cornaro Piscopia is celebrated as *venerabilis* (venerable) but the information is not reliable.[5]

For various reasons, a long and profound silence followed this period of great enthusiasm for Elena. First, with the death of Cornaro, there was no longer an untiring crusader to maintain enthusiasm for the memory of his daughter. Then, at the end of the eighteenth century, political and military events in the Lombardy-Veneto regions transformed Padua into an occupied city, as France and Austria vied for control of the region.

On January 20, 1798, the Austrian troops occupied Padua and were welcomed by the population as liberators and harbingers of a prosperous and peaceful era. The French, guilty of plundering and extortion of every kind, had become loathsome to the Venetian people.

From the first days of their occupation, the Austrians took certain measures to remedy the sad conditions of the city. There were many unemployed workers and the rich, impoverished by the events of the last few years, did not have capital to invest in laborers. Those who were able to find jobs in public works had to be content with half of the usual salary. Government clerks did not receive any pay. At the university, the professors received their stipends intermittently, and the institution, which had been for so many centuries the glory of Padua, was neglected by the government.

To provide for the needs of the occupying troops or of those passing through, the Austrians resumed the requisitions imposed during the French invasion. The burden of these military expenses fell entirely on private families, worsening their economic condition. The rich, then, could not help the poor because they had to turn over their surplus of clothes and household goods to the Austrian army. Even the slightest refusal was considered a discourtesy to the sovereign. Farmers continually saw their harvests and animals taken from them.

In addition to these grave hardships, troops were quartered in every possible place, so that convents, private homes, and public offices were transformed into barracks, warehouses, hospitals, and prisons for the soldiers. The Austrian collection of taxes was no less rigid than the French. Indeed, expenses for general living quarters in Padua were a burden on the public treasury while private citizens had to provide lodging for numerous officers of higher rank. This meant, therefore, a huge taxation, if we consider that in Padua several thousand soldiers were housed, a number often doubled either by the infirm and the wounded or by prisoners of war or by troops passing through.[6]

When more than 11,000 Russian soldiers with 4,500 horses passed through Padua in June 1799, the citizens had to close their shops and stay in their homes so as not to be robbed. In the countryside, the farmers were subjected to all sorts of raids and left in misery among the ruins.

The Austrian government, heedless of the people's needs, was interested only in money to continue the war. The discontent of the people had reached intolerable limits. The Austrians turned to force, imprisoning accused politicians, men of letters, scientists, priests, artisans, the rich and the poor. Some were exiled, some punished with the suspension or privation of work due to a mere suspicion or trivial accusation, since informing was not only permitted but rewarded as was the case at the time of the French occupation.[7]

In January 1801, after the Austrians were defeated, the Venetians hoped for a general improvement. But when the French reoccupied Padua on January 16, 1802, nothing changed because the military requisitions immediately resumed. The people, disappointed in their expectations, had practically resigned themselves to seeing their own land invaded by foreigners.[8]

These events had repercussions in the monastery of Santa Giustina, which was deeply involved with the completion of its new church, the current one, and the reclaiming of Corezzola and Cive.[9] Compounding its problems was the first expulsion of the Benedictines from the monastery in 1797–1798 by French troops occupying Padua, and then again after the passage of Napoleonic laws regarding the suppression of religious corporations (1810). In 1942, in a small part of the old monastery, the monastic community was reconstituted. It had to face numerous difficulties which were exacerbated by the persistence of the war.[10]

If these events were not the principal cause of the long silence surrounding Elena's memory, they certainly contributed to it.

AWAKENINGS

The long silence was gently broken from time to time by a few writers who, even if they only repeated material already known about Elena, were nevertheless able to keep her memory alive. One of these was the noble

Venetian Caterina Dolfin Tron (1736–1793). Intelligent, cultured, an assiduous reader of modern books, a patron of letters and poetry,[11] she obtained in 1772 an annulment of her marriage to Marcantonio Tiepolo and married Andrea Tron (1712–1785) with whom she had been having an affair for sixteen years.

Tron, a man of keen wit and so powerful that he was called *el paròn* (the master), had been elected a Reformer of the University of Padua. From then on, Caterina tried to live in the university's halo of glory. When her husband was named procurator of San Marco and she became "lady procurator," she schemed to appear almost the mistress of the University of Padua. But her shameless conduct, which had hindered her husband's ascent in Venetian political officialdom,[12] did not win her many friends in the university community. Perhaps to ingratiate herself with the community and also to render homage to an illustrious Venetian woman—a lover of scholarship and the glory of that university—in 1773 she donated to the university a statue of Elena Lucrezia Cornaro Piscopia which, at the direction of the Reformers, was placed at the foot of a great staircase with a dedication engraved on the base.[13]

The statue came from the grand funeral monument which, as described in the preceding chapter, the Bassanese sculptor Bernardo Tabacco had created for Elena. In 1727, the work was demolished with the consent of Girolamo Cornaro, Elena's brother, who retained ownership of all the statuary. How did the statue donated to the university become the property of Caterina Dolfin? It may be that Girolamo, who was having economic difficulties when the monument was demolished, sold the statues; they may have passed through many hands before this one came into her possession. Another possibility is suggested by Caterina Dolfin's will. Among the objects left to her nephew, Alvise Barbarigo, son of Luisa Tron, are books, bookcases, antique vases, paintings, stamps, and antique and modern statues.[14] Among these there may have been one from Elena Cornaro's monument. At any rate, we know nothing for certain of the fate of the other statues, more than twelve, which comprised the cenotaph.[15]

After a century of neglect, interest in Elena Cornaro revived in 1895. On the evening of September 8, while the feast of the Nativity of the Blessed Mother was being celebrated in the basilica of Santa Giustina, two English people arrived: Monsignor James Austin Campbell, rector of the Scottish College of Rome, and a Benedictine, Mathilda Pynsent, abbess of the "Sancti Benedicti de Urbe" (Saint Benedict of Rome) Monastery. They came in search of Elena Cornaro's tomb in the funeral chapel of the Benedictine monks of Padua. They found it after inspecting the entire pavement by the light of torches held by the brothers of the Blessed Sacrament who had gathered there to await the procession. It must have looked like a scene from a Rembrandt painting.

Having paid homage at the tomb, the abbess expressed to the pastor of Santa Giustina her desire to undertake a verification of the body. He told her to contact the ecclesiastical authorities in writing, that is, the vicar general of the diocese of Padua, since in those days the bishop was absent.[16] The same evening, Monsignor Campbell, in the name of Abbess Pynsent, wrote to the vicar general to obtain permission.[17] The next day, Father Giovanni Campeis, coadjutor of the bishop's curia, was delegated to perform the verification, subject to the agreement of the municipal authorities. Campeis presented the petition and obtained permission to open the Cornaro tomb in the presence of the municipal inspector.[18] On Wednesday, September 11, 1895, at twelve noon, they proceeded with the exhumation. Besides Monsignor Campbell and Abbess Pynsent, Doctor Giuseppe Petich, representing the prefect of the province; Doctor Gaetano Varda of the municipality of Padua; Father Domenico Puller, pastor of Santa Giustina; Commendator Carlo Ferraris, vice-chancellor of the University of Padua; and Father Giovanni Campeis were present.

When they took away the tombstone and removed also a second one, they discovered the well-preserved cypress casket, but, prudently, they did not move it from its place for fear that the underside might be rotten. In fact, once they had carefully removed the part that was intact, the completely pulverized body lay uncovered.

Michelangelo Vivaldi, a physician, entered the tomb to examine the mortal remains and declared that no part of the body was well preserved. It was easy to recognize the color and shape of the Benedictine habit and a few shreds of the religious veil. Near her head lay a zinc leaf, deteriorated on one side, on which a biographical and laudatory inscription was very legible.[19]

After Father Puller recited the prayers for the dead, the remains were placed in a new larch case, closed with the wax seal of Monsignor Callegari (1841–1906), the bishop of Padua, and inserted in a zinc coffin. The pieces of the original casket were placed near the new one, and the tomb was closed. The witnesses, to whom were added the Benedictine Father Marino Frattin, superior of the monastery of San Giorgio Maggiore of Venice, and Sister Maura Watson, a Benedictine postulant, signed the report of the verification drawn up in duplicate, one copy for the bishop's curia, the other for the municipality of Padua.[20] The cost of the exhumation and the new tombstone were borne by Abbess Pynsent.

De Santi is very imprecise when he states, without quoting documents, that the commission charged with the restoration of the tomb, as a tribute to the munificent abbess, wanted a few brief words to be added to the tombstone inscription in remembrance of Pynsent's interest in the matter.[21] But nothing more was written, and the tomb slab bears witness to it, still visible and recently affixed to the south wall of the chapel.

After these events, Pynsent returned to Rome. The following year she published, anonymously, her biography of Elena Lucrezia Cornaro Piscopia, which she hoped would make the noble Venetian woman better known and awaken her memory in an ever-expanding circle of people.

REVIVAL

The silence that surrounded the tomb and the memory of Elena Cornaro returned again for over seventy years. It was interrupted on April 3, 1968, when, during a radical restoration of the burial chapel under the auspices of the Italian Ministry of Public Education, the tomb was opened and the coffin, the great zinc casket made in 1895, was moved temporarily to the small crypt of the paleo-christian shrine of San Prosdocimo adjacent to the basilica of Santa Giustina.[22] On the morning of September 25, 1975, when the new floor of the chapel was finished, Elena's coffin was returned to its tomb.[23]

At this point we must go back to the first decade of this century to speak about a young American, Ruth Crawford, a student at Vassar College, the first college for women in the United States, located in Poughkeepsie, New York. Crawford recounts that beginning in her freshman year in college, she would often stop to admire the stained-glass window in the college library, a work by Dunstan Powell, 1904, that depicted, among other things, a young woman surrounded by professors who were conferring the doctoral symbols upon her. She learned that the woman was Elena Lucrezia Cornaro Piscopia, the first woman in the world to receive a university degree. She was profoundly disappointed to realize that this glorious female scholar was almost completely unknown, even in educational circles. She promised herself that, once her studies were completed, she would take on the mission of making this young and exceptional woman known in every way possible.

In 1912, having just graduated with a degree in sociology, Crawford quickly began work for the cause she had proposed for herself. Her interest—as well as that of other Americans—in Elena Cornaro was manifested in the Italian Nationality Room at the University of Pittsburgh, which in 1949 installed a large mural by the Italian Giovanni Romagnoli depicting Elena Cornaro.[24]

Then came the first visits by prominent Americans and later those of the female students of the University of Pittsburgh, organized especially to see the Cornaro tomb and the University of Padua.

In 1955, Ruth Crawford Mitchell was able for the first time to render homage at the tomb of Elena Cornaro, which she repeated in 1969 and in 1976.

A fervent admirer of Elena, Crawford Mitchell became the untiring promoter of an American campaign to make her better known and to commemorate the third centennial of her degree. For this purpose she contacted many institutions and organizations who gave their moral and material support to the restoration of the tomb and the burial chapel in the basilica of Santa Giustina.[25]

In Padua, in 1954, there was a small revival of interest in Elena Cornaro. The municipality passed a resolution on December 1, 1954, naming a small street (far from downtown with no possibility of development) in honor of Elena Cornaro Piscopia, alumna of the University of Padua.[26]

In 1967, an intense correspondence by letter was begun between Ruth Crawford Mitchell and the Benedictine monks of Santa Giustina regarding, for the most part, the restoration of the Cornaro tomb. In 1969, the University of Padua conducted research in all the universities of the world to verify the primacy of Elena Lucrezia Cornaro Piscopia's degree and published the results.[27]

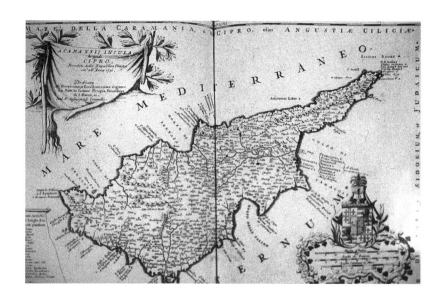

1.   The Island of Cyprus, from V. CORONELLI, *Atlante dell'isolario veneto*, I, Venezia 1696, p. 249.

The map contains the following place names and labels:

Salamua · Vrelio · Vassa · Saica
S. Cusma · mi · ni
ba · Masmi · Leruasa · Homoelos · Curis F.
rit · Marona · Chilan · Chiliaco
nara · Maneta · Musoro · Schinica · Miglia · S Z
hlia · Clora · S A · Taranpo
Amogna · Patra · Corimati · Diachinisa · Voni · Euresti
Ancimat · Pocano · Siria
Chavo · ciale · Z.S. · Chivida
Risato · S.E.
Audimo · Zabaca
Pisuri · Piromati · S. Chitino · Vlassa
Mandalati · M.
Cata · Critiui
Porphyrium P. · Cosol
Lago Elace
Piscopia · Curias · Anni · Fab: 1595 · auanti Cristo · S X
Da questa prese la denominatio ne la Prosapia detta nara, cia · o Gauate, la Grada, Gate, trema · Acroti

2. The Island of Cyprus (detail), from V. CORONELLI, *Atlante dell'isolario veneto*, I, Venezia 1696, p. 249. At the southern point we find the castle of Piscopi, fief of the Cornaros, which gave rise to the last name of the Cornaro Piscopia family.

3. CODEVIGO, Erle House (already a Cornaro villa). View facing the
    public street (photo of the Consorzio for the development of the
    Piovese). The sixteenth-century villa built by Falconetto for Alvise
    Cornaro as it is currently seen.

4. CODEVIGO, Erle House (already a Cornaro villa). East wall: signs of a double window which has been bricked up to close it off permanently (photo of the Consorzio for the Development of the Piovese).

5. VENICE, Correr Civic Museum Library, Gherro collection 2978. Engraving by G. A. Battisti (1779): Portal, no longer in existence, for access to the Cornaro villa (work of Falconetto) in Codevigo.

143

6. PADUA, L. Uggeri collection. Engraving by M. Marieschi (1694-1743). Venice: St. Mark's Square with the old "Procuracy" (left) and the new (right) built as the official residence of the Procurators of St. Mark's.

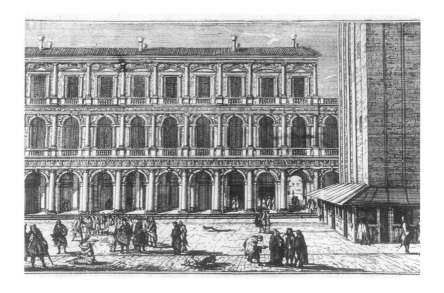

7. PADUA, L. Uggeri collection. Engraving by L. Carlevaris (1665-
   1731). Venice: The new "Procuracy" (detail). For several years, Elena
   Cornaro Piscopia lived in an apartment on the first floor of this
   building with her family.

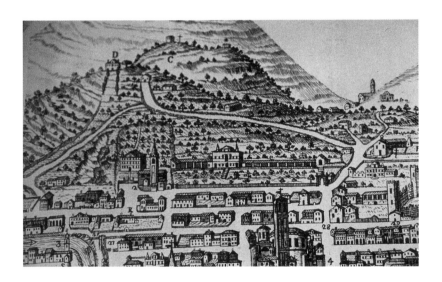

8. The city of Este (detail). Engraving by G Franchini (1775), from I. Alessi, *Ricerche storico critiche delle antichità di Este*, Padua 1776. The villa of Alvise Cornaro is visible in the center, with the greenhouse and the arched entrance to the garden (work of Falconetto, 16th century).

9. ESTE, Benvenuti Villa (already Cornaro). Renaissance arch (Falconetto) at the entrance to the garden.

10. ESTE, Benvenuti Villa (already Cornaro) is the 1848 radical transformation (architect G. Iappelli?) of sixteenth-century villa of Alvise Cornaro.

VERONA Antonio (1702 - 1754):
Busto di E.L.C.P. - Basilica di S. Antonio.

11. PADUA, Basilica of St. Anthony. G. Bonazza (active 1695-1730). Portrait bust of Elena Cornaro Piscopia placed (1727) in substitution of the funereal monument erected for her in 1684-1689 and demolished in 1727 because of its cumbersome nature.

149

12. VENICE, St. Luke Parish Archive, Baptisms 1633-1647, by name and by date. Elena Lucrezia Cornaro Piscopia's baptismal certificate.

13. VENICE, Loredan Palace (already Cornaro Piscopia) 12th century. Façade facing the Grand Canal.

14. Carlo Rinaldini, professor of philosophy at the University of Padua,
    who guided Elena Cornaro Piscopia in her philosophical studies until
    she obtained her degree (June 25, 1678). Engraving by M. Desbois
    (1630-1700) from C. PATINUS, *Lyceum Patavinum*, Patavii 1682, p. 52.

15. Professor Felice Rotondi, professor of theology at the University of
Padua, taught this subject to Elena Cornaro Piscopia. Engraving by
M. Desbois (1630-1700), from C. PATINUS, *Lyceum Patavinum*,
Patavii 1682, p. 47.

16. The University of Padua (Main façade), by I. PH. TOMASINI,
Gymnasium Patavinum, Utini 1654, p. 40.

VEN. SERVVS DEI
GREGORIVS S.R.E. CARD. BARBADICVS
EPISCOPVS PATAVINVS.

17. PADUA, Civic Museum Library, Racc. Icon. III, 518. Engraver I. Frey (1681-1752). Cardinal Gregorio Barbarigo, Bishop of Padua and Chancellor of the University.

18. PADUA, Ancient Archive of the University, ms. 365, f. 25^{r-v} - 26^{r-v}. Regular record of Elena Lucrezia Cornaro Piscopia's degree granted by the College of Philosophers and Physicians of the University of Padua.

19. PADUA, Civic Museum Library, Paduan Iconography 718.
Engraving by G. Langlois (1649-1712), Elena Cornaro Piscopia at the
age of twenty-two.

20. Elena Lucrezia Cornaro Piscopia. Engraving by D. Rossetti (1650-1736), from M. DEZA, *Vita di Helena Lucrezia Cornaro Piscopia*, Venice 1686.

21. Elena Lucrezia Cornaro Piscopia. Engraving by Sister I. Piccini (active
    1665-1692), from A. LUPIS, *L'eroina veneta, ovvero la vita di Elena
    Lucretia Cornara Piscopia*, Venetia 1689.

22. PADUA, Civic Museum. Elena Lucrezia Cornaro Piscopia. Portrait on
    canvas executed in 1673 and attributable more to Giovanni Battista
    Molinari (1638-1682) than to his son Antonio (1665-after 1727)
    barely eight at that time.

Elena Lucrezia Cornaro Piscopia. Engraving by A Portius (active
1686-1700), from M. Deza, *Vita di Helena Lucretia Cornara Piscopia*,
Venice-Genova 1687.

24. PADUA, Civic Museum Library, Paduan Iconography 719.
Engraving by C. Agostini from an engraving by G. Langlois, of Elena
Lucrezia Cornaro Piscopia.

25. VENICE, Correr Civic Museum Library, cod. Gradenigo 49, p. 156. Elena Lucrezia Cornaro Piscopia. Drawing from G. GREVENBROCH, (1731-1807), *Gli abiti de' veneziani di qualsiasi età con diligenza raccolti e dipinti.*

26. Elena Lucrezia Cornaro Piscopia. Engraving by A. VIVIANI (1797-1854) from drawing by M. FANOLI (1807-1876) in L. CARRER, *Anello di sette gemme o Venezia e la sua storia*, Venice 1838, p. 697.

27. The family of Carlo Patin, professor of medicine at the University of
Padua, who attempted to have his own eldest daughter graduate.
Engraving from CARLA PATIN, *Tabellae selectae et explicatae*, Patavii
1691, p. 201.

EMMANVEL THEODOSIVS EP̃VS OSTIENSIS S.R.E.
CARDINALIS BVLLIONIVS GALLVS
SACRI COLLEGIJ DECANVS
CREATVS DIE V. AVGVSTI MDC.LXIX.
Obijt die 2. Martij 1715.

Equus Hieron. Troppa Pinx.   *R. V. Auden. Aerd. Sculp.*

Romæ ex Chalcographia Dom.ti de Ruheis hæræÐis Io. Iacobi Ðe Ruheis, ad Templ. S. M.æ de Pace, cum Priuil. Sum. Pont.

28. VATICAN APOSTOLIC LIBRARY, Cardinals, sheet 6, I, 109.
Engraving by R. van Audenaerd (1663-1743), Cardinal Emanuel
Théodore de La Tour d'Auvergne de Bouillon (1643-1715), sent by
the King of France to Venice (1677) in order to verify the cultural
formation of Elena Cornaro Piscopia.

CAESAR S·R·E·ĒPVS CARD·DESTROEVS
GALLVS·XXIV·AVGVSTI MDCLXXI.

Obijt die 18.Decembris 1714.

Ferd.Voet pinx.   Alb.Clouwet fecit

Io·Iacobus de Rubeis formis Romæ ad Templ·Pacis cũ Priu· S·P·

29. VATICAN APOSTOLIC LIBRARY, Cardinals, sheet 6, I, 121.
Engraving by A. Clouwet (1636-1679), Cardinal Cesare d'Estrées
(1628-1714), Ambassador of France, who came to Padua in 1680 to
visit Elena Cornaro Piscopia.

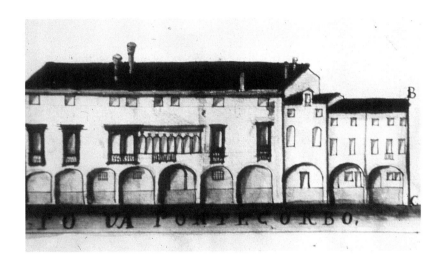

30. PADUA, State Archive, St. Anthony, Confessor, vol. 320. Drawing by
    L. MAZZI (1735). Alvise Cornaro's "La Casasa Vechia" [The Old
    House] in the district of the Saint in Padua.

31. PADUA, Civic Museum Library, Engraving by G. Valle (1784), The
    Cornaro "courtyard": the loggia in the background and on the right
    the odeon (work of Falconetto), to the left the "casa nova" [new house]
    to even out the "corte."

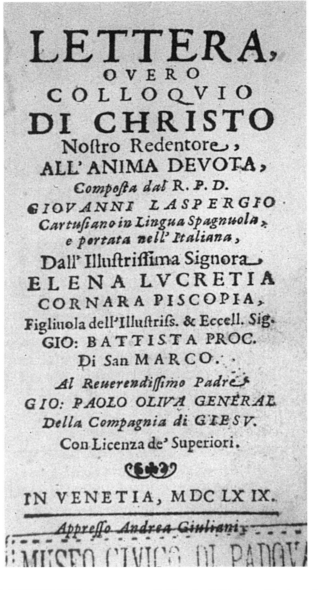

LETTERA,
OVERO
COLLOQVIO
DI CHRISTO
Noſtro Redentore,
ALL' ANIMA DEVOTA,
Compoſta dal R. P. D.
GIOVANNI LASPERGIO
Cartuſiano in Lingua Spagnuola,
e portata nell' Italiana,
Dall' Illuſtriſſima Signora
ELENA LVCRETIA
CORNARA PISCOPIA,
Figliuola dell'Illuſtriſſ. & Eccell. Sig.
GIO: BATTISTA PROC.
Di San MARCO.
Al Reuerendiſſimo Padre
GIO: PAOLO OLIVA GENERAL
Della Compagnia di GIESV.
Con Licenza de' Superiori.

IN VENETIA, MDC LX IX.

Appreſſo Andrea Giuliani

MUSEO CIVICO DI PADOVA

32. G. LANSPERGIO, *Lettera overo Colloquio di Christo all'anima devota...*,
a translation by Elena Lucrezia Cornaro Piscopia, Venetia 1669 (title
page), the first literary work of Elena Cornaro.

FRANCISCVS EPISCOPVS OSTIEN. SACRI COL. DE
CANVS CARD. BARBERINVS S·R·E·VICECANC. ET SVM
MISTA FLORENTIN. CREAT. DIE II. OCTOB. MDCXXIII.
Obijt die 10 Decembris 1679.

Valer·DA·Sad Jo. Jacobus de Rubeis Formis Romæ ad Templum Pacis Cum Priuil. S. Pontif.

33. VATICAN APOSTOLIC LIBRARY, Cardinals, sheet 6, I. Engraving
by G. Vallet (1632-1704), Cardinal Francesco Barberini (1597-1679),
to whom Elena Cornaro Piscopia wrote various letters.

171

INNOCENTIVS XI
PONT. MAX.
XXI. SEP
MDC
Obijt die

ODESCALCHVS
CREATVS DIE
TEMBR.
LXXVI
2. Augusti

34. VATICAN APOSTOLIC LIBRARY, Popes, sheet 7 (5), 104-105. Engraving by A. Clouwet (1636-1679), Pope Innocent XI (1611-1689), to whom Elena Cornaro Piscopia addressed a literary composition in gratitude for words of praise.

SECONDA CORONA

Intrecciata da varij Letterati co' fiori de' loro
ingegni , per coronar di nuouo

IL MOLTO REVERENDO PADRE

GIACOMO LVBRANI

DELLA COMPAGNIA DI GIESV.

*Predicatore nella Chiesa del Venerando Monistero di
San Lorenzo, e Corifeo trà gli Oratori sacri di
Venezia nell'anno 1675.*

D E D I C A T A

ALLA NOBILTA' VENETA

Dall'Illustrissima Signora :

ELENA LVCREZIA
CORNARA PISCOPIA.

VENETIA , M. DC. LXXV.

Appresso Antonio Bosio .
Con Licenza de' Superiori .

---

35. *La seconda corona intrecciata da vari letterati per il p. Giacomo Lubrani,*
Venetia 1675 (title page), promoted and published by Elena Cornaro
Piscopia.

Electus in Congrega: Generali   11 :
7: July. 1661   Obyt   26:
Nouem : 1681   ętatis   81 :

36. ROME, Archivum Romanum Societatis Iesu. P. Gianpaolo Oliva (1600-1681), Superior General of the Society of Jesus, who exchanged frequent correspondence with Elena Cornaro Piscopia and with her father.

37. Domenico Marchetti, professor of medicine at the University of
Padua, one of Elena Cornaro Piscopia's personal physicians. Engraving
by M. Desbois (1630-1700), by C. PATINUS, Lyceum Patavinum.
Patavii 1682, p. 39.

38. Giorgio Calafatti, professor of medicine at the University of Padua, cared for Elena Cornaro Piscopia during all of her illnesses until her death. Engraving by M. Desbois (1630-1700), by C. PATINUS, Lyceum Patavii 1682, p. 123.

39. PADUA, State Archive, Health Department n. 483, by name and Elena Lucrezia Cornaro Piscopia's civil death certificate.

40. PADUA, Civic Museum Library, BP. 914, Plate 114, Engraving by V. Coronelli (1650-1718), The Basilica of S. Giustina in Padua.

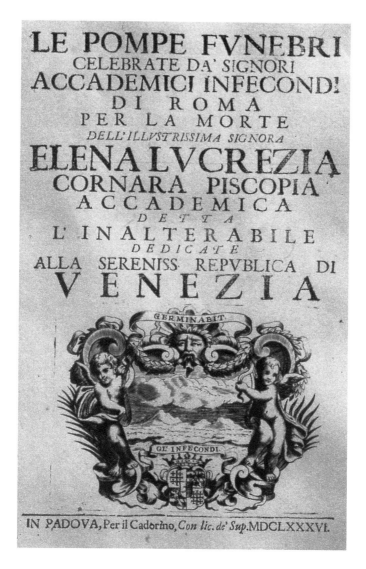

LE POMPE FVNEBRI
CELEBRATE DA' SIGNORI
ACCADEMICI INFECONDI
DI ROMA
PER LA MORTE
DELL'ILLVSTRISSIMA SIGNORA
ELENA LVCREZIA
CORNARA PISCOPIA
ACCADEMICA
DETTA
L'INALTERABILE
DEDICATE
ALLA SERENISS. REPVBLICA DI
VENEZIA

GERMINABIT

GL'INFECONDI

IN PADOVA, Per il Cadorino, Con lic. de' Sup. MDCLXXXVI.

41. *Le pompe funebri celebrate all' Accademia degli Infecondi di Roma per la morte di Elena Cornara Piscopia* [The funeral ceremony celebrated at the Accademia degli Infecondi of Rome on the death of Elena Cornara Piscopia], Padua 1686 (title page): collection of literary compositions for the observance.

42. Funeral monument to Elena Lucrezia Cornaro Piscopia erected in
1684-1689 (architect B. Tabacco) in the Basilica of St. Anthony in
Padua and demolished in 1727. Reconstruction (1974) by A. Calore
from the description of M. Deza, *Vita di Helena Lucretia Cornara
Piscopia*, Venice 1686, Appendix.

43. PADUA, Bottacin Museum. Engravor G.F. Neidinger (active 1678-
1692). Bronze medal of Elena Cornaro Piscopia which the College of
Philosophers and Physicians of the University of Padua had minted
(1685).

APPENDIX

DOCUMENT 1

MARRIAGE CONTRACT
BETWEEN GIOVANNI CORNARO PISCOPIA, SON OF FANTINO
AND CHIARA CORNARO, DAUGHTER OF ALVISE

A.S.V., Avogaria de Comun, reg. 143/4, f. 126r-v.

DIE VI IULII 1537

Consituti coram omnibus tribus magnificis dominis advocatoribus infrascriptis viri nobiles ser Ioannes Cornelio domini Fantini quonddam domini Hieronymi sponsus, ser Iacobus et Aloysius Cornelio quondam ser Antonii fratres nomine sponse infrascripte et ser Hieronymus Quirino quondam ser Saverii mediator nuptiarum infrascriptarum et in executionem legis presentaverunt dictis dominis advocatoribus contractum infrascriptum inter partes ipsas celebratum et per eos nunc ipsis dominis presentatum esse verum et autenticum contractum nec ullam aliam extare promissionem, pactum seu intelligentiam nisi quantum in contractu ipso continetur. Qui quidem contractus subscriptus fuit per dominos consiliarios et secretarium die XXII dicti mensis iulii iuxta formam legis. Cuius tenor sequitur et est talis videlicet.

1537 on the XVI of June in Venice

The magnificent Mister Iacobo and Mister Alvise Cornaro, of the late magnificent Mister Antonio, finding themselves without other heirs except for one daughter of said Mister Alvise and niece of the aforementioned Mister Iacomo, named Lady Chiara, and desiring with new offspring to renew and confirm his authority for the greater satisfaction of the Cornaro house, as it is a natural instinct that each one love his own family, after much consideration, they have chosen as son-in-law and son the nobleman Mister Giovanni Cornaro, son of the excellent Mister Fantin of the Episcopia, and by word of these present they have given the aforementioned Lady Chiara for his legitimate spouse as God and Holy Mother Church command and to obtain that which they desire as mentioned above. To which, for this marriage contract, the aforementioned Mister Iacomo and Mister Alvise promise and give on account as a dowry 4000 ducats cash, including 500 ducats of items.

Which same are content that the husband be free DE TUORLI in as much cash, declaring that, in the case of restitution, that God not permit it, it is understood that the loss is only 1000, as established by the latest law of this glorious city which they do not wish to disobey nor violate, again that the intention of the aforementioned magnificent Mister Iacomo and Mister Alvise and also that the aforementioned Mister Giovanni must be their son no less than the aforementioned Lady Chiara, neither one having other offspring as stated above. And thus both sides will undersign by their own hand. May it be pleasing to the majesty of God to give long life and happiness to both sides. And I, Fantino Cornaro, have received 500 ducats on account for clothing.

I Iacomo Cornaro of the late Mister Antonio am content with what is written above.

I Alvise Cornaro of the late Mister Antonio am content with what is written above.

I Fantino Cornaro am content with what is written above.

I Hieronymus Querini of the late Mister Saverio, as proxy, was present to what was written above.

Franciscus Maurocenus advocatus comunis.

Hieronymus Pisaurus advocatus comunis.

Marinum Iustinianus advocatus comunis.

DIE V IULII 1537

Philippus Zambonius notarius advocatoriae subscripsit.

1537 DIE XXII IULII

Polo Vallaresso consiliarius
Federicus Rhenerius consiliarius
Pandulphus Maurocenus consiliarius
Nicolaus Theupolus dominus consiliarius
Consilii Cavanius secretarius.

DOCUMENT 2

ORDINARY CEREMONIAL
FOR THE CONFERAL OF THE DOCTORATE IN THEOLOGY UPON MEN
BUT MODIFIED IN PART EXPRESSLY FOR THE BESTOWAL
OF THE DOCTORATE IN THEOLOGY ON ELENA LUCREZIA CORNARO PISCOPIA

PADUA, Biblioteca Antoniana, Opuscula varia Latina et Italica, ms. XXII-588, Prodoctoratu in sacra theologia nobilis et doctissimae virginis Elenae Corneliae Piscopiae Venetae, fasc. no. 8.

Authoritate omnipotentis Dei, Patris, Flii et Spiritus Sancti, sanctissimi domini nostri Innocentii divina providentia papae XI, eminentissimi et reverendissimi domini Gregorii Barbadici, sanctae Romanae Ecclesiae cardinalis amplissimi et episcopi Patavini vigilantissimi, annuente eius illustrissimo et reverendissimo domino pro-antistete Alexandro Mantuano, generali vicario iuris vice antecessore eximio.

[NORMAL CEREMONIALE]	[MODIFICATIONS OR VARIATIONS]
a) Creo, instutio atque declaro te magistrum et doctorem in sacra theologia cum omnibus honoribus, privilegiis, indultis, exemptionibus, immunitatibus atque prerogativis et gratiis, quibis per orbem christianum ceteri huiusmodi sacrae theologiae magistri et doctores de more, iure et approbata consuetudine fruuntur, potiuntur et gaudent; et ista sint tui doctoratus insignia	a) Pronuncio atque declaro te nobilem virginem Helenam Corneliam Piscopiam magistram laureatam in sacra theologia cum omnibus honoribus, gratiis atque indultis, quorum respective ad coeteros doctores sacros, ratione sexus es capax, et in signum
b) Accipe birettum pro sacra corona, Christi cruce insignitum, ut eamdem in pectore serves ad exemplum, sicit in capite geris ad gloriam.	b) Accipe sertum pro sacra corona veluti dignam divinae Sapientiae lauream, quam servare deves in via, donec angelicis vocibus audies: Veni, sponsa Christi, accipe coronam, quam tibi Dominus preparavit in eternum, celestem simul suscipiendo laureolam.

c) Annulum fidei tibi trado, ut sis fidelis doctor, fidusque magister in Ecclesia Dei.

c) Annulo fidei despondeo tibi christianam sapientiam, ut sis fidelis Dei sponsa, et virgo orthodoxa nullo non tempore in Ecclesia sancta Dei ad catholicae fidei ornamentum et incrementum.

d) Librum porrigo clausum et apertum cum facultate interpretandi, exponendi, glossandi, declarandi, aperiendi divina mysteria oportune fidelibus.

d) Librum porrigo clausum atque apertum

e) Sede in cathedra Christi ad publice docendum, ceteraque verbis et factis exequendum ad catholicae religionis incrementum.

e) ad divina meditanda atque describenda mysteria: non tamen ad publice predicandum atque docendum, iuxta Apostoli monitum, qui docere mulieribus in Ecclesia non permittit.

f) Amplexum sancto te excipio et osculo illibato te prosequor, ut caritate erga Deum et proximum coruscante prefulgeas.

f) Deinde divinus Sponsus quondam suae sponsae mistice edixit: Leva eius sub capite meo et dextera illius amplexabitur me, te quoque idem Sponsus caritate coruscans sancte aplexetur, dum ego

g) Tandem benedicto te, ut Dei opera maneant benedicta in aeternum.

g) benedico te in nomine sanctissimae Triadis, Patris Filii et Spiritus Sancti, ut Dei opera Iesu Christi domini nostri maneant in eternum obsignata sigillo.

DOCUMENT 3
REPORT OF ELENA LUCREZIA CORNARO PISCOPIA'S
DOCTORAL PRESENTATION

A.A.U., ms. 365, ff. 25r-v, 26r-v.

DIE SABBATI 25 MEMSIS IUNII 1678

Convocato sacro Collegio pro examine in philosophia illustrissimae Elenae Lugretiae Corneliae Piscopia, ob multitudinem gentium locique soliti angustiam, necesse fuit adire catthedralem ecclesiam, et in sacello beatissimae Virginis Mariae denuo convocare Collegium coram illustrissimis et excellentissimis civitatis rectoribus Hieronymo Basadona praetore, Aloysio Mocenico praefecto, reverendissimo vicario Alexandro Mantuano, et generosissimo vice sindico, ubi interfuere infrascripti nobiles et excellentissimi patres videlicet

Promotores {
Hieronymus Fizimelica Ruberti comes et eques
Carolus Renaldinus
Angelus Montagnana
Ermegildus Pera

Ioannes Petrus Saviolus sindicus
Ioannes Dominicus de Tessariis
   vice prior
Ludovicus Saxonia
Ermegildus Pera
comes Petrus Franzanus
Vincentius Anselmus
Franciscus Bosellus
Prosper Thedeschi
Ioannes Pompilius Scotto
Hercules Saxonia
Franciscus Zacco nobilis Venetus
Hieronymus Vergerius
Iacobus Cadenedus
Aloysis Speronus
Hieronymus Capivatius senior
Iacobus Bonzaninus
comes Alexander Borromaeus

Georgius a Turre
Sebastianus Scarabitius
Palmerinus Ianua
Nicolaus Campilongus
Marsilius Papafava
Iulius Mussatus
Iacobus Trentus
Franciscus Bonbardenus
Antonius Maria Ursatus eques
Carolus Patinus
Nicolaus Frascata
Vincentius Pasqualigo nobilis Venetus
Hieronymus Bradiolus
Ioannes Baptista Bradiolus
comes Franciscus Silvaticus
comes Bartholomeus Silvaticus canonicus
Prosdocimus Bosellus
Marcus Antonius Mussatus

Hillarius Spinelli
Dominicus de Marchetis
Ioannes Cicalla
Albanius Albanensis
Alexander Mussatus
Antonius de Marchettis
Aldrighettus Aldrighetti
Ioannes Antonius Perotius
Ioannes Capilisteus
Alverius Zacco
Marcus Antonius Franchinus
Severinus Bellini
Antonius Manzonius
Horatius Brentanus
[32] Ioannes Ursatus

Alexander Vigontia
Hieronymus Capivatius iunior
Alexander Bellafinus
Ioannes Augustus Scotus
Ioannes Franciscus Frangina
Carolus Mussatus
Ioannes Christophorus Massimus
Sulimanus Bradiolus
Tissus Bellafinus
comes Nicolaus Tebaldi
Angelus Casale
Marcus Antonius Peregrinus
Ioannes Vicentius Albanensis
[32] Hanius Falaguasta

- Ex una -

- Ex alia -

[64 total]

Et in praedicto sacello pleno Collegio iamscripta illustrissima Elena Lucretia Cornelia Piscopia recitavit in philosophia, more nobilum, duo puncta heri mane illi sorte assignata; in quorum explicatione tam egregiae ac excellenter se gessit, ut absoluto eiusdem nobilis viriginis examine, raro et admirabili exemplo, fuerunt de more suffragationis urnolae delatae ad nobilem et excellentissimum dominum Ioannem Dominicum de Tessariis vice priorem caeterosque de banca suffragationis gratia peragendae. Cum autem omnes Collegii doctores alta voce pronunciaverint tam sublimem punctorum recitationem nobiliori forma, quam per suffragia subiiciendam esse, propterea hoc audito illustrissima praedicta, reiteratis vocibus reverenter tamen, instetit ut iuxta consuetudinem ad secretam omnino suffragationem deveniretur. Et in eam opinionem abierunt ut honestum ac decens arbitrarent examen. Propterea illustrissimus dominus Ioannes Dominicus de Tessariis vice prior insurrexit dicens: quamvis dispositio statutorum decernat, ut examen secretae suffragationi exponatur, quia nihilominus haec heroina tam excellenter tamque excelse se gessit, praestat ob id suffragatione praeterissa insuetum modum explorandi mentem vestram, patres, adhibere. Unde proposuit ipsis ac universo Collegio, num communis acclamatio placeret, et omnes uno ore responderunt: placet, atque hunc in modum communi consensu acclamatione et vivae vocis oraculo illustrissima et excellentissima Helena Lucretia Cornelia praedicta philosophiae magistra et doctrix acclamata fuit coram universo doctorum coetu maxima nobilium populique frequentia.

Mox accissit praedicta nobilis virgo (cum prius more solito recessisset), ad lauream doctoralem suscipiendam, quam selectis ornatisque verbis petiit ab illustrissimo domino Carolo Renaldino promotore suo, patritio Anconitano, Cosimi III magnifici ducis Etruriae philosopho ac mathematico et <in> hac celeberrima Academia Patavina philosopho primae sedis. Qui statim surrexit et coram omnibus supraditis ornata et erudita quidem oratione nobilitatem atque virtutis heroinae praedictae commendavit summo cum audientium plausu, atque tandem corona ex lauro tempora ipsius redimivit, libros eidem exibuit, digito annulum inseruit et epinotion pelliceum humeris eiusdem induit.

Et dissolutum Collegium . . .

Document 4

Testament and codicil
of the most illustrious and most excellent Mister
Giovanni Battista Cornaro Piscopia,
Procurator of St. Mark's

A.S.V., Notary Document Testaments [Wills], b. 773, nos. 163–164.

Jesus Mary

In the name of God, the Father, the Son, and the Holy Spirit, and of the Blessed Virgin Mary, our Lady and my Advocate.

In Venice in my residence in St. Mark's Square in the Procuracy, the fifth of August on Saturday in the year 1690.

There being nothing more sure or certain than death, nor the more uncertain than the hour of it, for this reason we are obligated by reason of true Christian piety not to neglect anything which might get in the way of keeping us ready and prepared in that last hour and at that point to render us worthy of divine mercy, so that far from all mundane thoughts, we may be disposed to a fruitful beginning of our journey toward the port of eternal tranquility and toward the attainment of the glory of paradise. There being nothing, however, which troubles us more seriously, so as to divert us from our path toward that goal as much as the thought of mundane and domestic affairs, to organize them which one would do with difficultly and in great confusion during those final days and hours in which nothing else should occupy our soul except the thought of its being healthy, for this reason, I, Giovanni Battista Cornaro Piscopia, Procurator of St. Mark's, (thanks to divine grace I am sound both of body and of mind), wanted to make this my current testament (will) by my own hand for greater validity so that there can never be any doubt cast upon it at all.

Since, however, there are so many and such events of this world and that they are so subject to changes and new occurrences, because of this, our days are not filled solely with completing our lives, and therefore, we must always renew the established proposal, as has happened to me many times with great regret, and much more so with the death of my dearly beloved daughter, Lady Elena Lugretia {sic} still of eternal and glorious memory, mourned by all the world for her rare qualities, singular virtues, goodness of life and angelic habits, for which she was applauded by all the world and honored everywhere, as appears in the works of many great writers who speak of her and give ample testimony of it to posterity, for all the above mentioned reasons, and now particularly because of the recent death of Mister Francesco, my most delightful son of happy memory, having several times and for many sudden occurrences, misfortunes and reasons, and at different times, I had to change and make new testaments (wills) and codicils, which, if my memory serves me right, I have removed from where I kept them before presenting the revised versions, in any case for greater validity and security, and to eliminate every error and confusion which for this reason could arise, I cancel and annul all and every other testament (will), testamentary agreement and codicil which for whatever cause, time and place, and for whichever occasion I would have made previously, for whatever reason they exist, and be it understood that they are of no value and as if they had not been made, and let only this have its full execution by means of which I declare my last will.

In the first place, I commend my soul to the Lord God, to the Blessed Virgin Mary, our mother and my advocate, and to all the celestial court, beseeching St. John the Baptist, my guardian angel and all the saints that they kindly assist me at the time and point and hour of my death that in that last and tremendous step, I not lose divine grace, but that they intercede for me that His Divine Majesty be merciful.

I order and want to be brought for burial without ceremony and placed in the Church of St. Luke, in my family tomb, and that my heirs have said for me after my death, 2000 masses according to my wishes, as soon as is possible, within the span of one year, and this as soon as possible and for the most part by the Capuchin Fathers, and that at the same time and on the day of my funeral and burial, in which I want to be brought and laid to rest at night, that as many as possible of the masses be said, in the Church of St. Luke and in that of Frari, and particularly, in the family chapel, and that four large candles be given to them to place on the tomb, and all the candles necessary for all the altars to keep them lighted, as also with the candles during the time that said masses are celebrated and that as many as possible be said in the Church of St. Luke on the same day, and those remaining to be celebrated of the 2000, I want them to be said according to my wishes and in the aforementioned time span of one year, that on the same day 200 ducats be given to the poor of the district of St. Luke.

To the four Hospitalers, which will have to accompany me to my tomb, I leave twelve ducats V.C. [Venetian gold coins] for each one and for one time only.

To Nicolosa and to Catarina Bonoli, long-time chambermaids of Madame Procurator, my wife, I leave fifty ducats V.C. each [Venetian gold coins] once and for all; and to the other servants and maids, both mine and Mister Geronimo's, my son, who are in my service, and also to Dorotea, I leave twelve ducats each, and that they be outfitted in mourning clothes, and this, once and for all.

To the illustrious gentleman Doctor Georgio Calafati, public lecturer at the University of Padua, who with so much courtesy and assiduous labor took care of Lady Elena Lugretia, my daughter of glorious memory, only as a testimony of gratitude, not to satisfy what he deserves and what I owe him, I leave 100 cechini (gold coins) in cash and sixty ounces of wrought silver.

To Mister Francesco dal Re, my attorney and godfather of my child, I leave 40 ounces of wrought silver as a testimony of my affection.

And since it is about 27 years that Madalena has been in my home, as organist and in service to Lady Elena Lugretia (sic), my daughter of happy memory, until the day of her death, playing for her when she sang, therefore I order and I want that she always be kept in our home by my heirs, expenses paid and kept at their own table, well dressed and well treated, as long as she would like to stay, in the manner in which she is living at present in my home, and that she be given as a salary fifty ducats a year V.C. [Venetian gold coins] and dressed honorably according to her needs, as long as she lives in the home of the above mentioned and named heirs, such as they were at this time, and in the case that she not be able nor desire to, or would not be able to stay in the home of said and named heirs, in such case, I want her to be given one hundred and twenty ducats V.C. [Venetian gold coins] a year for the rest of her life, that is, ten ducats a month, and I mean even after the death of Madame Procurator, my aforementioned wife, while as long as she is alive, I desire that she not expect any more than that which is given to her now; that these ducats be paid to her as 120 every six months, that is, sixty ducats at a time paid in advance in cash, without even the slightest contradiction, and that all her furniture be given to her, those pieces which she brought with her and those which were given to her while staying in my house and all those which she would say in good conscience were hers; anyway, I believe they would be sufficient for her, while never having manifested the disposition to marry, I am persuaded that not even now, even though she is getting on in age, does she ponder such thoughts.

To Sister Catarina, my sister, a nun in the Monastery of Santa Maria of Bethlehem in Padua, I leave fifty ducats V.C. [Venetian gold coins] for one time only, since she has her own means with which to manage comfortably.

To the most illustrious and most excellent Mister Bertuci Contarini, my most beloved nephew, I leave 100 ounces of wrought silver for his satisfaction, and this only as a testimony of the esteem and affection which I have always born for him, as he has experienced in the course of time, having myself cared for the most excellent Mister Gerolimo his father and my brother-in-law, in a most loving fashion, well known to the excellent Mister Bertuci and to all the world, and to the utmost in the most troublesome circumstances during his public service in various important positions, to which he lent himself in the past war in Candia, which by unwarranted persecutions were fabricated against him and helped and assisted him in diverse guarantees made for him by me and other well-known things, so as to be able to put himself in the position to accept the order to go on to be the captain of ships; but I beg that in all cases he be allowed to execute and to fulfill the desires of the fond memory of Lady Isabella, his mother and my sister which are well known to him and his conscience, since she could not fulfill what she had ordered in her will which was made by her in her serious illness by which my house would have benefited which she took from the notary to revise and improve it, as is well known to the excellent Mister Bertuci, since it, the said will, happened into his hands and which could not be revised and fulfilled as she wanted because of her sudden death, while he knows with what affection and what fervor I have always procured by serving him, and not holding back at all in assisting him as much as his most excellent father. With all the greatest warmth and affection though I beg him to heed his conscience when not having heirs and to have under his protection and patronage the aforementioned Madame Procurator, my wife and all of my children and heirs.

To Lady Catarina, my beloved daughter, whom I have given in marriage to the illustrious Mister Antonio Vendramin, son of Sir Andrea and of Sir Zuanne, with a dowry of 40,000 ducats, as appears in her dowry papers in the notary acts of Mister Andrea Porta, Notary, the acts which she made also of her renouncement, the renouncement which I do not intend to take effect but that nothing be intended. This has no bearing on things her mother may leave her, Madame Procurator, Lady Catarina, anything which may be of use to her, declaring that she may always be able to receive it and enjoy it, as her mother were to order notwithstanding the said renouncement made to me, wherefore she has also to enjoy whatever I leave to her in this my testament (will), intending in such case the said renouncement as null, in witness though of that affection that she has always deserved and that I bear for her, I leave 200 ducats V.C. [Venetian gold coins] for one time only and all of the few fields, which I find myself to have under Lendenara, which are rented for five ducats and five sacks of wheat per year, with the condition that she be held to pay nine lire per year, that they be paid to the Contarina house at the steel doors at S. Francesco, on some of the fields given by me as a dowry to her, while I have forgotten to place such a condition on them in her dowry contract, and I further leave to her my house in Padua near Ponte Corbo and also the other little house attached to it, which houses at present time bring in eighty ducats and were acquired by me; I also leave her the piece of land of the Bassanelo with the small amount of ground which currently is rented with said parcel to the Danieleti, and furthermore, I want Mister Geronimo, my son, and his heirs and perpetual descendants to pay to the aforementioned Lady Catarina, and to her perpetual heirs, to whomever she were to leave it, 400 ducats V.C. [Venetian gold coins] per year, free and exempt from any tax, no exceptions, and in the case of default, and that they were not to pay for them, she could seek payment by legal means, and even when it would seem to her in the lack of such payment, she may take for herself as many goods or property, which would render to her these 400 ducats, always with the exception of my palace at St. Luke's; furthermore, I leave to her the house at S. Geronimo acquired by me from the lord governors of the INTRADE, and so that she may live in said house at Pontecorbo immediately and without inconvenience or expense to her, I desire that she be given all the furniture, which will be described by me on a sheet of paper and compiled by my own hand, which will be inserted in the copy of this my testament (will) which I keep near me, those properties, cash and furniture are to go to the possession of Lady Catarina after the death of Madame Procurator, her mother and my wife, free and at her disposition, declaring further, that when, at any time or for any reason, no exceptions, the fields or property be taken away from Lady Catarina, which were given to her by me as a dowry, I again mean and want that it be made up by my nominated heirs, whoever they be at the time, with all other properties of equivalent price and rent of those which would be taken and evicted from her, and all this I leave to her as a sign of my continued affection, having given me great honor for her great goodness, virtue and admirable outcome, as is evident, being ever most virtuous, since besides Lady Elena Lugretia (sic), of whom she has a fond memory as her sister, has no other as an equal.

Of all the rest of my means and things, goods and property, present and future, if movable, in decay or in disrepair and therefore not written, gold articles, jewelry, silver and cash monies which I were to have in and out of the city of Venice, as with all my other possessions, credit or effects of each one which is owed me or were to be owed to me and to my inheritance, now in life as after my death, for any cause or reason and action, no exceptions, and especially those which by the testament (will) of the late noble gentleman Sir Geronimo, my father, with things being as they are and circumstances arising, remain free in me, and I may dispense of them freely, as also with the portion of the donation of the late noblewoman Isabella Cornaro made in the year 1603, on the third of the month of February in Padua, Notary Antonio Cossavechia, presented and corroborated in the same year 1603 of May in Padua, mayor Sir Francesco Bernardo, by which I remain beneficiary and free heir, owner and absolute heir of all these my things and aforementioned means, I leave to Madame Procurator Zanetta Boni, my beloved wife, as long as she lives, declaring to be freely hers the proceeds acquired by her capital [of gold coins], whose proceeds are reduced to two percent, and in capital at the time of the evaluation of the coin, of which I desire that she may as pleases her make use, which she may never be asked to account for, neither for these nor for my aforementioned goods, gold items, jewelry, silver, cash monies, nor for any other sort or thing or of such conditions, nor from whomever and in the case where others were to do so, that they be deprived of all of mine and of all the benefits to which I have called them in my present testament (will), beseeching her to govern with love and charity all in this family, as I have done until now, being a woman of valor, known to the world, and mother of such virtuous and highly esteemed daughters, and as has been my experience for so long a time, to be prudent, virtuous and knowing how to govern, to whom I profess infinite depth, even of life, but I beg her and my children and heirs to love her and leave everything up to her, being able in handling great governing and management, I am very sorry that she be frequently troubled by gout.

I find myself to possess a very beautiful library of numerous volumes, part of which was left to me by my father whom I pleasantly remember, as appears from the inventory, which was drawn up to the blessed memory of my mother, in the notary act of Mister Giovanni Picini, to which act I also submit, but I declare that it has been greatly amplified and more than doubled by books and manuscripts, as much as a third of the columned compartments, which are still not sufficient, there having been added to at the top and at the bottom, without which it was unseemly and not uniform, since by acquisition of many books, excellent and of great quality, which clearly appears from the inventory of the Notary Picino aforementioned, with many other ornaments and purchases made by me of heads, busts of stone, mathematical instruments, globes, spheres and more. I declare, though, that a part of said inventory may be missing, being that much of it may have been stolen, not having been delivered and received by me, but those items of my father are for the most part simple and now remain free in me, as one can understand by the reflections which can be made in the testament (will) of the aforementioned gentleman, my father; I considered it necessary to express this to my heirs by this notation.

After the death of Madame Procurator, my said wife, residual and universal heir of all my goods and properties, present and future, both in Venice and outside of Venice, levels, gold coins, cash and all else that there be after the death of the said Madame Procurator, my wife, I leave to Mister Geronimo, my son, and to his male children, and to their perpetual male descendents, born in legitimate wedlock and born elegible for the Most Serene Major Council on the condition that if any one of them were to be without sons of the aforementioned conditions or if they were to die, their daughters sucede, and if there were no daughters even, of any one of those who are legitimate and of the said conditions stated for the males, the possessions and faculties pass to the others and the legitimate sons and able-born of the Most Serene Great Council, as above; and should there not be sons of said conditions with this declaration and conditions, that the administration be left to said mother Madame Procurator, all these things also conditions, during her life, while she has always maintained him and all his household, as he until now has experienced and experiences to the present as is well known to all, while if the contrary were to be and there should be the desire to move immediately to possession, after my death, with all the descendants, the exception in such case being the legitimate one, who belonged to him, when he left my home and separated, may my things go to her as I have stipulated in this my testament in the cases which I have expressed, with the declaration that at the time when possession is to be taken of these conditioned goods, he, Geronimo, though still after the death of his mother, of these goods which he expects and which were truly conditioned and were to go to him (these goods I again intend that they remain purified of the debts of the testator and by the bequests left by the same, while *non dicitur ereditas nisi detractis debitis et legatis*); but I intend and desire that in such case these goods be, which my lord father could not condition, figured in all my means, united with all said free means, of which I freely may dispose, prohibiting him, Geronimo, and his descendants and perpetual heirs, to argue even the slightest or to contest to the aforementioned Madame Procurator, his mother and to Lady Catarina, his sister and to her heirs, and other beneficiaries and substitutes in this my testament (will), for any reason or pretext, nor in court or out, not even with the slightest citation, or with any other act, no exceptions; otherwise doing so, he be deprived of all that is mine, as well as his, and his perpetual heirs, and in such case may these things of mine and my means be for Lady Catarina, my daughter and his sister, with all the conditions expressed above and ordered to him Geronimo, and in the case that he, Mister Geronimo, or his discendents, should have no sons or daughters, or that they should become religious, in such case I leave all these my things and faculties to her Lady Catarina, my daughter and her sons and male descendants, and in their absence to the daughters with all the conditions, clauses and orders etablished by me for the sons and daughters and descendants of him, Mister Geronimo, which

I would order in this my testament (will).

And since certain buildings cannot and should not suffer division for such purpose, I declare and desire that Mister Geronimo and his sons and heirs and perpetual descendents aforementioned cannot ever for any reason be paid for his legitimacy, if the occasion should come to pass that he wanted it notwithstanding the things mentioned above and ordered by me, during the life of Madame Procurator, his mother, as also for the things passed, for the palace in Venice, nor for any other credit, because I want this to remain entire in its inheritence, nor can he at any time, nor for any reason, with no exceptions, nor by anyone else, may it be divided, but only may it be divided regarding the rent received from it when they do not live there, though I am convinced that no such step will be taken, since it would be a loss to his reputation and good taste, nor also will he want after my death to be ungrateful for all the benefits I have bestowed upon him, which are known to all the world, while he still has the opportunity to learn from my example and fondly remember his father, the inheritence which I did not want to refuse, after having left his guardianship, not even accepting it with the benefit of the law and of the inventory, while I knew well that it is not ever called inheritance *nisi detractis debitis et legatis*, as is well known, and it is and will be just to reclaim all of my credits, as the expenditure of my mother, and by my commissaries, or by me on account of his debts, so as to satisfy those necessitated by my mother to have recourse to petition the magistrate from which the termination was effected in the year 1625 on the first of March, as can be seen, to be able to take the leveled monies, as has happened with much of it, and particularly 10890 ducats V.C. [Venetian gold coins], as an instrument made in Pesaro on January 26, 1626, Notary Allessandro Vaiani, by my father, by means of which I was left free heir, and all that I have used for the sole purpose of not diminishing their value and worth, which with such generous ways lent in public regiments and services had been earned, and so as not to cast any doubt on the salvation of his soul, not wanting in this part to follow the example nor the manner in these cases as such, because many are even more conspicuous and well-off and of rich families who by this means exempted themselves from a similar piety, generous and religious expenditure and example.

Further I order and desire that he, Mister Geronimo, and his descendants and heirs aforementioned and called by me and given benefits, as above, pay punctually all the public debts, and with all punctuality, as I have always done, and have the houses kept in good repair and all the buildings, both in Venice and ouside of Venice, and even in the villa, so that they not fall into disrepair, as usually happens for the most part to those buildings which have conditions attached to them and are not governed well, doing otherwise, he and they can be forced to do so by my heirs and beneficiaries, with all the force mandated by the courts, nor can they even pawn these my possessions and means to anyone, not even during their lives, nor can they make even the slightest guarantee, nor obligate my possessions during their lives for any reason, no exceptions, for in so doing, may they be obligated for each one of these guarantees to pay 200 ducats V.C. [Venetian gold coins] per year to the Pietà Hospital, and may each one of these nominated heirs continue to pay them until the obligation of this guarantee ceases.

Should it happen that Mister Geronimo, my son, after my death were to leave young sons and daughters and therefore incapable of managing and governing their possessions, for this reason and for the utmost caution and respect, I order and desire, in such case, that Madame Procurator, my wife and his mother, if she is alive, remain the administrator together with Lady Catarina, sister of said Mister Geronimo, and in the absence of these administrators, in such case, that the three most excellent senior procurators of the Procuracy of Upper St. Mark be the administrators.

To the most illustrious Lady Isabeta, my daughter-in-law, wife of the late and fondly remembered Mister Francesco, my beloved son, I leave 100 ounces of silver wrought to her liking, and this solely as a gesture of that affection and esteem which I profess for her, since she has many possessions, nor has the need of them but she may very honorably deal with them. Moreover, I declare and desire that she, the illustrious Lady Isabeta by her own choice, remain in my house, thus being treated as would please and satisfy her and in a manner and way with which she has always been treated when her husband and my son, Mister Francesco, was alive, which I am certain will be done by Madame Procurator, my wife, and after her death I also want such obligation to rest with Mister Geronimo, my son and her brother-in-law, the most illustrious to Lady Isabeta whom I commend to him, Mister Geronimo and Lady Catarina, my daughter, and I beg her to keep them under her care and to love them as she shows, having seen Lady Catarina and Mister Geronimo be born, while at the time she was living in my house, and having raised them as if they were her own children. Indeed, I desire even more, that after my death, Madame Procurator, my wife go to live on the upper level of my palace at St. Luke, that at such time those rooms which are most pleasing to her be given to her, Lady Isabeta, and after the death of Madame Procurator, my wife, I want her to be allowed to make her own choice of the rooms and the chambers which are most pleasing to her, for her to enjoy for the rest of her life, nor can any of this be denied her, nor precluded by anyone. This much I have wanted to express and order in this my testament and last will so that the world and she, the most illustrious

Lady Isabeta, my daughter-in-law, may know the great esteem I profess for her and the affection which I bear for her.

And because I purchased and reclaimed almost all of my aforementioned palace of St. Luke with my own money, and rebuilt the inside at the great expense of about 50,000 ducats, while it was practically falling down, and reduced to modern form, except the facade above the Grand Canal, which after the many centuries during which our family possessed it, only in recent years had it in large part passed to other houses and families, wherefore, to preserve in my house as much as possible this building which is as old and decorous as my family, I wanted this too to be subjected to a rigorous, perpetual trust as is so with all my remaining means as above, returning it to great splendor because of the very ancient symbols one can see engraved on our house and particularly, those of the King of Cyprus, donated by King Pietro Lusignano to our family, when he stayed in it with the perpetual Knight of the Order of Cypress, who, as a sign of which, had his sword engraved and sculpted in the middle of our antique coat of arms with the oath of the order, in very antique Longobardi characters and in the French dialect precisely of the Lusignana house, whose characters were used in those times, as one can still see, about whose order authors have written in giving an account of military orders and in particular, in writing about Francesco Menenio.

Therefore, when they wanted to bring forward the facade above the Grand Canal, as I had planned, when I had rebuilt and modernized the inside of this, my palace, because it was so old and falling down, to which I also exhort them, in such case, though, I want and order that they have all these arms, symbols and hieroglyphics as they are and are layed out at present, since these are the things which clearly make known the privilege of the Knight of Cypress and the perpetuity of the same, conceded and donated by the king to our well-deserving house, as I clearly made known in the writings I myself presented in the most excellent Pien Colleggio and Serenissima Signoria in the year 1683, on the third of the month of July; doing otherwise and not puting them there, may they be deprived of my inheritence, and may the Hospital of the Pietà enjoy all of my possessions and means, until they have it put there, leaving them though free to carry on with the façade, not wanting to obligate them to this.

This is my last will and testament, made by my own hand, I, Giovanni Battista Cornaro so called by the Piscopia, Procurator of St. Mark's, with which I cancel and annul all the other testaments (wills), testament coupons and codiciles, which in any other time or place I may have made, and let only this be executed and have its place, made in the house where I reside in Venice in the Procuracy on the square, found in the district of St. Mark, this fifth day of the month of August, Saturday, in the year 1690.

I Giovanni Battista Cornaro Piscopia, Procurator of St. Mark's, confirm all I have expressed in my above written testament and again by my own hand I confirm it ([a])

Die mercurii nono mensis augusti 1690, indictione decima tertia, Rivoalti.

I, Giovanni Battista Cornaro Piscopia, Procurator of St. Mark's, of the late most excellent Gerolamo, by the grace of God, of sound mind, senses and intellect and body, I had Don Andrea Porta, Venetian Notary, called and come to my home and residence, located in this city above the new Procuracies of St. Mark's, to whom in the presence of the undersigned witnesses I gave and presented this my present testament (will), firm and last will written and undersigned by my own hand and also sealed, and I asked said notary to accept it, take custody of and preserve it, in case of my death, which will follow when pleasing to His Divine Majesty, that he open it, publish it, execute it, and corroborate it according to the laws of this city.

Questioned by said notary of others similar, to present in the Chancellary, as also of the Hospital of the Pietà, other hospitals, Riscato de Schiavi (Ransom of Slaves), Poveri Vergonosi (the Shameful Poor) and other pious places of the city, I answered him: I do not want other to create coupons nor to leave anything else.

Praeterea etc. Si quis etc. Signum etc.

I doctor Giorgio Calafatti of the late Stefano, public professor of medicine in the University di Padova, was present as witness to the said presentation and deed, summoned and sworn.

I Bortolo Seffani di Marco, servant in the house of the above written most excellent Mister Procurator, was present as witness to the above written presentation and deed, summoned and sworn.

---

[a] The annotation follows:

On the day of March 15, 1692

The present testament (will) was published for me, Notary, along with a codicil, given the death of the above named most illustrious and most excellent Mister Procurator Giovanni Battista Corner Piscopia (*viso prius cadavere*), at the instance of the noble Lady Zanetta, his wife and heir, by whom said notice was given to me on behalf of the Aque.

CODICIL
JESUS MARY

In the name of the Lord God, Father, Son and Holy Spirit, and of the Blessed Virgin Mary, our Mother and my advocate, in Venice at my residence in the Procuracy of St. Mark Square, on the 13th of the month of May, Sunday, of the year 1691.

I, Giovanni Battista Cornaro Piscopia, Procurator of St. Mark's, having made my testament (will) by my own hand, on the fifth of the month of August of the past year, 1690, and presented it to the Notary Mister Andrea Porta, and wanting to add to same a few things which I consider necessary and worthwhile, but I wanted to make this present codicile, by my own hand, so that there can never be any doubt at all.

Therefore, loving very much Lady Catarina, my daughter, married to the most illustrious Mister Antonio Vendramin, for her rare virtues, qualities, goodness and exemplary life, I want and order that, should Mister Geronimo, her brother, or his sons, or his heirs and descendants seek to cause her worry or begin an argument with her for any reason, no exceptions, the aforementioned Lady Catarina is free from the renouncement made to me when she married, wherefore she may in all aforesaid situations and incidents, have at her disposal all that which was available to her before said renouncement, from which in said cases I declare her entirely free and absolved.

Furthermore, I order and want that Mister Geronimo, my son, be free to pay to said Lady Catarina, his sister, 400 ducats V.C. [Venetian gold coins] per year ordered by me in my will, and in their place I leave to Lady Catarina, my aforesaid daughter, the Valle dell'inferno and Moraro [Val del Moraro] in the lower lagoon in the Conche villa, and the Petrobello field made by me with the happy memory of Sir Petrobello Petrobelli, as shown by the instrument, all free and at her free disposal, as also as much as I left her in my aforesaid will, and in the case where for any accident of water or other things and at any time that the valley were to be lost, or the rent were to diminish, which the renters now pay, I declare and desire that she be able to seek compensation for losses upon my goods of any kind which she pleases, except, though, the palace of St. Luke, all this, however, after the death of Madame Procurator, my wife and her mother.

I Giovanni Battista Cornaro Piscopia, Procurator of St. Mark's, made the present codicil by my own hand, this year 1691, on the 13th day of the month of May, Sunday([a])

A The annotation follows:

On the day of March 15, 1692

The present codicil was published together with the testament (will).

Wednesday, the 23rd day of the month of May 1691, at the Rialto.

I Giovanni Battista Cornaro Piscopia, Procurator of S. Marco, of the late most excellent Gerolamo, by the grace of God, of sound mind, senses, intellect and body, had called and had come to my house and residence, located in this city of Venice in the new Procuracies above St. Mark Square, Don Andrea Porta, Venetian Notary, to whom, in the presence of the undersigned witnesses I gave and presented the present codicil, written and undersigned by my own hand and also sealed and I beseeched said notary to accept it, take custody of it and preserve it, and in the event of my death, which will take place when it pleases His Divine Majesty, to open it and publish it together with my will in accordance with the laws. Having been interrogated by said notary to present in the chancellery, as also with the four hospitals, Riscato de schiavi (Ransom of Slaves), Poveri Vergognosi (Shameful Poor) and other pious locations in the city, I responded to him: I do not want to do anything else, nor leave anything else.

Praeterae etc. Si quis etc. Signum etc.

I Doctor Nicolò Bubulli de Antonio present witness to the aforesaid presentation and deed, summoned and sworn.

I Alvise Agusti of the late Marin, barber, was present as witness for the above, summoned and sworn.

Document 5

Testament and Codicil
of the Noble Lady Cattarina Cornaro, Widow of the Late
Antonio Vendramin

Venice, April 21, 1705

Venice, Biblioteca del Civico Museo Correr, mss. PD-C. 1324/2.

Die vigesima prima
mensis aprilis 1705, indictione 13a, Rivoalti.

The noble Lady Cattarina Cornaro Piscopia of the late Mister Giovanni Battista, Procurator of St. Mark's, widow of the late nobleman the most excellent Antonio Vendramin, sound, praised be God, of mind, senses, intellect and body, being in the house of her residence in the district of Santa Giustina in the district of S. Francesco, presented to me, Girolamo Marcello, Venetian public notary, in the presence of the here undersigned witnesses, the present testamentary coupon written and undersigned, she stated, by her own hand and sealed with two seals, requesting me to take custody of it, in the event of her death, to open it, make it public, and corroborate it according to the law.

Upon questioned by me, the Notary de interrogandis, she replied: I want nothing more.

I Giovanni Barbazza, of the late Christoforo, was witness to said presentation, summoned.

I Giovanni Vincenzi, of the late Vincenzo, was a witness, was present at said presentation, summoned.

Cuius quidem cedulae testamentariae tenor sequitur:

Jesus Mary

At the location of my residence in Venice in San Francesco in the district of Santa Giustina, on April 13, 1705.

Finding myself, the survivor of the late nobleman Sir Antonio Vendramin, sound of mind and body, but bearing in mind that no one is certain of the hour of death, I therefore wanted in all respects to put into order all my affairs with this my testament (will) and free testamentary coupon which I, myself, have drawn up and signed.

First of all, I cancel, revoke and annul each and every testament (will), testamentary coupon, and codicil that at any time and any place I have made, intending that they have no value, bearing or efficacy, as if they had not existed or been presented. Encountering this testamentary coupon, which I am now writing, I want it to be of binding force in all its parts, and that after my death, it be opened by a public notary, read and corroborated according to the laws and orders practiced in our dominating city.

I commend my soul to Almighty God, to the Blessed Virgin Mary, to my guardian angel, to St. Catherine and St. Elizabeth whose names I unworthily bear, and all my saints of the month and to all the celestial court, beseeching them to assist me at the hour of my death and that they intercede for me that I may enjoy the fruits of the very precious treasure of the blood of Jesus Christ which has redeemed me.

When it so pleases the Lord to call me into His hands, it is my wish that my mortal remains, with the usual customs and nothing more, be buried in the Vendramina alli Servi family tomb, where the body of Mister Antonio, my beloved husband, was buried, and that I be dressed in the habit of Our Mother of the Seven Sorrows; I want 1000 masses to be said for me immediately at the time of my death, the majority of them taking place on privileged altars and in dedicated churches, and that a mass be sung for me at the Pute of the Pietà, and for this a contribution of twenty five ducats be made, for one time only and that one scudo [antique coin] be given to the chaplain, and one ducat to the sacristan and these also for one time only. I want also a mass to be said right away in Rome, as is usually done for departed souls.

After this, I want another 1000 masses to be said in the span of one year, and all in dedicated churches and for the most part on privileged altars, and for ten more years, 300 masses to be said per year, also on privileged altars, after which my heirs have no other obligations. I want also some good religious to be sent to Perdon d'Assisi, and should Doctor Leogani, a priest of Santa Fosca, desire to go there, he shall be given 50 ducats as alms, and he shall go there at a time of the year of his choosing, beseeching him to perform this act of charity for my soul.

To Mister Girolamo Cornaro, my beloved brother, as a sign of my love I leave 50 ounces of silver once and for all. To Mister Lorenzo Contarini, my dearest son-in-law, as a sign of my affection, I leave 50 ounces of silver once and for all, recommending my daughter and his wife to him.

To the most excellent Mister Giovanni Bernardo, my revered cousin, who with such charity aided me in all things, in my most afflicted time when I lost my husband, as a small sign of my gratitude, I leave my diamond ring bound in the center with three large diamonds and four small ones, hoping that he will receive from God a reward for his charity toward me and my daughter, being myself a widow and she, orphaned, and if I be judged worthy to enjoy celestial glory by the merits of the blood of Jesus Christ, I promise to pray always for his health, both of soul and body.

To Abbot Contarini, brother-in-law of my daughter, I leave, once and for all, 40 ounces of silver, begging him to pray for my soul, entrusting my daughter and his sister-in-law to him.

To the most excellent Princess Lady Pia, survivor of the most excellent Mister Cavalier Contarini, always my revered Lady to whom I profess uncountable debt, as a sign of my heartfelt devotion I leave, once and for all, 50 ounces of silver.

I leave to all my dearest sisters-in-law and brothers-in-law 20 ounces of silver once and for all.

I leave to my dearest nieces Elena and Lucretia Cornaro, and to my dearest nephews, their husbands, to each one, 30 ounces of silver, once and for all.

I leave my Vendramin nephews and nieces, children of my brother-in-law Mister Alvise, males and females alike, 12 ounces of silver each, once and for all.

I leave to my beloved aunt Elisabetta Dandolo Zustinian, sister of my dearest mother-in-law, so beloved by me, 20 ounces of silver as a sign of my love, once and for all.

I leave to my dearest aunt Faustina Grimani Malipiero, as a sign of my heartfelt love, 20 ounces of silver once and for all.

I leave to my confessor, Doctor Vedoa, 50 ducats, for one time only, beseeching him to remember my soul in his sacrifices and prayers.

I leave to Mister Professor Georgio Calafatti, as a sign of my gratitude in aiding me in my affairs, 30 ounces of silver for one time only.

I leave to Mister Iseppo Boselli, as a sign of my being so pleased for all he did with my interests in mind, 30 ounces of silver for one time only.

I leave Doctor Litegato da Lendinara 20 ounces of silver for one time only.

I leave to the most illustrious Mister Bellin and to Abbot Gennari da Lendinara 20 ounces of silver each.

I leave to the man of God, Father Giovanni Battista Leogani 20 ducats once and for all, beseeching him to pray to God for me.

I leave to Mister Pietro Rubinato, agent of Ca' Vendramin, 20 ducats once and for all.

I leave to Prudenza della Pietà, whom I brought up, 20 ducats once and for all.

To Cattina, a Turkish woman whom I had baptized, raised and whose marriage to Rinaldo Pazon, a furrier in Padua, I arranged with 800 ducats as a dowry, I leave, for the rest of her life, 12 ducats per year, and if her husband should die before her, or should she be abandoned or mistreated by him I want my daughter Elena to take care of her and not abandon her. I leave to Catte and Nicolosa, currently chamber maids of Madame Procurator, my mother, and also to Caterina, who is in my brother's service and who took care of my father, the Procurator in his final illness, six ducats each, once and for all.

I leave to Elena Borosini, my chambermaid, 16 ducats per year, for the rest of her life, obligating my Daughter Elena to keep her on and to have her cared for in her old age.

I leave to all the servants and maids, who will be employed in my home and the Contarini home at the time of my death, two ducats each, for one time, so that they pray for my soul.

I leave to my gondoliers, for one time only, four ducats each.

I leave to the four hospitals and to the Catechumens five ducats each, for one time only.

I order and desire that with my remaining monies, the rest of my husband's debts be quickly paid, those which I may not have finished paying in my lifetime, about which I leave among my papers a detailed notice, as Doctor Giovanni Battista Leogani knows, and another registry, also in the hands of Mister Pietro Rubinato, agent of Ca' Vendramin, and these debts alone I desire to be satisfied because they are legitimate, but if God grant me the time, I will pay since I consider them more pressing than anything else, and until now, if there had not been the circumstance of so many extraordinary debts, I would have paid.

The remainder of all my goods and property, present and future, which in any way are owed to me and pertain to me, or which could be due me or expected to come to me, I leave to Elena, my daughter, wife of Mister Lorenzo Contarini, by my agreement, married to him, with my having given her completely her dowry, without any assistance at all from the paternal family, with the obligation of having to pay to Isabella, my other daughter and her sister in the Third order of the Franciscans in Murano, 300 ducats per year, for the rest of her life; and I desire also that one thousand ducats be given one time only to the sisters of Santa Maria Maggior of Venice, should I not have given them myself either in their entirety or in part during my lifetime, so that, should I have already given them, she will no longer be obligated to do so, and also I want them to be given at more than one time, whenever she is able, beseeching these sisters to remember me in their prayers.

I further desire that my daughter Elena leave for rent the two Valli dell'Inferno e Moraro (Valleys of Inferno and Moraro) to the most excellent noble gentleman Bortolo and to the Galli brothers, that is, Felice and Giovanni Battista, for the rent that they pay me at present, as appears by the writing done by them under October 2, 1704, written by the hand of Mister Bortolo, with the obligation, however, that they always keep company with Mister Antonio dall'Acqua, valesan, but when they want to lower the rent, she is no longer obligated to allow them to continue.

Next, I recommend to my daughter Elena that she love equally all of her children, the two little girls she has at present as much as the boys whom God might be pleased to send her in the future, finding herself to be about eight months pregnant, that, not making any distinctions, but treating them with equality in the vocation and state to which God may call them, I not leaving anything in particular to these little girls who are born because, leaving all that I have to my daughter and their mother, whom I know to be of extraordinary prudence, I am sure that in the same way she will govern them, and, if God should grant me a longer life, I will do in due time for them that which resources will allow.

And this I further want and order of my daughter, that she give to the elderly women of Padua, when in said location a daughter of Doctor Francesco Gasparini, a lawyer in Padua and godfather of my child, should enter there, whom I am at present attempting to get accepted in such place for all the time she will be staying there, 12 ducats per year, as is customary to pay in such place for each spinster.

And so I leave, order, and want and institute that truly this be my last will and testament, declaring that all the obligations be met from the income, not from the capital, and thus everyone will be content to receive them as my residual funds will cover them, but which I recommend to be paid as soon as possible, leaving to the notary for his payment 20 ducats and the desire that this be my last will and testament, revoking and annulling every other testament which I may have made as I said above.

I Cattarina Cornaro Piscopia Vendramina wrote and I undersign the present testamentary coupon of mine by my own hand.

Et hic est finis supradictae cedulae testamentariae.

Praeterea etc. Si quis etc. Signum autem et +([a])

CODOCIL

Die quarta mensis maii 1707, indictione decima quinta, Rivialti.

The noble Lady Cattarina Cornaro Piscopia of the late Mister Giovanni Battista, Procurator of St. Mark's, survivor of the late noble man,

---

[a] Note follows:

Die undecima mensis maii 1707, publicatum, viso cadavere testatricis, ad instantiam nobilis mulieris Elenae, eius filiae et heredis, cui intimata fuit pars offirii illustrissimi Aquarum.

the most excellent Antonio Vendramin, son of the late most excellent Andrea, known by me, of sound mind, senses and intellect, though indisposed lying in bed in her residence in the district of Santa Giustina, has presented to me, Girolamo Marcello, Venetian public notary, in the presence of the undersigned witnesses the present codicillary coupon, which she had me write as her confidant, to which, though, when read to her, the two of us alone, she had me add a few lines, and then confirmed all of it in the presence of these same witnesses which were recalled, and she stated that it contained her last will and beseeched me to take custody of it, seal it, and in the event of her death, to open it, make it known, execute it and corroborate it together with her testament according to the law. When questioned regarding the same, she replied: I want nothing more. When questioned regarding all the pious locations and charitable works according to the law, she replied: I have already taken care of it.

I Domenico of the late Zuane Storti was present as witness to said presentation, summoned and sworn.

I Domenego of the late Antonio Orti was present as witness to said presentation, summoned and sworn.

Cuius quidem cedulae codicillariae tenor sequitur:

The 4th day of May 1707. Venice

I, Cattarina Cornaro Piscopia of the late Mister Giovanni Battista, Procurator, survivor of the late most excellent Antonio Vendramin son of the most excellent Andrea, wanting to add and revise my testament which I previously handed over to the Venetian notary Girolamo Marcello, I have called for the same notary to come to me and I asked that he, as my confidant, write this my codicillary coupon, so that he may then accept it as a public notary; that though, ever more invoking the help of God and never begging of him enough pardon for my sins, I recommend and place by soul in his wounds and in the bosom of the Most Blessed Virgin Mary, that they grant me a place in eternal glory.

Having instituted as my universal and residual heir with my testament my most delightful daughter Elena, wife of the nobleman the most excellent Lorenzo Contarini, son of the late, most excellent Tomaso, whence, if in said testament I had not expressed myself well in the institution of said heir of mine, again I order and desire that my said most beloved daughter be my sole heir, universal and residual, freely of all my goods and effects of any sort wherever they exist for whatever reason and action, that in any case or time could ever be due me or come to me, without any contradiction, brand or bond, obligation or condition, but at her total and free disposition, and if in said testament I have expressed or remembered the memory of her children, I protest that such expressions have been simple bursts of affection, but never can one deduce or interpret conditions or obligation added to them [by these expressions] regarding my inheritance, replicating that I mean and want that my absolute and free heir, and to dispose of as she likes of my means as I said above, obligating though to correspond with Isabella, by other daughter and her sister, who lives with the Third Order Franciscans, the three hundred ducats annually, as long as said Isabella is alive, and no more, according to what I declared in my testament and furthermore, to fulfill the other additions made and which I will declare here.

Declaring, though, that she is not held to keeping Elena Boresini, my former chambermaid, in her home, according to what I ordered in said testament of mine, since she has desired to retire with a niece of hers, my said daughter and heir must, however, send her the annual lifelong sum left to her in my said testament without other obligation. I leave to the Reverend Father Michiel Angelo from Borgo del Santo in Padua, my confessor during the period that I live in said city, twenty-five ducats once and for all.

As a sign of my esteem for the most excellent Mister Zuan Francesco Loredan, father-in-law of my niece Lucretia Cornaro, I leave to the same as many ounces of silver as I leave in my testament to my aforementioned niece and her husband.

I leave to Alba, daughter of my godfather, Francesco Gasparini, a lawyer in Padua, whom I have under my custody, fifty ducats and twelve tunics immediately, and at the time of her marriage or entrance into monastic life, one hundred ducats for one time only.

I leave to Bastian, my waiter, twenty-five ducats once and for all, and I recommend my husband's chamberlain to my daughter, to keep him in mind, to aid him in all his needs because he has been a good servant.

I leave to Laura, the widow of my house, besides all that I leave to my servants in my testament, two ducats per year as long as she lives and another ten ducats once and for all.

I leave to Mister Giorgio Naghel, who assisted me in so many ailments and currently aids me, two hundred ducats as a remembrance I profess for his great assistance, being a small part of all that I owe to his worthiness.

I leave to the physician Lorando twenty ducats once and for all.

To Francesco, my boatman, besides what I leave in my testament, I want him to be given six ducats once and for all.

I want the debt with Gobetti and also Francesco Sartor to be forgiven.

I leave to the home for poor sinners on Canal Reggio five ducats once and for all.

I leave to Don Andrea Boni twenty ducats once and for all.

I leave to the priest Domenico of Santa Fosca five ducats once and for all.

I leave to the reverend Jesuit fathers fifty ducats once and for all.

I leave to the noble Lady Paolina Contarina, my most beloved, twenty ounces of silver once and for all.

I leave to the vice prioress of doctrine at Santa Fosca six ounces of silver and to Lady Laura Petrachina another four ounces of silver once and for all, beseeching her to continue full of zeal and love the good work of instructing the little girls in Christian Doctrine, and to beg their forgiveness for my past omissions.

I leave likewise to the women teaching said doctrine at Santa Fosca twenty-five ducats once and for all, with the provision that Madame vice-prioress divide them among said teachers and the other workers as she sees fit.

I leave to my beloved German sister Eletta Maria Contarini, a nun at Santa Catterina, thirty ounces of silver once and for all.

I leave twenty ducats once and for all to Lady Marina Bortoletti who was my teacher, and since she is old and feeble, if she were to die before me I want said bequest to be given to Lady Antonia, her daughter.

I leave to Lady Maddalena Capelli, who was my sister's organist, ten ounces of silver once and for all.

To Seraffin, known as Iseppo in Hebrew, whom I had baptized by Mister Sarat the Armenian, I leave a cot, a straw mattress, and a pair of sheets and twenty-five ducats, once and for all and any other household items which to my daughter and heir seem suitable; wanting, furthermore, that if any devout person should put up a shop or store of some sort for the above mentioned Seraffin with the approval of said Mister Sarat and of the noble gentleman, the most excellent Crestin Marinelli, and when the same Mister Sarat should appraise favorably the store that was proposed for him and which he would organize, that once and for all another one hundred ducats be paid out for engaging in said store the assistance of said Seraffin; again beseeching, as I have done before, said Mister Sarat to aid and assist said poor Seraffin.

I desire that the heart of gold that was at S. Basso be found and that it pass as creditor of my late husband for certain hearts of gold, which Salvador Treves, the Jew, says were returned to him; and I want this affair to be verified and punctually paid, when becoming creditor.

Similarly, I want the pedestal of stone made on my behalf at the Santo of Padua to be paid for, according to the appraisal of the work, Don Calafatti of Padua having some money of mine for that purpose.

I order furthermore that one thousand masses be celebrated for me as my daughter and heir should see fit, besides those already ordered in my testament.

And since Laura, widow, has always desired to go to Loretto, I desire that she be sent there to pray for my soul and that she be assisted with all that she may need for said trip and that she be recommended in Ancona to the Reverend Don Giovanni Bubuli.

I declare that all the bequests, expressed as much in my testament as in this present codicil, are my intention, once and for all, except those which I have declared lifelong. And so be it for the praise and glory of God.

Et hic est finis supradictae cedulae codicillariae.

Praeterea etc. Si quis etc. Signum autem et +

Die undecima mensis maii 1707, publicatum, viso cadavere testatricis, simul cum testamento ad instantiam ut in eo.

(S) Ego Hieronymus Marcello publicus Venetus notarius publicavi, complevi, roboravi et in fide me subscripsi et signavi.

DOCUMENT 1

JULY 6TH, 1537

Appearing in the presence of all the three undersigned distinguished lawyers, the nobleman Giovanni Cornelio son of Fantini, once sponsor of Girolamo, noblemen Giacobbe and Luigi Cornelio, brothers of nobleman Antonio in the name of the bride mentioned below, and nobleman Girolamo Quirino once intermediary of the marriage of Saverio mentioned below, for the purpose of executing the law, they presented, to the aforementioned lawyers the contract written below, carried out between the parties themselves and through them now presented to these attorneys, declaring it to be a true and authentic contract and that no other promise, agreement or understanding exists, except what is contained in the contract itself.

This contract was signed by the counsellors and the secretary on July 22nd according to the dictates of the law.

Its content follows.

240-243a
English translation of
Latin

DOCUMENT 2

By the authority of the almighty God, Father, Son and Holy Spirit, of our holy Father Innocent XI, pope by divine providence, of the most reverend Father Gregorio Barbadici, distinguished cardinal of the holy Roman Church and most vigilant bishop of Padua, with the approval of his representative, the most reverend Father Alexandro Mantuano, general vicar and distinguished vice-professor of law,

a) (left) I make, establish and declare you Master and Doctor in Sacred Theology with all the honors, privileges, indulgences, exemptions, immunities, prerogatives and favors, which all the Masters and Doctors of this sacred theology use, possess and enjoy throughout the Christian world, by custom, law and common practice. These are the marks of your doctorate:

a) (right) I proclaim and declare you, noble young lady are Helena Cornelia Piscopia, Laureate Master in Sacred Theology, with all the honors, favors, indulgences of which, compared with all the other Doctors, you are capable by virtue of your sex. And, as a mark,

b) (left) Take the academic cap in place of the sacred crown, marked by Christ's cross, in order that you may keep that (cross) in your heart for an example to be followed, as well as on your head as a sign of glory.

b) (right) Take the wreath in place of the sacred crown as a worthy laurel sign of that divine Wisdom, which you must keep on your way, until you hear from the angelic voices: "Come, bride of Christ, take the crown which the Lord has prepared for you forever, adding a heavenly laurel wreath."

c) (left) I give you the ring of faith, that you may be a faithful Doctor and a faithful Master in the Church of God.

c) (right) By the ring of faith I pledge the Christian Wisdom to you, that you may be a faithful bride of God, and an upright virgin in the holy Church of God for a long time for the honor and increase of the Catholic faith.

d) (left) I offer you the book open and closed with the power of interpreting, explaining, making comments, proclaiming and unveiling at the proper time the divine mysteries to the faithful.

d) (right) I offer you the book open and closed.

e) (left) Sit on the authoritative chair of Christ, to teach in public and to explain with your words and actions all (his) other teachings, for the increase of the Catholic religion.

e) (right) For meditating upon and expressing the divine mysteries: not for preaching or teaching in public, however, according to the admonition of the Apostle [Paul], who does not permit women to teach in the Church.

f) (left) I welcome you with a holy embrace, and I greet you with a chaste kiss, that you may shine forth with your gleaming love toward God and neighbor.

f) (right) The divine bridegroom once inspired his bride with a mystic language: "His left hand (is) under my head and his right arm will embrace me." May the same bridegroom, gleaming with love, holily embrace you too, as I.

g) (left) Finally I bless you, that God's works may be blessed forever.

g) (right) I bless you in the name of the most holy Trinity, Father, Son and Holy Spirit, that God's works may remain forever sealed with the seal of our Lord Jesus Christ.

DOCUMENT 3

Saturday, June 25th, 1678

After the venerable Academic Committee was assembled for the examination in Philosophy of the distinguished Elenae Lugretiae Corneliae Piscopia, because of the crowd and the narrowness of the usual place, it was necessary to go to the Cathedral Church and to assemble again the Committee in the Chapel of the Blessed Virgin Mary. Present were the honorable and distinguished leaders of the city, the governor Girolamo Basadona, the prefect Luigi Mocenico, the most reverend Vicar Alexandro Mantuano and the Vice-Mayor. The gentlemen and the Father mentioned below were also present, namely;

Sponsors

(32) J.U.
column one

(32) H.D.
column two

(64 total)

p. 199   "unless the debts and the bequests have been subtracted"

p. 203   Wednesday, August 9th, thirteenth declaration, at R.

In the chapel mentioned above, in the presence of the entire Academic Committee, the above-mentioned most distinguished Elena Lucretia Cornelia Piscopia discussed two philosophical topics, which had been chosen by lot the morning before, availing herself of the privileges of the nobles [they were exempt from questioning after their presentation].

In the presentation of these two topics she performed in such an excellent and extraordinary manner that, at the end of the examination, extraordinary and astonishing, according to custom the urns for the secret ballot were brought to the distinguished Vice-Prior Giovanni Domenico de Tessariis and all the other Committee Members for the purpose of carrying on the voting process.

But all the professors of the Committee claimed in a loud voice that such a brilliant discussion of the topics had to be judged in a more noble way than the voting process. Having heard this, the noble young lady in a respectful manner insisted repeatedly that, according to custom, the vote be completely secret. They concurred with this opinion in order to formulate a proper verdict on the examination.

Then the distinguished professor Giovanni Domenico de Tessariis, Vice-Prior, rose up and said: "Although the statutes of the University decree that the examination be subject to a secret ballot, since this heroine has performed in such an excellent and brilliant manner, it is preferable that you, fathers, omitting the secret ballot, employ a different way of ascertaining your minds." Therefore, he asked them and the entire Committee whether they would be pleased with a unanimous acclamation, and all of them unanimously answered: "It is acceptable." Thereafter, in this manner, by unanimous consent, that is by acclamation and by solemn utterance of living voice, the noble Elena Lucretia Cornelia was proclaimed Master and Doctor of Philosophy before the entire assembly of professors and a great crowd of nobles and common people.

Then the above-mentioned young lady, who had previously left the place, according to custom, came forward to receive the doctoral degree which, with fitting and gracious words, she had requested from her Sponsor, the distinguished professor Carolo Renaldino, a patrician from Ancona, philosopher and mathematician of Cosimo III Duke of Tuscany and chaired philosopher in this illustrious University of Padua. He immediately arose and before all the people, with an eloquent and scholarly speech, praised the nobility and the virtues of the lady. This was followed by the most vigorous applause on the part of the audience.

Finally, he crowned her head with a laurel wreath, offered her the books, put the ring on her finger and covered her shoulders with the ermine cape.

NOTES

1. It gave to the Republic a queen, Caterina of Cyprus (1454–1510), and four doges: Marco (July 21, 1365–January 13, 1368); Giovanni I (January 4, 1625–December 23, 1629); Francesco (May 17–June 5, 1656, only 20 days); Giovanni II (May 22, 1709–August 12, 1722). It also produced nine cardinals: Alvise (c. 1517 –Rome, May 10, 1584), son of Giovanni; Andrea (c. 1509–Rome, January 30, 1551), son of Giacomo and cousin of Cardinal Alvise; Federigo Senior (June 1531–Rome, October 4, 1590), brother of Cardinal Alvise; Federigo Junior (1579–June 5, 1653), son of the Doge Giovanni I, nephew of Cardinal Francesco Junior, studied at the University of Padua; Francesco Senior (d. Viterbo, September 26, 1543), son of Giorgio, grandson/nephew of Queen Caterina of Cyprus, brother of Cardinal Marco; Giovanni I, nephew of Cardinal Alvise and Cardinal Federigo Senior, uncle of Cardinal Federigo Junior; Giorgio (August 1, 1658–Padua, August 10, 1722), son of Federigo, brother of the Doge Giovanni II, graduate *in utroque* of the University of Padua (1677); Giovanni (June 30, 1720–Rome March 28, 1789), son of Nicolò, graduate *in utroque* of the University of Padua (1741); Marco (d. Venice, July 24, 1524), son of Giorgio, brother of Cardinal Francesco Senior, grandson of Queen Caterina of Cypress. In addition there were various bishops, abbots, and religious superiors. G. Musatti, Storia di Venezia 2:455–58; Ruysschaert, *Cornaro*, 886–90.

2. Amore, "Apostolicità delle chiese," 1695–96.

3. Battisti and Alessio, *Dizionario etimologico italiano*, 2:1114; Olivieri, *Toponomastica veneta*, 55; Prati, *Etimologie venete*, 49.

4. The reference is to Cornelio Musso, a Conventual friar, bishop of Bitonto. See also note 33 below.

5. Magagnò, Menòn, and Begotto, *Rime in lingua rustica padovana*, 95.

6. Du Cange, *Cornare, cornarius, cornicare, corniculare*, in *Glossarium*, vol. 2.

7. Blaise, *Dictionnaire latin-français des auteurs chrétiens*, 223.

8. Migliorini, "Onomastica," 378.

9. Padua, Biblioteca Universitaria, ms. 822, f. 117; Padua, Biblioteca del Museo Civico, mss. C.M. 16, f. 47; C.M. 232; C.M. 651/12, f. 16.

10. According to legend, the twelve apostolic families are the Contarini, the Tiepolo, the Morosini, the Michiel, the Badoer, the Sanudo, the Gradenigo, the Memmo, the Valier, the Dandolo, the Polani, and the Barozzi. The four evangelists are the Giustinian, the Cornaro, the Bragadin, and the Bembo. Tentori, *Saggio sulla storia civile*, 2:315; E. Musatti, *Storia d'un lembo di terra*, coll. 222, 1069; Roberti, *Le magistrature veneziane*, 1:33; Molmenti, *Storia di Venezia*, 1:58; Romanin, *Storia documentata di Venezia*, 4:420, 9:6; Cessi, *Storia della Repubblica di Venezia*, 1:50.

11. The Venetian nobles Bembo, Calbo, Corner, Donno, Foscari, Foscarini, Labia, Lion, Mairano, Molin, Morosini, Serzi, Steno, Vendramin, Ziani, and Zorzani

were merchants. Padua, Biblioteca Universitaria, ms. 822, f. 505; Cicogna, *Delle inscrizioni veneziane*, 2:26, 270, 371; Lestocquoy, *Aux origines de la bourgeoisie*, 76, 89; Cessi, *Storia di Venezia*, 2:391; Cracco, *Società e Stato nel medioevo veneziano*, 39–40, 389.

12. E. Musatti, *Storia d'un lembo di terra*, 382; Fontana, *Cento Palazzi di Venezia*, 393.

13. Those surveyed numbered 2,128 (1,209 nobles and 919 commoners). Luzzatto, *I prestiti della Repubblica di Venezia*, CXLIV; Cracco, *Società e Stato nel medioevo veneziano*, 451.

14. Caterina Cornaro (b. Venice 1454–d. Venice, July 10, 1510), a beautiful daughter of Andrea, was given in matrimony to the bastard son of the Lusignano, Giacomo II, king of Cyprus, who died shortly after turning thirty-three (July 6–7, 1473), leaving several bastard children and a legitimate unborn heir, Giacomo III, who died at the age of one; with him the direct line of the Lusignanos became extinct. After the death of her husband, Caterina reigned for almost sixteen years in the midst of political and military hostilities, in an atmosphere of intrigues, until the Venetian government, which had favored her marriage in order to carry out its own aims on Cyprus, recalled her in 1489. It annexed the island and allotted her the possession of the land at Asolo (territory of Treviso), preparing a small and magnificent court for her. Forced by the German invasion on the Venetian mainland at the time of the League of Cambrai (1509 and later) to take refuge in Venice, she died there in the palace where she was born and was buried in the Church of S. Salvatore (right transept) in a monument which was the work of the architect Bernardino Contino (16th–17th century). E. Musatti, *Storia d'un lembo di terra*, 584–85; Berruti, *Patriziato veneto. I Cornaro*, III; Lorenzetti, *Venezia e il suo estuario*, 387.

15. Lupis, *L'eroina veneta*, 8; Deza, *Vita di Helena*, 17; Tassini, *Alcuni palazzi ed antichi edifici*, 60; Pynsent, *The Life*, 9; Dalmazzo, *Lucrezia Cornaro*, 29.

16. Urban V (Guglielmo da Grimoard), beatified, pope from September 28, 1362 to December 19, 1370. From a noble family, he became a Benedictine monk and a doctor of theology and he taught at Montpellier and Avignon. At the insistence of the Romans, and especially of St. Catherine of Siena, he left Avignon and returned to Rome (October 16, 1367), but on the pretext of unhealthful weather, he soon returned to Avignon (September 24, 1370) where he died on December 19, 1370. Devout, a lover of the arts and sciences, he founded the University of Cracow.

17. Bacchini, *Helenae Lucretiae*, 4; Lupis, *L'eroina veneta*, 8–9; Deza, *Vita di Helena*, 17; Tassini, *Alcuni palazzi ed antichi edifici*, 60; E. Musatti, *Storia d'un lembo di terra*, 343, 366; Pynsent, *The Life*, 9; De Santi, "Elena Lucrezia," IV, 184–85; Fontana, *Cento palazzi di Venezia*, 393–94; Dalmazzo, *Lucrezia Cornaro*, 29–30.

18. Cessi, "Cipro," 936–938; Corradi, "Cipro," 625.

19. Coronelli, *Isolario dell'atlante veneto*, 1:249–250; Desio, "Piscopi, l'isola meno nota del Dodecaneso," 56.

20. Rossi, "Rodi," 555–556; Padua, Biblioteca Universitaria, ms. 255, f. 29.

21. Fontana, *Cento palazzi di Venezia*, 394. Valentina Visconti was one of the

fifteen legitimate children (five boys and ten girls) whom Bernabò had by his legal wife, Regina della Scala. He had, however, many illegitimate children, so that with both bastard sons and daughters he had to find positions for about thirty people in order to serve the political interests of his family. Cognasso, *L'unificazione della Lombardia sotto Milano*, 494; for the children fathered by Bernabò see Giulini, Memorie della città e campagna di Milano, 5:661.

22. E. Musatti, *Storia d'un lembo di terra*, 650–52.

23. A.S.V., Barbaro, *Arbori di patrizi veneti*, ff. 17–27.

24. Ibid.; Venice, Biblioteca Nazionale Marciana, Capellari Vivaro, *Arbori di patrizi veneti*, I, ms. It. VII (=8304); Bosmin, "Cornaro," 418, (see the family tree). A parallel example would be the Greek poet Vincenzo Cornaro (17th century), one of those of Venetian origin who were Hellenized during the long centuries of living together with the island population of Crete; in his poem *Erotocrito*, he reveals his very fine knowledge of the Italian language by his use of the *Orlando furioso* (Lavagnini, "Cornaro Vincenzo," 551; Lavagnini, "Erotocrito").

25. Berruti, *Patriziato veneto*, 24–26; Crollalanza, *Dizionario storico-blasonico*, 1:322. The small Venetian population, with typical wit, distinguished the various patrician families by attaching a nickname to each one suggested by the place where they lived or even from some physical or moral defect. For those which concern us there were the Corner della Regina (of the queen, i.e., Queen Caterina of Cyprus), the Corner della Ca' Grande (of the Ca' Grande, for the vast size of the structure), the Corner Piscopia, the Corner Taco (ignorant), the Corner Squaquera (liquid sewage) (Patriarchi, *Vocabolario veneto e padovano*, 225, 307, 323; Boerio, *Dizionario del dialetto veneziano*, 322, 465, 697). It is not out of the question to consider Fantina, born Episcopi and wife of the famous Venetian painter Jacopo Tintoretto (1518–1594), as being from and even given the last name of "da Piscopia" (from Piscopia) (A.S.V., Notarile, *Testamenti*, b. 157, no. 483).

26. The coat of arms: a shield divided into four sections—in the first and the fourth are five red Jerusalem crosses on a silver background; in the second and third are the emblem of the Lusignano bound horizontally with a silver and blue band and a red rampant lion, wearing armor, showing its tongue, and wearing a crown; at the center is a small shield divided in half vertically, the first part blue and the second part gold (of the Cornaros).

27. The Cavalier ranks of Cyprus or "Knights of Silence": an equestrian order founded by the Lusignano, the kings of Cyprus, under the Rule of St. Basil, with the mission of taking up arms against the infidel. These knights had as an insignia a necklace formed by many S's chained together, in the middle of which hung a gold sword upon which was intertwined the same letter S (symbol of silence) with the motto, "Pro fide servanda." Venice, Biblioteca del Civico Museo Correr, cod. Gradenigo, 49, 49.

28. Giovanni Domenico Cornaro, the son of the late Fantino and Marietta Foscari, was born on December 10, 1514, and registered with the public official on December 17; the witnesses were Alvise Foscari, son of the late Girolamo, and Sebastiano Loredano, son of the late Fantino. A.S.V., Avogaria de Comun, ms. 68, years 1506–54, pages not numbered.

29. The date of Alvise Cornaro's birth is uncertain; E. Menegazzo favors 1484. Menegazzo, "Altre osservazioni intorno alla vita e all'ambiente del Ruzante e di Alvise Cornaro," 260, 263.

30. See appendix, document 1. The marriage was celebrated in the church of S. Croce alla Giudeca on July 1, 1537; witnesses for the groom were the father, Fantino Cornaro, son of the late Girolamo, and Dario Pesaro, son of the late Taddeo. For the bride there were Giacomo and Alvise Cornaro, of the late Antonio. A.S.V., Avogaria de Comun, reg. 143/4, f. 126r-v.

31. Cornaro, *Discorsi intorno alla vita sobria*, 69. He mentions eleven grandchildren, eight boys and three girls, and in his will he also indicates their names (Sambin, "I testamenti," 382, 384); there were in fact twelve, of which the grandfather omitted Pietro Bernardo Giuseppe, who perhaps died as an infant (A.S.V., Avogaria de Comun, Indice delle nascite, cassetta 168). For names and vital statistics, see the family tree.

32. Cicogna, *Saggio di bibliografia veneziana*, 5:175–192; Molmenti, *Storia di Venezia*, 2:326.

33. For the relationship between Cornelio Musso and Alvise Cornaro see Sambin, "I testamenti," 337–39, 348–49, 358–64.

34. Of the three girls, Elena and Cornelia married Nicolò and Giovanni Contarini respectively. Isabella remained single, however, as her grandfather knew she would (Sambin, "I testamenti," 382). She lived in the house in the Santo district of Padua and died there on April 14, 1609, at the age of sixty-nine (A.S.P., Sanità, 466; A.C.P., Parrocchia S. Lorenzo, *Liber mortuorum*, 2, f. 51) in extreme poverty; even her mattress and sheets had been borrowed. She arranged in her will that her debts be paid with the various suppliers and that the money she borrowed from private individuals and from convents both in Padua and Venice be paid back. She also wanted to be buried dressed as a Capuchin in the family tomb in Venice at the Frari with just one priest and one torch of twelve pounds (A.S.P., Notarile, b. 2199, ff. 175–77v). This was a disconcerting and inexplicable situation. At this point, the entire dowry which was given to her by her grandfather had disappeared. Six years earlier she had made a donation of property which was due her from her mother's legacy to her brother Giacomo Alvise and his sons, Alvise, Francesco, and Girolamo (A.S.P., Notarile, vol. 3465, ff. 639–40). What was the cause then? Bad administration or rather voluntary deprivation in order to live like the Franciscans? Was there perhaps a spiritual commitment to the third order which she entered into in her youth and of which only her grandfather was aware? An examination of both of their wills would leave it to conjecture.

35. Girolamo Cornaro, son of Giacomo Alvise and grandson of the late Giovanni and Caterina Bragadin, daughter of the late Giovanni, was born in Venice on August 29, 1574. A.S.V., Avogaria de Comun, Nascite, cassetta 168.

36. Belotti, *Storia di Bergamo*, 4:486. The statue, the work of Domenico Tomezzoli (17th century), was removed from the piazza by a decree of the Venetian Senate which ordered the removal of all of the statues and inscriptions in honor of its public representatives (Zannandreis, *Le vite dei pittori*, 269–70; Brenzoni, *Dizionario di artisti veneti*, 278–79).

37. The betrothal was celebrated on June 30, 1610, at the Thilmans' residence (Giustiniani House) in the Ca' d'oro street. The marriage was celebrated on

November 22, 1610, in S. Sofia Church and was made officially known to the public on December 19, 1610. There were three witnesses for the bride, Flemish merchants living in the same street. Venice, Archivio Parrocchiale di S. Sofia in S. Felice, *Matrimoni*, no. 3, letter C; A.S.V., Avogaria de Comun, b. 82/2, years 1600–47, pages not numbered.

38. A.S.V., Notarile, b. 587, ff. 625v–26; b. 594 ff. 421v–22r-v; b. 595, ff. 269v–75v; b. 598, ff. 5r-v–6, 378v–81; b. 605, ff. 63v–65v; Venice, Biblioteca del Civico Museo Correr, mss. PD, C. 755/51, original parchment paper.

39. The body of Girolamo Cornaro was transported to Venice and buried in the family tomb in the parish church of S. Luca. A.S.P., Sanità, 469; A.S.L.V., Morti, no. 1, pages not numbered.

CHAPTER 2: A FAMILY

1. A.S.V., Notarile, b.57, no.335. Isabella, Paolina, and Cornelia were Augustinian nuns in the convent of Santa Maria di Bethlemme. Maria was in St. Stephen's Benedictine Convent in Padua, and Prudenza in "Zirada," an Augustinian convent in Venice.

2. Cocchetti, *Brescia e la sua provincia*, 3:290–91; Beltrami, *Forze di lavoro*, 12; Caccia, "Cultura e letteratura," 486–87, 511. Regarding the culture and the schools of Salò see Brunati, *Uomini illustri della riviera di Salò*.

3. A.S.V., Notarile, b. 756. No documentation of Caterina Thilmans's death has been found in the civil or ecclesiastical archives; it may be dated between October 25 (the date of the last will and testament) and November 3, 1629 (the date of the publication of this will and testament).

4. A.S.V., Notarile, reg. 10784, ff. 1–5v, 6, 9r-v, 10.

5. A.S.V., Notarile, f. 10789, f. 579r-v. The marriage between Isabella Cornaro, daughter of Girolamo, and Girolamo Contarini, son of Bertucci, was celebrated in the church of S. Samuele on July 11, 1634, and officially noted on July 27, 1634, the witnesses being the nobles Bernardo Loredan, son of Antonio, and Girolamo Zane, son of Francesco (A.S.V., Avongaria de Comun, b. 82/2, fasc. 16). Isabella died between the end of the year 1677 and the beginning of 1678, cared for in her infirmity by her niece Elena Lucrezia, daughter of her brother Giovanni Battista, as stated in a letter of the latter to Cardinal Francesco Barberini (Vatican City, Biblioteca Vaticana, Barb. lat. 6462, f. 192).

6. A.S.V., Notarile, f. 10788, ff. 312r-v, 313r-v, 314.

7. A.S.V., Notarile, b. 773, nos. 163–64.

8. Portenari, Della felicità di Padova, 475–76. The convent annexed to the church of S. Maria di Bethlemme, erected in 1441 by the Florentine humanist Palla Strozzi next to his palace, was built in the Prato della Valle at the beginning of what is currently via Luca Belludi (left side).

9. Bianchi-Giovini, Biografia di fra Paolo Sarpi, 1:214–15.

10. Here he was struck by a grave illness and was taken to Padua on his deathbed.

He expired in the Cornaro home on July 28, 1639, and the following day was buried in the church of S. Maria di Bethlemme (A.C.P., *Parrocchia S. Lorenzo*, Liber mortuorum 4, f. 59v). The palace at Codevigo, a work by Falconetto, was not very big. Temanza, who had seen it many times, wrote that it was of noble construction, two floors, the first vaulted and the second beamed. The adjacent grounds and courtyards were reached by a majestic arched portal held up by two Ionic columns and surmounted by a rectangular tympanum upon which was sculpted an eagle with open wings, also by Falconetto. Of the entire complex, Marcolini did not hesitate to say that, "if a gentleman or other private person, wants to know how to erect a villa he should go to see Codevigo" (Temanza, *Vite dei più celebri architetti*, 138–40). Later the palace became part of the dowry of the Foscari, after Elena Cornaro Piscopia, one of the two daughters of Girolamo, the last offspring of the family (see the family tree) married Sebastiano Foscari (1703). The edifice is not completely gone without a trace, as G. Fiocco wrote (Fiocco, *Alvise Cornaro e il suo tempo*, 87) although it has undergone, in various eras, horrible transformations and adaptations that have altered its original form. Nevertheless, on the external east walls the signs are still visible of closed up mullioned windows and the antique sundial; windowsills and decorative stone above the balconies still exist. The inside walls of the granary preserve the traces of stucco ornamentation. For two years now, in a ground floor room, through a gash in the collapsed roof, I was able to observe the beams, painted in sixteenth-century fashion. The architect, Gianantonio Battista, left an engraving (1779) of the majestic entrance portal at the courtyard (Venice, Bibliotheca del Civico Museo Corner, Collezione Gore, no. 2978, tavola I), presented erroneously by Fiocco as the portal of the church of Codevigo (*Alvise Cornaro e il suo tempo*, table 43), while even a layman would recognize the great difference between this portal and a church portal. In fact, the inscription in the engraving leaves no doubt: "main door of Ionic order connected to factory of rustic order of Giovanni Maria Falconetto, architect, erected in the year MDXXXVII in the territory of PADUA in the Codevigo villa of the district of the land of Piove di Sacco by the renowned Mr. Luigi Cornaro called *vita sobria* 'the sober life' now of the noble family Foscari."

11. Francesco Antonio, born January 19 and baptized February 11, 1635, was registered as the son of Signora Zanetta and had Cavalier Zaccaria Martini as his godfather. Caterina Isabetta was baptized January 13,1636, and registered as the daughter of Signora Zanetta, daughter of the late Anzolo "and of unknown father" (Venice, Parrocchia S. Polo, in the parish archive to the Frari, Battesimi 1624–41 ff. 145–47). On April 18, 1641, Giovanni Battista Cornaro, in the presence of the patriarchal vicar and of Anzolo Bon declared that Francesco and Caterina, baptized in the church of S. Polo, "are both his children procreated by him with the most illustrious Venetian lady Zanetta of the late Mr. Anzolo Bon; although in the notation of these baptisms the father's name is not mentioned, which is his; and because of his honesty, desiring that it should always appear that those children were his own, natural children" (ibid., document inserted between ff. 144–45).

12. Contarini, Dizionario tascabile, 51–52, 78; Romanin, *Storia documentata di Venezia*, x, 54.

13. Padua, Biblioteca Universitaria, ms. 295, f. 114; Cicogna, *Delle inscrizioni veneziane*, 4:442.

14. Padua, Biblioteca Universitaria, ms. 730, f. 51.

15. The palace section was acquired for 5,050 ducats. A.S.V., Notarile, b. 10802, year 1640, I. ff. 287–89v.

16. A.S.V., *Necrologio*, a. 1641, Provveditori alla Sanità, n. 870; A.S.L.V., Morti III (1638–65), to date.

17. Vatican City, Archivio Segreto Vaticano, Secr. Brevia, vol. 1543, f. 590. Unfortunately it is impossible for me to supply further information about this child, notwithstanding the minute research done in the archives of all the parishes of Venice. Therefore, she is indicated as "unnamed nun" in the family tree.

18. Angelini, *Catalogo cronologico de' rettori di Bergamo*, 63; Cicogna, *Delle inscrizioni veneziane*, 4:442; Belotti, *Storia di Bergamo*, 4: note 486.

19. Padua, Biblioteca Universitaria, ms. 730, f. 54.

20. Dalla Rovere had Andrea Balbi, son of Todaro, a noble Venetian, for a proxy at the baptism. A.S.L.V., *Battesimi II (1633–1647)*, atto no. 43, f. 45; Morti III (1638–1665), f. 29.

21. Padua, Biblioteca Universitaria, ms. 340, ff. 1, 5, 10.

22. Ibid., f. 10; Bianchi-Giovini, *Biografia di Fra Paolo Sarpi*, 1:204; Contarini, *Dizionaria tascabile*, 43; G. Musatti, *Storia di Venezia*, 1:230.

23. De Santi, "Elena Lucrezia," IV, 180.

24. Venice, Biblioteca del Civico Museo Correr, ms. Cicogna 1213, t. I, f. 24.

25. I find a Giovanni Battista Boni registered, a middleman, in the parish of S. Luca in Venice, and one Carlo Boni listed repeatedly in the register of hat makers in Venice (A.S.L.V., Battesimi, December 31, 1648; Padua, Biblioteca del Museo Civico, ms. C.M. 208, ff. 2, 18, 48, 62). For the significance of "volgare" in connection with the word "mechanic," we remember even at the time of Manzoni the words of the haughty noble spoken to Ludovico: "In the middle, vile mechanic" (Manzoni, *I promessi sposi*, 86; for more information, see Ventura, *Nobilità e popolo nella società veneta del '400 e '500*).

26. De Santi, "Elena Lucrezia," 179–80.

27. Others were from Valsabbia: Fabio Glisenti of Vestone (sec. XVI), who practiced medicine in Venice with honor and great financial gain; the Gianantonio brothers and Stefano Nicolini, from Sabbio, renowned printers (sec. XVI); Pietro Bellotti (Volciano 1627–Gargagnano del Garda 1700), a portrait painter who distinguished himself in painting old men and women, yet died in poverty (Molmenti, Storia di Venezia, 2:240, note 1, 370; Lorenzetti, *Venezia e il suo estuario*, 858; Corna, *Dizionario della storia dell'arte in Italia*, 2:79; Benezit, *Dictionnaire critique*, 1:540). For more in-depth information on the Valsabbia, see Comparoni, *Storia delle valli Trompia e Sabbia*; Vaglia, *Storia della valle Sabbia*.

28. Cantù, *Storia di Venezia*, 2:151.

29. The surname Boni (De Boni, Bono, Del Buono) occurs repeatedly in the parochial registries of Vestone from the fifteenth century to the present, leading me to believe that this is the place of origin of the Boni family. Even if it is sometimes found in Nozza, Sabbio, Vobarno, and in Gavardo, in the same valley, it is possible that a few Boni came down from Vestone to

establish themselves in these localities without more yielding ground.

30. Cocchetti, *Brescia e sua provincia*, 188.

31. A.S.V., Notarile, Testamenti, b. 773, no. 163–64; Caro, *Oratio parentalis*, 9.

32. Venice, Biblioteca del Civico Museo Correr, ms. 1213; De Santi, "Elena Lucrezia," IV, 180.

33. De Santi, "Elena Lucrezia," IV, 181; Dalmazzo, *Lucrezia Cornaro*, 32.

34. The aspirant was supposed to pay twenty thousand ducats (or more) in cash, putting down half in eight days and the other half fifteen days later. If he failed to do so, the nomination was withdrawn, but the individual had to pay a fine of 10 percent of the entire sum. Venice, Biblioteca del Civico Museo Correr, Miscellanea Correr, 1108, ff. 111–12; Cicogna, *Delle inscrizioni veneziane*, 4:443; E. Musatti, *Storia d'un lembo di terra*, 1137.

35. The basilica of San Marco, constructed at the expense of the state (9th-11th centuries), was always considered a chapel for use by the doge and the Venetian Senate for the functions of the Republic and as such was maintained and administered. It remained thus until the viceroy of Italy, after the fall of the Republic, declared it a cathedral church (Oct. 19, 1807), and just a few days later (Oct. 26) the patriarch Nicola Saverio Gamboni (1742–1808) transferred the patriarchal cathedral from S. Pietro di Castello to the ducal S. Marco, where until that time there had been a chapter of canons presided over by a *primicerio*. It was a canonically arbitrary transferral; the disgrace of it was relieved only by the papal bull *Ecclesias quae* (September 29, 1821) which abolished the ducal canonic chapter of S. Marco. It was then declared a metropolitan cathedral church replacing S. Pietro di Castello, and the cathedra, the patriarch, and the chapter were transferred to S. Marco. Cappelletti, *Storia della Chiesa di Venezia*, 1:565-66, 581.

36. Manfredi, *Dignita procuratoria di S. Marco*, 10–12; E .Musatti, *Storia d'un lembo di terra*, 294; Falaschi, "Procuratori di S. Marco," 1261–62.

37. Vatican City, Archivio Segreto Vaticano, Secr. Brevia, vol. 1693, f. 292; vol. 1409, f. 46; vol. 1581, f. 414; vol. 1564, f. 155; vol. 1694, f. 324; vol.1359, ff. 241, 249, 253.

38. Vatican City, Biblioteca Apostolica Vaticana, Vat. lat. 10419, g. 113; Ottob. lat., 2351, f. 24.

39. The total sum collected at various intervals up to 1715 from the Benedictine monasteries of Cassino was 117,968 lire, divided as follows: S. Nicolo del Lido, 7,200; S. Giorgio Maggiore, 23,900; S. Giustina (Padua), 37,800; Praglia, 9,253; Vicenza, 5,658; Verona, 5,566; S. Eufemia, 9,986; S. Faustino (Brescia) II, 655; S. Polo (Paolo d'Aragon), 2,857; Pontida, 4,093. A.S.P., Corporazioni Soppresse, S. Giustina, 384, f. 172.

40. Padua, Biblioteca Universitaria, ms. 186, f. 152.

41. A.S.V., Notarile, b. 10802, ff. 298r–300r; b. 773, nos. 163–64; b. 11200 (142); b. 11191, f. 8r-v; b. 11221, f. 2r-v; b. 11221, f. 9r.

42. The marriage was celebrated May 27, 1654, in the parish of S. Luca and blessed by the priest D. Giovanni Batista Fabris in the presence of witnesses Domenico Dal Re, lawyer, and Giuseppe Petrobelli Pizolo of Padua (A.S.L.V., Matrimoni III 1647–83, f. 26). The document regarding this marriage was

registered at the end of June at the bottom of the page in a corner, with very small and poor writing, as if to hide the late rectification of a rather embarrassing situation.

43. Venice, Biblioteca Nazionale Marciana, Capellari Vivaro, *Arbore Cornaro*, f. 332v; Bacchini, *Helenae Lucretiae*, 4.

44. Contarini, *Dizionario tascabile*, 36; Cantù, *Storia di Venezia*, 2:165; Molmenti, *Storia di Venezia*, 3:25; Lorenzetti, *Venezia ed il suo estuario*, 138.

45. A.S.V., Notarile, b. 11191, f. 8r-v.

46. A.S.V., Notarile, b. 11192, ff. 153r-v , 154, 167r-v, 11215, ff. 8–18.

47. A.S.V., Notarile, Testamenti, b. 773, nos. 163–64.

48. A.S.V., Notarile, b. 11225, fasc. marzo, f. 45.

49. A.S.V., Notarile, ref. 11212.

50. De Santi, "Elena Lucrezia," IV, 183.

51. Treviso, Biblioteca Comunale, ms. 774.

52. A.S.V., Avogaria de Comun, reg. 15 (nuova segnatura Miscellanea codice I, *Storia veneta* 44–45), ff. 198–201, 202–205, 218-21, 243–46, 247-48; Treviso, Biblioteca Comunale, ms. 774; Cicogna, Delle inscrizioni veneziane, 4:442–443; E. Musatti, *Storia d'un lembo di terra*, 1657, note 5. Of the four petitions of Cornaro, De Santi lists only three and he is not precise with the various dates (De Santi, "Elena Lucrezia," IV, 183–84).

53. Dalmazzo, *Lucrezia Cornaro*, 37.

54. Venice, Biblioteca Nazionale Marciana, ms. It. VII, 1522 (= 8825); Padua, Biblioteca Universitaria, ms. 255, ff. 29–30; Molmenti, *Storia di Venezia*, 1:222.

55. Cantù, *Storia di Venezia*, 2:150.

56. Bacchini, *Helenae Lucretiae*, 156; De Santi, "Elena Lucrezia," IV, 186.

57. A.S.V., Notarile, b. 11224, fasc. settembre; Venice, Biblioteca del Civico Museo Correr, mss. PD. C. 2377/XXVI; *La diocesi di Padova* 1972, 214.

58. Vatican City, Biblioteca Apostolica Vaticana, Vat. lat., 10419, f. 241; G. Musatti, Storia di Venezia, 2:25, n. 3; A.R.S.J., *Epistolae nostrorum*, no. 10, ff. 169v–70, 289v.

59. Venice, Biblioteca del Civico Museo Correr, Codd. Grimani 15, ff. 63–65.

60. A.S.V., Notarile, Testamenti, b. 773, nos. 163–64 (see document 4).

61. He died of fever and of old age after two months of illness, taken care of by several doctors including Giorgio Calafatti, physician and family friend. Venice, Archivio Parrocchiale di S. Marco, *Morti* V, f. I; A.S.V., *Necrologio a. 1692*, Provveditori alla sanità, no. 898; Molmenti, *Storia di Venezia*, 2:346.

62. A.S.V., Notarile, b. 11212; b. 11225; A.A.U., ms. 366, f. 113v.

63. Vatican City, Archivio Segreto Vaticano, Secr. Brev., vol. 1310, f. 283.

64. She died of dropsy after a year of illness. The funeral was arranged by her son Girolamo. A.S.L.V., *Morti* VI (1697), f. 71v; A.S.V., Necrologio a. 1697, Provveditori alla sanità, no. 901.

65. Padua, Biblioteca Universitaria, ms. 295, f. 114.

66. Codevigo, Archivio Parrocchiale, *Battesimi* 1654–73, f. IIv, Oct. 3, 1669; Molmenti, *Storia di Venezia*, 3:337.

67. A.S.V. , Notarile, b.11214, ff. 4–5.

68. A.S.L.V., *Morti* IV (1668), f. 68v; Bacchini, *Helenae Lucretiae*, 4–5; Ziegelbauer, Historia rei literarie, 3:516.

69. Caterina Isabetta, born February 20, 1655, was baptized the following March 1. A.S.V., Avogaria de Comun, Nascite, cassetta 168; A.S.L.V., *Battesimi* III (1648–1718); Bacchini, *Helenae Lucretiae*, 4–5; Ziegelbauer, *Historia rei literariae*, 3:516.

70. Leti, *L'Italia regnante*, 4:59; Mercure Galante, 1678, 93–94; Lupis, *L'eroina veneta*, dedication; Mabillon and Germain, *Museum Italicum*, 1:36; De Santi, "Elena Lucrezia," IV, 180. A sonnet about Caterina exists, composed for the graduation of Angelo Sumachi, a noble of Zante, published in the *Epantismatologia*, Padua 1668, II.

71. The marriage was celebrated in the church of S. Giorgio Maggiore, the witnesses for the groom being the nobles Battista Nani and Giovanni Grimani, and for the bride the nobles Andrea Vendramin and Gaspare Dandolo. A.S.V., Avogaria de Comun, b. 100. 4, fasc. XVI, f. 5; Notarile, b. 11192, ff. 153–54; b. 11215, ff. 8–18.

72. He died after being ill for only a month, assisted spiritually by a certain Jesuit father and clinically by the physicians Casale and Calafatti, a friend and physician of the Cornaros. The following day the body was brought to Portello and shipped to Venice. A.C.P., *Parrocchia S. Lorenzo*, Morti B (on the back 32), f. 28; A.S.P., Ufficio di sanità, 486 by name.

73. The inscription reads: "Ex pio Catharinae Corneliae Piscopiae Vendraminae legato anno Domini MDCCXII" (Gonzati, *La basilica di S. Antonio di Padova*, 1:172). Orazio Marinali (Bassano Veneto 1643–Vicenza 1720), son of Francesco, a wood sculptor, was apprenticed in Venice to the Flemish Giusto Cort (1627–1679) and worked in collaboration with his brothers Francesco and Angelo. As the Da Pontes were a family of painters, the Marinalis were a family of sculptors whose work appears in the churches, buildings, and gardens of Venice, Bassano, Verona, Brescia, Padua, Vicenza, Udine, and Treviso. Orazio had already sculpted the statue of Apollo and Diana, geometry and prudence, that decorated the atrium of the Cornaro palace in Venice. Brentari, *Storia di Bassano*, 721; Fontana, *Cento palazzi di Venezia*, 396; Tua, "Marinali scultori," 345.

74. Venice, Biblioteca del Civico Museo Correr, mss. PD-C. 1324. 2.

75. Venice, Biblioteca del Civico Museo Correr, mss. PD-1312. 2. Of this famous church, founded with the convent in the fourteenth century, rich in historical memories and works of art, suppressed in the beginning of the nineteenth century and almost completely demolished in 1862, pictorial ruins and architectural remnants still exist (windows and portals in the gothic Venetian style, fourteenth and fifteenth centuries) (Lorenzetti, *Venezia e il suo estuario*, 437).

76. A.S.V., Avogaria de Comun, Nascite, drawer 168; A.S.L.V., *Battesimi III (1648–1718)*, at letter G; Pynsent, *The Life*, 8.

77. Padua, Biblioteca del Museo Civico, ms. C.M. 247, f. 151; ms C.M. 715, ff

164–65.

78. Published in the *Epantismatologia*, 87.

79. The marriage was celebrated in the church of the Redeemer, witnessed by the nobles Ascanio Giustiniani, son of Antonio; Francesco Contarini, son of Benedetto; Lorenzo Zorzi, son of Mar' Antonio; Gian Domenico Tiepolo, son of Francesco (A.S.V., Avogaria de Comun, b. 83. 3, fasc. 23, 1675–1684). Of the daughters, Elena married (on November 29,1703, in the church of S. Maria della carità) the noble Sebastiano Foscari, son of Francesco; Lucrezia married (on January 7, 1703, in the church of S. Maria delle grazie) the noble Giovanni Battista Loredan, son of Francesco (A.S.L.V., *Matrimoni IV (1683–1732)*, g. 73; A.S.V., Avogaria de Comun, b. 84. 4, fasc. 26, 1703–1714).

80. Padua, Biblioteca Universitaria, ms. 730, f. 21; Tron, *Tributo d'ossequio*, 13.

81. He succeeded Gianfrancesco Pasqualigo (1692–1694) and was himself replaced by Nicolo Manin (1695–1697). Angelini, *Catalogo cronologico*, 68; Belotti, *Storia di Bergamo*, 4:487 note.

82. In the eighteenth century the villa belonged to the Farsetti, then to the Marchesa Centurione Scotto Benvenuti. In 1848 she had it remodeled by the architect Giuseppe Jappelli (?), together with the garden which in Alvise Cornaro's time had an open-air theater, where perhaps Ruzante had recited (Venice, Biblioteca del Civico Museo Correr, ms. BPC 507, fasc. 17/11; Cornaro, *Discorsi intorno alla vita sobria*, 64, 68; Mazzotti, *Le ville venete*, 94). Today the villa—the property of the local nursing home (via S. Stefano), by which one enters—is uninhabited and neglected and in danger of greater damage to the plaster ornamentation and the eighteenth-century frescoes in the upper hall.

83. A.S.P., Corporazioni Soppresse, S. Giorgio no. 5.

84. A.S.P., Notarile, b. 6057, ff. 69-70v; b. 6061, f. 79r-v; Gloria, "Nuovi documenti intorno la abitazione di Galileo," 146 note I; Sambin, "I testamenti," 315.

85. The act was drawn up in Venice by the notary Emilio Velano in the home of the lawyer Giulio Crivellari, witnessed by Francesco Ferrara, son of Antonio, and Gianfrancesco Badoer, son of Marcantonio (Padua, Archivio Antico dell'Arca del Santo, *Atti e parti*, vol. 28 [XXVII old enumeration], ff. 130v–31v). The Paduan historian Gennari errs when he writes of the monument, "since the Cornaro family was extinct, the necessary licenses having been obtained, it was removed" (Gennari, *Memorie inedite sopra le tre chiese di Padova*, 13–14).

86. This bust is one of the few surviving examples of Bonazza's portraits, since many portrait busts were lost in the fire (February 1798) that destroyed the Delia Academy of Padua (Ronchi, *Guida storico-artistico di Padova*, 125; Checchi, Gaudenzio, and Grossato, *Padova, guida ai monumenti*, 323–25; Bresciani Alvarez, *L'opera di Giovanni Bonazza al Santo*, 36). The inscription under the bust reproduces the error of the epitaph, assigning the year 1688 as the year of death of Elena Lucrezia Cornaro Piscopia instead of 1684. To the initial inscription were added the last five lines recalling the new entry (Gonzati, *La basilica di S. Antonio*, 2:309).

87. Girolamo Cornaro was buried by his daughter Lucrezia, married to Loredan, and his granddaughter Foscari (born of his daughter Elena, married to Sebastiano Foscari, perhaps both already deceased). A.S.L.V., *Morti VII (1733–1752)*, f. 14; Padua, Biblioteca Universitaria, ms. 882, f. 15.

CHAPTER 3. CULTURE IN THE CORNARO PISCOPIA HOME

1. A.S.L.V., *Battisimi II (1633–1647)*, to the letter E; Venice, Biblioteca del Civico Museo Correr, ms. Correr 2039, f. 577.

2. Pynsent, *The Life*, 8; Dalmazzo, *Lucrezia Cornaro*, 38–39.

3. Molmenti, *Storia di Venezia*, 3: 339.

4. Bacchini, *Helenae Lucretiae*, 5; Deza, *Vita di Helena*, 21; De Santi, "Elena Lucrezia," IV, 421.

5. Berruti, *Patriziato veneto*, 112. To Cornaro's munificence we also attribute the splendid wooden altarpiece of the triptych altar of San Marco with the Saints Jerome, John, Paul and Nicholas, a masterpiece of the budding gothic style signed by Bartolomeo Vivarini, 1474 (Lorenzetti, *Venezia e il suo estuario*, 582).

6. Cicogna, *Delle inscrizioni veneziane*, 6:569, 751; D'Ayala, *Bibliografia militare italiana*, 18. Marco Bragadin, a Cypriot and alchemist who came to Venice in 1590 for his experiments, elicited the envy of the princes against the Serenissima who had the good fortune of receiving a man who "made fine gold from live silver." Convicted of fraud, he was sentenced by the duke of Bavaria to in 1591. Before climbing the gallows, he confessed that he never knew how to "take the soul out of gold" (Molmenti, *Storia di Venezia*, 2:247).

7. A.S.V., Barbaro, *Arbori*, 17. *Dialogo della laguna con quello che si ricerca per la sua lunga conservazione, composto da ser Marcantonio Cornaro q. Zuanne che fu di ser Fantino* (Dialogue about the lagoon with research for its long-term conservation, composed by Mr. Marcantonio Cornaro q. Zuanne of Mr. Fantino): Venice, Biblioteca Nazionale Marciana, cod. It. IV, 164 (=5642); published by G. Pavanello, in *Antichi scrittori di idraulica veneta*, I (Venice, 1912).

8. Sambin, "I testamenti," 368, 378.

9. Cicogna, *Delle inscrizioni veneziane*, 6:751. The manuscript copy, in two folio volumes, of this work by Chiericati existing in the library of Girolamo Cornaro leads me to believe that it is the one examined and annotated by Giacomo Alvise and, inherited by his son Girolamo, passed subsequently into the hands of Giovanni Battista, his son and the father of Elena Lucrezia (A.S.V., Notarile, b. 10780, III, fasc. 2–3).

10. Martino Hasdale, born in 1570 in Germany, came to Padua to study and was later in the court of Emperor Rudolph II; Nicolò Nonstiz, also a German, was a student in Padua and testified in favor of Galilei in the Venice debate between Galilei and Baldassare Capra; Giovanni Eutel Zugmesser, Flemish, in 1620 was a student in Padua. Girolamo Spinelli, born in Padua around 1580, at age twenty professed his vows in the Benedictine order. In the early years of the seventeenth century he became a good friend of the Benedictine

Benedetto Castelli at the Monastery of S. Giustina in Padua; both were disciples of Galileo, taking the master's side on the new star of 1604. From 1627 to 1632 he was the ninety-seventh abbot of S. Giustina (not the sixty-seventh as Favaro wrote); during his tenure, Padua was stricken by the plague (1630), which nonetheless spared the monastery. His brother Andronico, a priest and jurist, defended the rights of the Monastery of S. Giustina in the Roman Curia, earning for himself well-deserved esteem; after his death (May 2, 1631) he was buried in the Basilica of S. Giustina and remembered with a memorial stone in the short passage (left wall) which currently leads from the aisle between the two choirs into the rectory. Don Girolamo died in 1647 after having been abbot also of S. Nicolo del Lido, of S. Giorgio Maggiore of Venice, and of S. Giovanni Evangelista of Parma. Fano, *Sperone Speroni*, 115; Borgherini Scarabellin, *La vita privata a Padua nel sec. XVII*, 164–65; Galilei, *Opere*, 20:460, 496, 540, 561; Favaro, *Galileo Galilei e lo Studio di Padua*, 1:231; Soppelsa, "Un dimenticato scolaro galileiano," 97–114; Soppelsa, *Genesi del metodo galileiano*, 41–43.

11. Galileo, *Opere*, 2:294, 520, 530, 536–537, 545–546, 560, 574, 576; 10:173–176.

12. *Lettere d'uomini illustri*, 24, 47; Angiolgabriello di S. Maria (Calvi), *Biblioteca e storia*, 5:CXCIII.

13. Modena, Archivio di Stato, Cancelleria ducale, Lettere e documenti di particolari, C. 373/25.

14. Giacomo Alvise Cornaro Piscopia, stricken with risipola and fever, died after eight days of illness and was buried in the church of the sisters of S. Chiara together with his wife Caterina Bragadin. A.S.P., Ufficio di sanità, 466, at the name; A.C.P., *Parrocchia S. Lorenzo*, Morti II, 1599–1617, f. 47; Galileo, *Opere*, 10:315.

15. A.S.V., Notarile, Testamenti, b. 37, 335. Collegio was the title of some assemblies of the Venetian Republic. For the formation and jurisdiction of each, see Contarini, *Dizionario tascabile*, 56–57.

16. A.S.V., Notarile, reg. 10784, f. I (marginal note).

17. A.S.V., Notarile, b. 10780 a. 1629, III, fasc. 2–3.

18. Mercure Galant, 93; Caro, *Oratio parentalis*, 4; Moroni, *Dizionario di erudizione storico-ecclesiastica*, 91:353; Fontana, *Cento palazzi di Venezia*, 395.

19. Ridolfi, *Le meraviglie dell arte*, 1:401, 2:286; Boschini, *Carta del navegar pitoresco*, 554–55; Sansovino and Martinioni, *Venetia città nobilissima*, 374; Cicogna, *Delle inscrizioni veneziane*, 4:443; Moroni, *Dizionario*, 91:353; Mutinelli, *Lessico veneto*, 61; Tassini, *Alcuni palazzi*, 63; De Santi, "Elena Lucrezia," IV, 423; Fontana, *Cento palazzi di Venezia*, 396–397; Lorenzetti, *Venezia e il suo estuario*, 484. For the libraries of the convents and of the patrician palaces of Venice, see Briois, *Voyage littéraire de Paris à Rome en 1698*, 25–30; Savini Branca, *Collezionismo veneziano*, 205–206.

20. Gar, *I codici storici della collezione Foscarini*, 427. Tommaso Gar described and ordered the historical manuscripts of the Foscarini collection already in the Imperial Library of Vienna and since 1868 in the Marciana National Library of Venice (ms. It. IV-164 [=5642]).

21. Mabillon and Germain, *Museum Italicum*, 1:35. Dalmazzo is imprecise

regarding the event, indicating April 29 as the day of Mabillon's visit to Cornaro, although on that date the Benedictine had not yet arrived in Venice; from April 26 to May 12 he was in Milan and the surrounding area (Dalmazzo, *Lucrezia Cornaro*, 90).

22. Vallery, *Correspondance inédite de Mabillon*, 2:32, 35. The two publications mentioned are: *Le pompe funebri celebrate da' signori accademici Infecondi di Roma*, and Deza, *Vita di Helena*.

23. A.S.V., Notarile, Testamenti, b. 773, 163, f. 6v; Tassini, *Alcuni palazzi*, 61; Fontana, *Cento palazzi di Venezia*, 395.

24. Selvatico, *L'architettura e scultura in Venezia*, 78–79; Marini, *Venezia antica e moderna*, 80; Molmenti, *Storia di Venezia*, 1:276; Lorenzetti, *Venezia ed il suo estuario*, 484–85.

25. Giovanni Battista Cornaro bequeathed the palace to his son Girolamo, who later gave it as the dowry of his daughter Lucrezia when she married (January 12, 1703) Giovanni Battista Loredan. It belonged to this family until October 19, 1816, when Lucrezia Maria, daughter of Cristoforo Antonio Loredan and widow of Zaccaria Valier, sold it to Giuseppe Arizzi, from whose hands it passed into the ownership of others, serving several different uses. The building became a lithographic press, an inn, a stagecoach dispatch office, a message office, a steam office, and a railway society office. Acquired then by the Countess Caterina Peccana Campagna of Verona, it was decorated, furnished, and restored from inopportune changes that it had undergone. Then Augusto Barbesi owned it, using it as a hotel with the name of Hotel de la Ville. On December 18, 1867, it was purchased by the cavalier Francesco Gossleth, who on January 5, 1868, sold it to the municipality of Venice which restored the façade and joined it by means of an overpass to the adjacent and almost twin palace, the Farsetti palace, of the same style and time, in order to use both as the municipal building of the city (such use remains to date). Tassini, *Alcuni palazzi*, 63; Fontana, *Cento palazzi di Venezia*, 397; Lorenzetti, *Venezia e il suo estuario*, 484.

26. Rinaldini, *De resolutione et compositione mathematica*, 157; Sumachi, *Enypnionsophiae panagrypnon*; Fiorelli, *Detti e fatti memorabili*, 40; *Pictura Venetae urbis*, 61; Muti, *La penna volante*, 157; Cicogna, *Delle inscrizioni veneziane*, 4:443.

CHAPTER 4. ELENA LUCREZIA'S EDUCATION

1. Venice, Archivio della Curia Patriarcale, *Liber collationum beneficiorum*, ms. senza segnatura; Cornelius, *Ecclesiae Venetae*, 12:253, 260; Cappelletti, *Storia della Chiesa*, 1:621; 3:234.

2. Richard and Giraud, *Dizionario universale delle scienze religiose*, 2:74; Alessi, *Vita del B. Gregorio card. Barbarigo*, 38; Bellinati, *S. Gregorio Barbarigo*, 43.

3. Bacchini, *Helenae Lucretiae*, 6–7; Lupis, *L'eroina veneta*, 18; Deza, *Vita di Helena*, 24; Pynsent, *The Life*, 14–15; De Santi, "Elena Lucrezia," 4:421; Dalmazzo, *Lucrezia Cornaro*, 50–51.

4. Graziani, "L'educazione della donna," 826.

5. Juan Luis Vives, a religious author, philosopher, and pedagogue (born in Valencia on March 6, 1492, and died at Bruges on May 6, 1540), wrote among other things *De ratione studii puerilis* (Paris, 1523) and *De institutione feminae christianae ad Catharinam Angliae reginam pro institutione filiae suae Mariae* (Bruges, 1523). Vives is considered one of the pioneers of modern pedagogy. Garin, *L'educazione in Europa*, 161.

6. Silvio Antoniano—cardinal, humanist, pedagogue (born in Castello, Penne Diocese, on December 31, 1540, and died in Rome on August 16, 1603)—represented the late humanist period in the Ciceronian Style; he was a prolific author of Latin hymns and prayers. To check the Protestant Reformation and to put regular instruction and upper level instruction on the level of the new educational trend by the Council of Trent, St. Charles Borromeo invited him to write the valuable pedagogical treatise *De christiana puerorum educatione*, which is a well organized exposition of the fundamental principles of the Counter-Reformation as applied to the field of education. The work was a great success. Published in Verona in 1583, it was reprinted several times until 1928, edited by L. Pogliani. Gamba, *Storia della scuola italiana nel Seicento e nel Settecento*, 301; Garin, *L'educazione in Europa*, 207.

7. Brignole-Sale, *Il satirico innocente*, 229; Spini, *Ricerca dei libertini*, 43.

8. Among the learned Venetian women of the seventeenth century we should remember: Lucrezia Marinelli Vacca (1571–1653), author of various works, among them *Nobiltà ed eccellenza delle donne* (Venice 1600); Veneranda Bragadin Cavalli, whose works were printed partly in Venice (1613) partly in Verona (1619); Sara Copia Sullan, correspondent with the Genovese writer Ansaldo Ceba (1565–1623) already a student in Padua. Among the Paduans: Isabella Andreini Canali, scholar and actress (1562–1604); Valeria Miani Negri (1560), who wrote verses, madrigals, and a tragedy; Beatrice Papafava Cittadella (1626–1729); the sisters Gabriella and Carlotta Patin, of French origin but residents in Padua, at whose university their father Carlo taught.

9. Fabris died on November 30, 1668, due to an apoplectic attack that struck him as soon as he finished celebrating Mass and caused him to drop dead in the sacristy. A.S.L.V., *Morti IV* (1668); Deza, *Vita di Helena*, 21, 26; De Santi, "Elena Lucrezia," IV, 422; Dalmazzo, *Lucrezia Cornaro*, 51.

10. Deza, *Vita di Helena*, 26–27; Bacchini, *Helenae Lucretiae*, 7; Lupis, *L'eroina veneta*, 18–19; Pynsent, *The Life*, 16; De Santi, "Elena Lucrezia," IV, 422; Dalmazzo, *Lucrezia Cornaro*, 51–53.

11. Rome, Archivio del Collegio Greco (Archive of the Greek College), t. XIV, f. 30.

12. Vatican City, Biblioteca Apostolica Vaticana, Barb. lat. 6462, ff. 173, 182; Legrand, *Bibliographie hellénique*, 2:257; 3:346–47.

13. Vatican City, Biblioteca Apostolica Vaticana, Barb. lat. 6462, f. 180r-v; Padua, Biblioteca del Museo Civico, ms. BP 124-XXXIV, F. 29v; Rinaldini, *Geometra promotus*, 60; Macedo, *Myrothecium morale*, 209; Bacchini, *Helenae Lucretiae*, 9; Deza, *Vita di Helena*, 29.

14. König, *Biblioteca vetus et nova*, 357; Colomies, *Opera*, 68; Morelli, *Della pubblica Libreria di San Marco in Venezia*, 2:305.

15. A.R.S.J., Vota Carlo Maurizio (biographical chart); *Sommervogel, Bibliothèque*

de la Compagnie de Jésus, 8:918.

16. Borsetti, *Historia almi Ferrariae Gymnasii*, 2:261; Sommervogel, *Bibliothèque*, 5:266; De Santi, "Elena Lucrezia," IV, 423.

17. Geymonat, *Storia del pensiero filosofico e scientifico*, 2:304.

18. In 1679 Father Vota was sent to the College of Turin, then to the College at Como (1681). On March 4, 1684, he was in the professed missionary house of Milan, ready to go to Linz as apostolic prefect of Innocent XI, to the Emperor Leopold (1640–1705), and to Warsaw to King Sobieski, to obtain their support in the alliance against the Turks. He arrived in Vienna on June 19, 1684, and in Moscow on August 14 where he opened a house for the Society of Jesus which remained until 1689. In Moscow he received news of the death of Elena Lucrezia. Leaving Moscow, he lived in Warsaw until 1710 when he returned to Rome (to the Gesù) where he died on December 9, 1715. A.R.S.J., Vota Carlo Maurizio (biographical chart); *Epistolae nostrorum*, 14; Sommervogel, *Bibliothèque*, 8:918–22.

19. Garin, *L'educazione in Europa*, 205–206.

20. Padua, Biblioteca del Museo Civico, ms. BP. 124-XXIV, f. 29; Facciolati, *Fasti Gymnasii*, 277; Patinus, *Lyceum Patavinum*, 55–56; Fabronius, Historia *Academiae Pisanae*, 3:393–98 passim; Vivani, "Rinaldini, Carlo," 788–89.

21. De Santi, "Elena Lucrezia," IV, 423.

22. Rinaldini, *De resolutione*, 157; Rinaldini, *Geometra promotus*, 59; Facciolati, *Fasti Gymnasii*, 277; Patinus, *Lyceum Patavinum*, 56; Fabronius, *Historia Academiae Pisanae*, 3:398; De Santi, "Elena Lucrezia," IV, 424.

23. Deza, *Vita di Helena*, 31; Pynsent, *The Life*, 63; De Santi, "Elena Lucrezia," IV, 424; Dalmazzo, *Lucrezia Cornaro*, 58.

24. Soppelsa, *Genesi del metodo galileiano*, 170–176.

25. Capone-Braga, *La filosofia francese*, 2:58; Soppelsa, *Genesi del metodo galileiano*, 115–200; Malusa, *Dall'umanesimo alla controriforma*, 248–53; Geymonat, *Storia del pensiero*, 2:191. See also: Poppi, *Casualità e infinità nella Scuola padovana dal 1480 al 1513*; Poppi, *La dottrina della scienza in Giacomo Zabarella*.

26. Rinaldini, *De resolutione*, 157; Rinaldini, *Geometra promotus*, 59; Rinaldini, *Commercium epistolicum*, 65.

27. Scardova, *Vita compendiosa di Elena Lucrezia*, Padua, Biblioteca del Museo Civico, ms. B.P. 125/I, 18; Rinaldini, *Geometra promotus*, 59; Bacchini, *Helenae Lucretiae*, 12; Deza, *Vita di Helena*, 32; Gonzati, *La basilica di S. Antonio*, 2:310-311; Pynsent, *The Life*, 64; Dalmazzo, *Lucrezia Cornaro*, 61.

28. "This day, February 15, 1662. The Reverend Hippolito Marchetti, age 72, from a five-month fever. Physician Lucatello. Buried by the Fraterna S. Luca." A.S.L.V., Morti III (1638–1665), f. 117v.

29. Vatican City, Biblioteca Apostolica Vaticana, Barb. lat. 6462, f. 184.

30. Father Rotondi was born in Monte Leone Sabino c. 1630 and died in Padua on February 7, 1702, buried under the floor in the entrance to the sacristy of the Basilica of St. Anthony. On December 20, 1704, the Conventual community decided to erect a statue in his honor according to the model presented by the Paduan sculptor, Giovanni Bonazza. But then, instead of a

statue, they placed a headstone with a cornice of Carrara marble finely worked in detail by the aforementioned artist, with a laudatory inscription in gold lettering, surmounted by an oval portrait in oils of the illustrious deceased (Gonzati, *La basilica di S. Antonio*, 2:321; E. Musatti, *Storia d'un lembo di terra*, 1790–1791, note 5). As a result of the restoration of the little antesacristy in 1939, the headstone was removed and set in the wall of the "cloister of paradise" behind the apse of the basilica where it remains to this day.

31. Padova, Biblioteca del Museo Civico, ms. B.P. 124-XXIV, f. 34v; Rinaldini, *Commercium epistolicum*; 84; Patinus, *Lyceum Patavinum*, 47–49; Facciolati, *Fasti Gymnasii*, 257–258; Rossetti, *Francescani del Santo docenti all'Università*, 178–179.

32. Marrano (from the Spanish *marrano*, pig, pork) was the name given to those Jews who had renounced Judaism to escape persecution and death (in fifteenth-century Spain) but who secretly continued to profess their former religion.

33. Cantù, *Storia di Venezia*, 2:276; Molmenti, *Storia di Venezia*, 1:80, note 3; Lorenzetti, *Venezia e il suo esuario*, 409–410; Milano, *Storia degli ebrei in Italia*, 312–317 passim; Sandri and Alazraki, *Arte e vita ebraica a Venezia*, 29–33. Venice's hospitality for the Marranos was displeasing to the pope who considered it a "marked offense toward his divine Majesty."

34. Aboaf had four sons: Abraham, David, Jacob, and Joseph. Joseph was so learned as to be able to act as rabbi of Venice during the brief periods of his father's exile, after which he emigrated to Palestine, establishing himself in the "sacred city" of Hebron where he died. David was the patron of the family. He paid for the publication of his father's Responsi. Jacob, versed in Jewish and civil culture and Biblical history, knowledgeable in Caraitic civilization and liturgy, was a rabbi in Venice and died in 1727. Roth, *Gli ebrei in Venezia*, 266–69; Ravenna, "Aboab Samuele," 54–55; Milano, Storia degli ebrei, 678; David Abraham, "Aboab Samuel Ben Abraham," 94–95.

35. Bacchini, *Helenae Lucretiae*, 44–45; Deza, *Vita di Helena*, 63–64; Pynsent, *The Life*, 29; De Santi, "Elena Lucrezia," IV, 425; Dalmazzo, *Lucrezia Cornaro*, 60–61.

36. Bacchini, *Helenae Lucretiae*, 29; Lupis, *L'eroina veneta*, 49; Deza, *Vita di Helena*, 54; Pynsent, *The Life*, 82; Dalmazzo, *Lucrezia Cornaro*, 82; Loewe, "Hebraists Christian (1100–1890)," 9–71.

37. The titles of the compositions are as follows: *Sacre ariose cantate a voce sola, dedicate all'illustrissima signora Ellena Cornera Episcopia. Opera quarta di Carlo Grossi* [Sacred arias for solo voice, dedicated to the illustrious Signora Ellena Cornera Episcopia. The Fourth Opera by Carlo Grossi] (Venice, care of Francesco Magni, the so-called Gardano, 1663). Among Elena's biographers, this opera, which had become rare, is included only by De Santi ("Elena Lucrezia," IV, 426). Performances of these works were planned for the tricentennial celebration of Elena's doctorate.

38. See appendix, document 4.

39. In the conservatories of the four major Venetian hospitals, or homes of charity—Pietà (Mercy), Incurabili (Incurables), Derelitti (Derelicts), Mendicanti (Beggars)—the inhabitants were taught to sing and to play

various musical instruments under the tutelage of the most celebrated masters, such as Antonio Vivaldi at the Pietà. Molmenti, *Storia di Venezia*, 3:78, 275; Della Corte and Pannain, *Storia della musica*, 2:942; *Dizionario musicale Larousse*, 1:418–19; 3:355–56.

40. A.S.V., Notarile, b. 773, nos. 163–64, f. 3 (see appendix, document 4).

41. Lupis, *L'eroina veneta*, 120; Deza, *Vita di Helena*, 65–66, 84; Pynsent, *The Life*, 90–91; Dalmazzo, *Lucrezia Cornaro*, 142–43, 147.

42. A.S.V., Notarile, b. 773, nos. 163–64, g. 3; Venice, Biblioteca del Civico Museo Correr, mss. PD-C. 1324/2.

43. A.S.V., Riformatori dello Studio di Padova, b. 409; Rinaldini, *Commercium epistolicum*, 88; Caro, *Oratio parentalis*, 6, 8.

CHAPTER 5. A DEGREE

1. Prodi, "Riforma cattolica e controriforma," 391–95; Taveneaux, "Il cattolicesimo post-tridentino," 312–14.

2. Congar, "Théologie," 429–430; Michel, "Trente (concil de)," 1505; Raner and Vorgrimler, *Dizionario di teologia*, 692, 734–35; Jedin, *Storia della chiesa*, 6:661; Garin, *L'educazione in Europa*, 204–205; Taveneaux, "Il cattolicesimo post-tridentino," 334–335.

3. Spini, *Ricerca dei libertini*, 143, 146–48; De Bernardin, "La politica culturale," 459–60; Cessi, *Storia della Repubblica di Venezia*, 2:148, 159; Benzoni, *Venezia nell'età della controriforma*, 54.

4. De Bernardin, "La politica culturale," 464–65; Rossetti, *L'Università di Padova*, 28.

5. Rossetti, *L'Università di Padova*, 30.

6. Borgherini Scarabellin, *La vita privata*, 160–161, 167.

7. Tagliaferri, *Podestaria e capitanato di Padova*, 378–379.

8. Pychowska, "A Learned Woman," 47.

9. Vatican City, Biblioteca Apostolica Vaticana, Ottob. lat. 2479, f. 55r-v.

10. A.S.V., Riformatori dello Studio di Padova, b. 75.

11. Vatican City, Biblioteca Apostolica Vaticana, Barb. lat. 6462, ff. 169–173, 179–180, 182–185, 191–192; Bacchini, *Helenae Lucretiae*, 163; De Santi, "Elena Lucrezia," IV, 182.

12. A.S.V., Riformatori dello Studio di Padova, b. 75; A.A.U., ms. 707, f. 101r; Caro, *Oratio parentalis*, 8.

13. The Festa della Sensa (dell'Ascensione)—Feast of the Ascension when Christ ascended into heaven 40 days after Easter—was the first of the official ceremonies in which Venice celebrated its symbolic marriage to the sea, marking its dominion over the Adriatic. The Doge, at the entrance to the harbor, tossed a ring into the sea, pronouncing the words, "As a sign of eternal dominion, we, the Doge of Venice, marry you, oh sea." With this official symbolic ceremony, a series of spectacles and festivals began which

lasted several days and culminated in a traditional bazaar, a sort of exposition in the Piazza S. Marco, where all the Venetian arts, all the artistic industries, exhibited their products in separate booths. E. Musatti, *Storia d'un lembo di terra*, 896, 1876–79; Molmenti, *Storia di Venezia*, 3:223–27; Cessi, *La Repubblica di Venezia e il problema adriatico*, 47–66; Lorenzetti, *Venezia e il suo estuario*, 20.

14. Bacchini, *Helenae Lucretiae*, 166; Lorenz, *Analecta literaria*, 17.

15. Facciolati, *Fasti Gymnasii*, 1–2. The Reformers of the University of Padua were elected from the most worthy and cultured men of the nobility; they served a two-year term that could not be prolonged for any reason. They exercised their authority directly in educational and administrative matters (contracts with professors, regulations, exams, discipline, etc.). They supervised the scientific and literary academies, both public and private, and together with a representative from the Venetian inquisition, oversaw pre-publication censorship of books and printed materials and license concessions. Since almost all the reformers had previously held positions of great responsibility in the government, they brought with them an experience of the world that conformed to the high office to which they were elected. (E. Musatti, *Storia d'un lembo di terra*, 883 and note 2; Favaro, *L'Università di Padova*, 27–28; Rossetti, *L'Università di Padova*, 18).

16. Padua, Biblioteca Antoniana, Miscellanea, Ms. XXII, 588, fasc. 8, ff. 43–44, 56r-v. These three anonymous documents, preserved by the Conventual Friars in Padua, to whose order and friary of St. Anthony Father Felice Rotondi belonged, were found after his death among his papers. The handwriting is identical to other documents by Rotondi and therefore may be attributed to his hand and remain to document this event. Padua, Biblioteca Antoniana, Collezione autografi, under the heading Rotondi (see appendix, document 2).

17. Serena, *Lettere inedite*, 4–5; Serena, *S. Gregorio Barbarigo*, 1:198–199.

18. See note 16 above.

19. De Santi, "Elena Lucrezia," IV, 178–180; Serena, *Lettere inedite*, 9–13; Serena, *S. Gregorio Barbarigo*, 1:215.

20. De Santi, "Elena Lucrezia," IV, 178.

21. Serena, *Lettere inedite*, 22; Serena, *S. Gregorio Barbarigo*, 1:216.

22. These observations are the result of two meetings which took place in Rome on May 28 and on June 18, 1973, with Monsignor Giovanni Papa, vice rector-general of the Historical-Hagiographical Office of the Sacred Congregation for the Causes of Saints, to whom I express my cordial thanks.

23. A.S.V., Riformatori dello Studio di Padova, b. 75; A.A.U., ms. 707, f. 101r; ms. 716, f. 121v.

24. Bacchini, *Helenae Lucretiae*, 21; Deza, *Vita di Helena*, 46.

25. The request was presented to Angelo Montagnana, prior of the college, to Giacomo Trento, trustee, to Carlo Mussato, vice procurator, and to Gian Pietro Saviolo, auditor. A.A.U., ms. 365, ff. 24v–25r.

26. The witnesses were the Marquis Carlo Dondi Orologio and Antonio Mussato, both Paduans. A.C.P., Diversorum II, f. 103v.

27. A.A.U., ms. 365, f. 25.

28. Dalmazzo, *Lucrezia Cornaro*, 18.

29. Dalmazzo proves to be misinformed when she writes that at the request to award the doctorate to Elena Cornaro, the professors of the university divided into two opposing parties for almost a year, threatening to sink the project. Things unfolded instead quite differently as shown by the ceremony of the conferral of the degree in which the opinion of the professors was unanimous. Dalmazzo, *Lucrezia Cornaro*, 8; see also appendix, document 3.

30. Rinaldini, *Commercium epistolicum*, 85–88.

31. A.A.U., ms. 365, ff. 25r–26v; see appendix, document 3; Tonzig, "Elena Lucrezia Cornaro," 183–84. Capellari Vivaro is incorrect in giving 1680 as the date of Elena Lucrezia Cornaro's degree (Venice, Biblioteca Nazionale Marciana, Capellari Vivaro, *Arbore Cornaro* [Cornaro Tree], ms. It. VII, 15 [=8304], ff. 328v , 332v). Bacchini, having copied from Pynsent, carries as a formulary used for the proclamation of the doctorate of Elena Lucrezia Cornaro Piscopia one which does not correspond to the original, which shows that he was unaware of it (Bacchini, *Helenae Lucretiae*, 23; Pynsent, *The Life*, 68).

32. A.C.P., *Diversorum II*, ff. 103v.

33. After the first day of this visit of the cardinal, the document states: "Post haec discessit et se recepit in aedes nobilis viri domini . . . Cornelii divi Marci Venetiarum procuratoris pernoctaturus ibidem cum tota familia" (A.C.P., Visitationes, vol. LI, f. 311v). It is not known why (difficult reading on the part of a copyist or other?) the well-known name of Cornaro is missing from this document.

34. Padua, Biblioteca del Museo Civico, ms. B.P., 126-XIV. Attached to the document are two printed invitations, sent to the members of the College of Philosophers and Physicians of the University of Padua for (a) Elena's degree and (b) for her induction into the same College:

>   a) Die mercurii 22 iunii 1678.
>   Domini, vinite ad Collegium
>   die sabbati 25 currentis hora 13,
>   cum veste et pelle, pro examine
>   in philosophia more nobilium
>   ilustrissimae et excellentissimae
>   dominae Elenae Lucretiae Corneliae nobilis Venetae.
>
>   b) Die martis V iulii 1678.
>   Domini, venite ad Collegium
>   die sabbati 9 currentis hora 12
>   pro ingressu illustrissimae et excellentissimae
>   dominae Elenae Lucretiae Corneliae Piscopiae
>   nobilis Venetae.

35. See appendix, document 3.

36. *Da so posta*: that is by her alone, by herself. Contarini, *Dizionario tascabile*, 256; Boerio, *Dizionario del dialetto veneziano*, 528.

37. He refers to the work by Tomasso Garzoni (1540–1589), *L'hospitale de' pazzi incurabili*, which describes many types of madness and incurably insane

individuals.

38. The scornful term *babuazzo* is a variation of blockhead, idiot, stooge, fool, dolt. In the only phrase book of Milanese dialect babuas has more than ninety meanings, one worse than the other. "Cherubini, babuas, badee," in *Vocabolario milanese-italiano*, 1:52, 54; Tommaseo and Bellini, "babbuasso," in *Dizionario della lingua italiana*, 1, pt. 2:826; Battaglia, "babbuasso," in *Grande dizionario della lingua italiana*, 1:919; Devoto and Oli, "babbuasso," in *Vocabolario illustrato*, 1:263; Devoto, "babbuasso," in *Avviamento alla etimologia*.

39. Deza, *Vita di Helena*, 49; Lupis, *L'eroina veneta*, 38; De Santi, "Elena Lucrezia," IV, 187–188; Dalmazzo, *Lucrezia Cornaro*, 21. Among the congratulatory writings, see: Venice, Biblioteca del Civico Museo Correr, ms. Cicogna 1216, f. 104; Bronckhorst, *La Dama di Lettere*; *Applausi accademici*; Macedo, *Panegyricus dominae Helenae Corneliae*; *Distichon ad virginem Helenam Corneliam*; Rinaldini, *Commercium epistolicum*, 88 ff.

40. *Manuel de bibliographie biographique*, 189–90.

41. Vatican City, Archivio Segreto Vaticano, S.S. Venezia, 119, f. 554.

42. A.A.U., ms. 365, ff. 27r–28v.

43. Dalmazzo, *Lucrezia Cornaro*, 65.

44. Malaguzzi made repeated supplications to the duke of Modena and Reggio, to whom he was also indebted for accepting into the religious life or marrying some of his daughters (he had eight) and for fiscal exemptions. Modena, Archivio di Stato, Carteggi particolari, 624, under the title "Malaguzzi."

45. Guasco, *Storia litteraria*, 353–54; Tiraboschi, *Biblioteca modenese*, 3:129-37 passim; Tiraboschi, *Storia della letteratura italiana*, 4:558. A printed work exists by Veronica Malaguzzi Valeri, *L'innocente riconosciuta*, published in Bologna in 1660, dedicated to Laura Martinozzi (1635–1687) duchess of Modena.

46. Padua, Archivio dell'Accademia Patavina, Giornale A, 290r-v. Ottone Bronckhorst published *La dama di lettere* for the occasion.

47. *Mercure Galant*, 95–97; *Journal des Sçavans de l'an 1678*, 399–400; Neocorus and Sikius, *Bibliotheca librorum novorum*, 496; "Piscopia (Lucrecia Cornelia Helena)," 47.

48. Bacchini, Helenae Lucretiae, 160–161, 163–164.

CHAPTER 6. ELENA CORNARO PISCOPIA: SCHOLARLY WOMAN

1. Carlo Patin, antique dealer, numismatist, son of the famous physician Guido, was born in Paris on February 23, 1633. Having earned doctorates in jurisprudence and medicine, he taught medicine until, accused of slanderous libel against a princess of the court, he had to flee France. Condemned in absentia to be hanged, his goods were confiscated. After wandering through Germany and Switzerland, he sought refuge in Padua where, also for personal interests of Giovanni Battista Cornaro, he taught medicine at the university.

A member of the Accademia dei Ricovrati (1674) and then president (1678), he wrote about twenty works. He died in Padua on October 10, 1693, and was buried in the cathedral. Padua, Biblioteca del Museo Civico, ms. B.P. 124-XXIV, ff. 32, 34; Facciolati, *Fasti Gymnasii*, 354, 382, 392; Patinus, *Lyceum Patavinum*, 79–106 passim.

2. A.S.V., Riformatori dello Studio di Padova, b. 75; A.A.U., ms. 707, f. 101r; Facciolati, *Fasti Gymnasii*, 237.

3. De Santi, "Elena Lucrezia," V, 190.

4. Maddalena Hommetz, wife of Carlo Patin, was a daughter of Pietro, a physician. By some she is considered a member of the Accademia dei Ricovrati of Padua with the name "Modesta," but her name does not figure in the registry of the inductees of the academy. She wrote an ascetic-moral treatise entitled *Riflessioni morali e cristiane cavate per lo più dall'epistole di s. Paolo* (Moral and Christian reflections taken for the most part from the epistles of St. Paul), (Padua, 1680). Gabriella Carlotta, the eldest daughter, was born in Paris (not in Padua as Bandini Buti wrote) and inducted into the Accademia dei Ricovrati in 1679 with the name "la Deserta." She published a *Dissertation sur le phénix d'une médaille d'Antoine Caracalla* (Discussion of the phoenix of a medal by Antoine Caracalla), (Venice, 1683). Carla Caterina, the youngest daughter, also born in Paris, married Francesco Rosa in Padua and was inducted into the Accademia dei Ricovrati in 1683 with the name "la Rara." She published *Mitra ou la démon mariée, nouvelle hébraïque et morale* (Mitra or the married demon, Hebraic and moral news) (Demonopolis, 1688), and *Tabellae selectae ac explicatae* (Patavii, 1691). Padua, Biblioteca del Museo Civico, ms. B.P. 124–XXIV, ff, 36, 38; Patinus, *Lyceum Patavinum*, 101–102; Vedova, *Biografia degli scrittori padovani*, 2:65–66; *Nouvelle biographie*, 39:332–33; Bandini Buti, *Poetesse e scrittrici*, 2:118.

5. De Santi is incorrect when he writes that Delfino was patriarch of Venice ("Elena Lucrezia," V, 193, note 1). In fact, Cardinal Giovanni Delfino (Venice 1617–1699) was first senator, then titular bishop of Tagaste (1656) and coadjutor of the patriarch of Aquileia, Girolamo Gradenigo, whom he succeeded in 1657. The patriarch of Venice at the time was Giovanni Francesco Morosini, from 1644 until his death in 1678. Ritzler and Sefrin, *Hierarchia catholica*, 4:90, 362; Ruysschaert, "Delfino Pietro," 179-90.

6. A.S.V., Riformatori dello Studio di Padova, b. 490.

7. Ibid.

8. Ibid.

9. Ibid., b. 75.

10. Ibid., b. 490.

11. Gamba, *Storia della scuola italiana*, 302. The various statements of the Paduan Academy on the topic were gathered in the *Discorsi accademici di vari autori viventi intorno agli studi delle donne* (Academic discourses of various living authors regarding studies by women).

12. Bandiera, *Trattato degli studi delle donne*.

13. Muratori, *Lettere inedite*, 365, 487; Catoni, "Bandiera Giovanni Nicola, 687.

14. Tonzig, "Elena Lucrezia Cornaro Piscopia," 184.

15. Padua, *Archivio dell'Accademia Patavina*, Giornale A, ff. 209, 211; it is found also in Padua, Biblioteca del Museo Civico, ms. B.P. 124-XXIV, f. 29. Elena's thank-you letter to the Accademia dei Ricovrati was published by Menin, *Cenni storici della R. Accademia*, XXVIII.

16. The palace of Federico Cornaro, first home of the Accademia dei Ricovrati, already Cornara, was on Via Santa Sofia and later became Priuli Palace. Ronchi, *Guida storico-artistica di Padova*, 61, 99.

17. It lasted until March 18, 1779, when by a decree of the Venetian Senate, together with that of the Agraria, it merged with the present Accademia di Scienze, Lettere e Arti [Academy of Sciences, Letters and Arts]. Other Paduan academies, of which most were short-lived, were: *Affettuosi, Amatori, Arditi, Avveduti, Avvinti, Desiosi, Elevati* (c. 1550), *Eterei* (1564), *Giustiniani* (early seventeenth century), *Incogniti, Infiammati* (1540), *Invigoriti, Orditi, Serafici, Sitibondi, Spensierati* (first half of the seventeenth century). Padova, Biblioteca del Museo Civico, ms. B.P. 617/I; Vedovo, *Biografia degli scrittori padovani*, 1:33–34, 2:151–52; Gloria, *Lucrezia degli Obizzi*, 27–28.

18. I will cite a few significant names: *Addormentati* (Genoa), *Agiati* (Rovereto), *Alterati* (Florence), *Assorditi* (Urbino), *Buon gusto* (Palermo), *Caliginosi* (Ancona), *Erranti* (Fermo), *Freddi* (Lucca), *Insensati* (Perugia), *Nascosti* (Milan), *Offuscati* (Cesena), *Ostinati* (Viterbo), *Oziosi* (Naples), *Sfaccendati* (Roma), *Umoristi* (Rome). Valery, *Correspondence inédite de Mabillon*, 3:96 note 1.

19. "To give credence to the ancient chroniclers, in Siena the first academy probably emerged in the middle of the thirteenth century. . . . But in reality, we have mention of true academic activity only in 1415, with the cultural gatherings promoted by Enea Silvio Piccolomini." C.P.B., "Gli 'Intronati' di Siena," *L'Osservatore Romano*, December 6, 1953, 5.

20. At that time, the Accademia dei Pacifici had its seat in the home of Antonio Loredan, son of Gianfranco. Occioni Bonaffons, *Brevi cenni sulle Accademie in Venezia*, II.

21. Vatican City, Biblioteca Apostolica Vaticana, Ottob. lat. 2479 (I), f. 55. Lupis and Fontana are incorrect when they report that this debate took place in the Cornaro palace in San Luca during the solemnity of "the Sensa," since it occurred instead in the Procuratie in the Piazza S. Marco on the Sunday after the Ascension, which in that year fell on Thursday, May 27. Lupis, *L'eroina veneta*, 32; Fontana, *Cento palazzi*, 396.

22. Bacchini, *Helenae Lucretiae*, 25; Deza, *Vita di Helena*, 50–51; Dalmazzo, *Lucrezia Cornaro*, 69. Federico von Hessen-Darmstadt, territorial count of Assia, became titular cardinal of Santa Maria in Acquiro (1655), later of San Cesario (1661), of Sant'Eustachio (1667), of San Nicola in Carcere (1688), and of Sant'Agata (1670); he died outside Rome on February 19, 1682. Ritzler and Sefrin, *Hierarchia catholica*, 4:30.

23. Rinaldini, *Geometra promotus*, 59; Bacchini, *Helenae Lucretiae*, 25; Deza, *Vita di Helena*, 50; Armellini, *Bibliotheca Benedictino-Cassinensis*, 196; Valery, *Correspondance inédite de Mabillon*, 2:39, note 4; Dalmazzo, *Lucrezia Cornaro*, 78. Emmanuel Théodore de La Tour d'Auvergne de Bouillon was born August 24, 1643, in the castle of Turenne to an ancient and noble family related to almost all the reigning families of Europe. He graduated in theology (1664), skilled in Greek and Hebrew, became canon of Liège at

fifteen years of age in 1658, and cardinal in 1669. He had a determining role in the conclave of 1670 in the election of Clement X and of 1676 of Innocent XI, and in his capacity as almoner for the king was the most influential ecclesiastic in France. In 1697 he established himself in Rome as the king's chargé d'affaires and died there on March 2, 1715 (Lesort, "Bouillon Emmanuel," 43–45).

24. César d'Estrées was born in Paris on February 5, 1628, and died there on December 18, 1714. The third child of Duke François, he received a doctorate in theology at the Sorbonne and was named bishop of Laon in 1658. Having proved himself an able diplomat, he held posts for the king in Germany and Spain and was ambassador to the Holy See where he defended the interests of the French crown. Made a cardinal (1671, announced in 1672), he participated in four conclaves. He had a part in the composition of the so-called *pace clementina* (Clementine Peace) of 1669 and in the condemnations of Miguel Molinos and the Quietists. A member of the Academie Française, he was in contact with the most illustrious men of his time, exercising among them a notable influence. In 1681 he renounced the position of bishop of Laon in favor of his nephew Jean, and the king made him abbot of Saint-Germain-des-Prés where he died and was buried. Cistellini, "Estrées César," 652–53; De Morembert, "Estrées César," 1087–88.

25. "Regalìa" was the right, specific to the feudal system, of state appropriation in a jurisdictionalistic regime of the administration of vacant ecclesiastical benefices and of receiving the rents from them.

26. Padua, Biblioteca del Museo Civico, ms. B.P. 125/I, ff. 55–56.

27. Rinaldini, *Geometra promotus*, 59; Bacchini, *Helenae Lucretiae*, 26–32; Deza, *Vita di Helena*, 52–55; Lupis, *L'eroina veneta*, 49–52; Armellini, *Bibliotheca benedictino-Cassinensis*, 196; Ziegelbauer, *Historia rei literariae*, 3:522; Valery, *Correspondance inédite de Mabillon*, 2:39, note 4; Pynsent, *The Life*, 79–82; Dalmazzo, *Lucrezia Cornaro*, 79–82.

28. Padua, Archivio dell'Accademia Patavina, Giornale A, ff. 317r–318.

29. A.S.P., Notarile, vol. 4847, ff. 99–107; vol. 4823, f. 539; Moschini, *Guida per la città di Padova*, 176; Fiocco, *Alvise Cornaro*, 35, 37–38; Sambin, "I testamenti," 303.

30. Sambin, "I testamenti," 304. The façade no longer exists, and to recognize it we must cautiously consult the drawing made in 1735 by the architect Lorenzo Mazzi. We do not know, however, if this represents the old house Alvise Cornaro inherited from his uncle Angelieri or the one totally redone by his heir Giacomo Alvise after the spring of 1566 according to the plans of his deceased grandfather Alvise (A.S.P., Sant'Antonio confessore, vol. 320; Fiocco, *Alvise Cornaro*, 36; Sambin, "I testamenti," 313; Fiocco, "La Casa di Alvise Cornaro," 7.

31. In this new house, specified as the residence of Cornaro, several notarized papers were drawn up by him: "Padue in domo magnifici domini constituentis (=Aloysius Cornelio quondam magnifici Antonii habitator Paduae in contracta divi Antonii confessoris) in loco qui vocatur la casa nuova in statione inferiori" (August 23, 1558); "Paduae in domo solite habitationis in loco qui vocatur la casa nuova in quandam camera anteriori" (January 7,

1559); or even with terminologiy which is more appropriate to a notarized document: "Paduae in contrata Sancti Antonii confessoris in domo soliae habitationis infrascritte magnifice domine constituentis (=Veronica Cornelia filia quondam magnifici domini Ioannis Agugie et uxor magnifici domini Alovisii Cornelii) in domibus novis inferioribus" (May 9, 1559); "Paduae in vicinia Sancti Antonii confessoris in domo infrascritti magnifici domini constituentis (=Alvise Cornaro) in quadam camera superiori domus novae (December 4, 1559). Sambin, "I testamenti," 322.

32. A.S.P., Notarile, vol. 4847, ff. 99–107.

33. A.S.P., Notarile, vol. 4166, ff. 309–311; Sambin, "I testamenti," 315.

34. Fiocco, "La casa di Alvise Cornaro," 15. Traces of an entrance to the underground tunnel are still visible on an internal wall of the lodge as is a vault "at the little house" decorated with stucco.

35. See below, chapter 7, section 2.

36. Even this artistic building was demolished in the eighteenth century to make room for homes of little worth. There remains only the image engraved by G. Valle in 1784. Moschini, *Guida per la città di Padova*, 176; Sambin, "I testamenti," 323; Fiocco, "Alvise Cornaro," 37.

37. Rinaldini, *Commercium epistolicum*, 88.

38. Bacchini, *Helenae Lucretiae*, 143.

39. Rinaldini, *Commercium epistolicum*, 65–67. The incomplete work was *Philosophia rationalis, naturalis atque moralis*, a two-volume work, of which only the first was published in Padua in 1681.

40. Rinaldini, *De resolutione*, 157. A copy of this work preserved in the Biblioteca Antoniana in Padua (BO-IX-6) bears a handwritten inscription of ownership on the inside front page: "Ex libris magistri Felicis Rotundi de Monte Leone theologi publici Patavini munus auctoris." This is another evident sign of the friendship between Rinaldini and Father Rotondi.

41. Bacchini, *Helenae Lucretiae*, 142.

42. Ibid., 143–45. Elena was unable to keep this promise because the second volume was published much later (Padua, 1688), four years after her death.

43. Ibid., 146–47.

44. Ibid., 148–50. Because of this postal delay even the Venetian ambassador in Paris, Sebastiano Foscarini, apologized to Elena (Paris April 8, 1682).

45. Ibid., 149. The work, in fact, appeared as: Caroli Renaldini, *Philosophia rationalis, naturalis, atque moralis. Tomus primus rationalem philosophiam complectens. Pars prima. Ad magnum ac semper invictum Ludovicum XIV Francorum regem christianissimum.*

46. This is the Italian translation of Rinaldini's work, *Ars analytica mathematum in tomos III distributa*, of which two volumes had appeared (vol. 1 in Florence, 1665; vol. 2 in Padua, 1669), while the third appeared in Padua in 1684, perhaps toward the end of the year, having been granted permission for publication on April 19, 1684. Therefore, in all probability, Elena was unable to see it because she died on July 26, 1684. This volume, like the preceding two, is dedicated to Cosimo III, grand duke of Tuscany.

47. Caro, *Oratio parentalis*, 6.

48. Rinaldini, *Commercium epistolicum*, 65–67.

49. Bacchini, *Helenae Lucretiae*, 156.

50. Ibid., 43; Deza, *Vita di Helena*, 66, 84; Lupis, *L'eroina veneta*, 120; Dalmazzo, *Lucrezia Cornaro*, 143.

51. This first Spanish translation, done by a Carthusian monk, Andrea Capilla (or Capiglia), bishop of Urgel (d. 1609), was published in Lerida in 1572.

52. The first translation is by Father Serafino Torresini, published around 1550; the second is by a certain Father Girolamo, printed in Venice in 1575. Tanquerey, *Compendio di teologia ascetica e mistica*, XL; Autore, "Lansperge," 2608.

53. Bacchini, *Helenae Lucretiae*, 179–86.

54. Venice, 1669 (Giuliani); Venice, 1673 (Giuliani); Venice, 1681 (Hertz); Parma, 1688 (Rosati); Venice, 1706 (Hertz). Lorenz is incorrect in citing 1673 as the first edition; it is the second (Lorenz, *Analecta literaria*, 23).

55. Bacchini, *Helenae Lucretiae*, 51–73.

56. Ibid., 74–88; Occioni Bonaffons, *Brevi cenni sulle Accademie in Venezia*, 11.

57. ". . . quis enim virtutem amplectitur ipsam, praemia si tollas?" (Satira X, 141–142).

58. Like Elena, Santinelli belonged to the Accademia dei Ricovrati in Padua and the Accademia degli Infecondi in Rome. His lengthy ode in honor of the liberation of Vienna (1683) was printed together with a few literary compositions by Elena Lucrezia for the same occasion in *Poesie de' signori accademici Infecondi di Roma* (Venice, 1684), 88–93. Padua, Biblioteca del Museo Civico, ms. 124–XXIV, f. 34.

59. Bacchini, *Helenae Lucretiae*, 89–106.

60. Claudianus, *Eidylia*, II Histrix, 28–31; Lucanus, *Pharsalia*, VI, 210.

61. Vatican City, Biblioteca Apostolica Vaticana, Barb. lat. 4502, ff. 98r–103v. Dalmazzo is mistaken when she says that this discourse was published by Bacchini in *Helenae Lucretiae* (Lucrezia Cornaro, 161, note 40). In fact, neither in this nor in other works by Bacchini does this discourse appear.

62. De Santi, "Elena Lucrezia," IV, 680–681; Dalmazzo, *Lucrezia Cornaro*, 74–75.

63. Vatican City, Biblioteca Apostolica Vaticana, Barb. lat. 6462, ff. 169r–73, 179–80v, 182–85, 191–92.

64. Venice, Biblioteca del Civico Museo Correr, ms. Morosini-Grimani, 442-XVII.

65. Vatican City, Archivio Segreto Vaticano, Secr. Brevia, vol. 1454, f. 369; vol. 1543, f. 590.

66. Bacchini, *Helenae Lucretiae*, 151–156.

67. Ivanovich, *Minerva al tavolino* (Minerva at the table), 1:84–85, 94–95, 99, 195–96.

68. Rinaldini, *Commercium epistolicum*, 65; Bacchini, *Helenae Lucretiae*, 143–45, 157–58, 175–77; Menin, *Cenni storici*, XXVIII.

69. Bacchini, *Helenae Lucretiae*, 113–31, 139–41; *Poesie de' signori accademici Infecondi di Roma*, 31–47, 49–53.

70. Bacchini, *Helenae Lucretiae*, 109–12, 132–35. Silvestro Valier, remembered as a meritorious individual of the university even by Salomonio (*Inscriptiones Patavinae*, 114) was the doge of Venice from 1694 to his death in 1700 and was buried in the doge family mausoleum of the Valiers in the Church of Sts. Giovanni and Paolo in Venice (Lorenzetti, *Venezia e il suo estuario*, 341–42).

71. *Epantismatologia*, 8–10.

72. *Seconda corona*, lettera-prefazione, 50–64.

73. Dragoni, *Oratione di A.D. e componimenti*, 138–139.

74. *Epantismatologia*, 7.

75. They were published under the direction of the Accademia dei Ricovrati of Padua for the occasion together with the writings of other academy members, among whom were Ottavio Ferrari, Carlo Dottori, Carlo Rinaldini, Alvise Gradenigo, Carlo Patin, and Father Felice Rotondi. *Compositioni degli accademici Ricovrati*; Bacchini, *Helenae Lucretiae*, 136–37.

76. Guyonnet De Vertron, *La nouvelle Pandore*, 437. The preceding year (1678) De Vertron turned to Elena to have her interpret six monosyllables written on a serpent's egg found near Montpellier (July 1678). She deciphered them as containing a sort of prognosis for the peace concluded later that same year by Louis XIV in favor of France (ibid., 343–436). The Treaty of Nijmwegen put an end to the long and involved war between France and the Dutch Republic.

77. Bergalli, *Componimenti poetici*, 2:169; De Santi, "Elena Lucrezia," IV, 684.

78. Bergalli, *Componimenti poetici*, 169, 280–281.

79. Bacchini, *Helenae Lucretiae*, 183–186.

80. Ibid., 186.

81. Mabillon and Germain, *Iter Italicum*, 35; Lorenz, *Analecta literaria*, 22.

82. Oliva, *Lettere* (Venice, 1681), 4, 159–60; Oliva, *Lettere* (Rome, 1681), 2:9, 35–36, 69–70, 218–19, 316, 382–83, 400–401, 429–31.

83. A.R.S.J., *Epistolae nostrorum*, n. 10, f. 289v.

84. I owe this information to the courtesy of Father Edmund Lamalle, director of the central archive of the Society of Jesus in Rome, to whom I express appreciation and esteem.

85. Bacchini, *Helenae Lucretiae*, [X]. We must remember that this collection of Bacchini, though praiseworthy, is incomplete.

86. *Spicilegium Benedictinum*, 4:79–80.

87. Armellini, *Bibliotheca benedictino-Cassinensis*, 1:198.

88. Ziegelbauer, *Historia rei literariae*, 3:514–528; François, *Bibliothèque générale*, 1:218–19.

89. For the principal works that praise Elena's writings, see: Deza, *Vita di Helena*, 127–31; Lupis, *L'eroina veneta*, 54–58; Armellini, *Bibliotheca benedictino-Cassinensis*, 199; Ziegelbauer, *Historia rei literariae*, 3:527–28; De Santi, "Elena Lucrezia," 67–68. I have a list of more than three hundred works,

carefully compiled during my research.

90. Giovanni Battista Becci, born in Castiglione Fiorentino in 1613, a professed Benedictine (1629), was abbot in Foligno and in Arezzo, where he died in 1687. Gifted with wittiness, he dedicated himself to the literary genre of anagrams for which he became famous. He published *Veritas anagrammate explorata ad varia texenda encomia*, (Padua, 1668). Armellini, *Bibliotheca benedictino-Cassinensis*, 2:20–23; Valery, *Correspondance inédite de Mabillon*, 1:25, 241; François, *Bibliothèque générale*, 1:101.

91. Lorenz, *Analecta literaria*, 23–24.

92. Bacchini, *Helenae Lucretiae*, [X]; Tiraboschi, *Storia della letteratura italiana*, 8, pt. 3:648–49.

93. Cantù, *Storia di Milano*, 1:214–15; Pompeati, *Storia della letteratura italiana*, 3, pt. 3:19–20; Sapegno, *Disegno storico della letteratura italiana*, 331–63; Canepari, "Secentismo" [Sixteen -hundredism], 673–674; F. Croce, "Critica e trattatistica del barocco," 471–518; Calcaterra, "Il problema del barocco," 408–410, 418, 429, 434; Getto, "La polemica sul barocco," 469–71, 501–502.

94. B. Croce, "Appunti di letteratura secentesca," 471–72.

95. Belloni, *Il Seicento*, 24.

96. B. Croce, "Appunti di letteratura secentesca," 471–72.

97. Tiraboschi, *Storia della letteratura italiana*, 8:646–48.

98. Barbiera, *Italiane gloriose*, 257.

CHAPTER 7. ELENA LUCREZIA AND THE DEMANDS OF THE SPIRIT

1. Deza, *Vita di Helena*, 27.

2. Ibid., 41. Deza is incorrect when writing that Elena was eleven years old at the time of the vow, March 25, 1657; she would not have been eleven until June 5, more than two months later (ibid., 27).

3. Mabillon and Germain, *Iter italicum*, 36; Bacchini, *Helenae Lucretiae*, 10; Armellini, *Bibliotheca benedictino-Cassinensis*, 1:196–197; Ziegelbauer, *Historia rei literariae*, 3:517; Morery, *Grand dictionnaire historique*, 4:138–39; Lorenz, *Analecta literaria*, 22; Pychowska, "A Learned Woman," 664; Pynsent, *The Life*, 17, 34; De Santi, "Elena Lucrezia," IV, 430; Zimmerman, *Kalendarium benedictinum*, 2:498; Dalmazzo, *Lucrezia Cornaro*, 44; Simon, *La règle de s. Benoît commentée pour les oblats de son ordre*, 25. As noted previously, this list could be lengthened with the names of over three hundred authors.

4. Paolo Laymann (1574–1635), famous moralist and canonist, taught successively in the universities of Ingolstadt, Monaco, and Dilinga. His lectures were very much sought after by scholars, and his responses to inquiries sent to him from near and far were considered definitive. His work in moral theology was judged to be unequaled. Sommervogel, *Bibliothèque de la Compagnie de Jésus*, 4:1582–94.

5. *Codex iuris canonici*, canons 89, 1312.

6. Laymann, *Theologia moralis*, 561–62, 573–78 passim.

7. Bacchini, *Helenae Lucretiae*, 15–16; Deza, *Vita di Helena*, 41–42; Lupis, *L'eroina veneta*, 24–26; Pynsent, *The Life*, 33-34; De Santi, "Elena Lucrezia," V, 434–435; Dalmazzo, *Lucrezia Cornaro*, 87–89. Notwithstanding the research I completed from May 17 to June 20, 1973 in the Secret Vatican Archive (Penitenzieria apostolica, Segreteria dei Brevi e Segretaria di Stato di Venezia), I did not find a papal dispensation relative to the supposed vow of Elena Lucrezia Cornaro Piscopia. I proposed the question to expert canonists of the appropriate Vatican departments, and they responded that there was no reason to grant such a dispensation.

8. Bacchini, *Helenae Lucretiae*, 14; Deza, *Vita di Helena*, 40; Dalmazzo, *Lucrezia Cornaro*, 93.

9. De Santi, "Elena Lucrezia," IV, 437; Gaeta, *S. Lorenzo*, X–XI.

10. Lorenzetti, *Venezia e il suo estuario*, 364.

11. Regarding this, there are four letters from Cecilia Cornaro to the duchess of Modena requesting her mediation in obtaining the Jesuit priest Giuseppe Perini as a preacher for the church of S. Lorenzo, which had been denied her by the Superior General of the Society of Jesus (Modena, Archivio di Stato, Cancelleria ducale, Lettere e documenti di particolari, C. 373/25). De Santi is imprecise when he mentions only two of these letters, saying that they were addressed to the duke instead of the duchess of Modena (De Santi, "Elena Lucrezia," IV, 437, note 2).

12. Bacchini, *Helenae Lucretiae*, 13–14; Ziegelbauer, *Historia rei literariae*, 3:518.

13. E. Musatti, *La donna in Venezia*, 168.

14. Hoefer, *Nouvelle biographie générale*, 11:842.

15. Bacchini, *Helenae Lucretiae*, 155.

16. Cornelio Codanini, a Venetian, was an alumnus of the S. Giorgio Maggiore Monastery since 1622, an abbot of the same monastery, and later at the S. Giustina Monastery of Padua (1673), the monastery in Praglia (1675), and finally at S. Faustino Monastery in Brescia where he died in 1680. A scholarly prelate who led an exemplary life, he wrote the ascetic work *Breve e metodica istruzione per l'orazione mentale di D. Celidaro Nonciano (anagramma di Cornelio Codanini) dedicato a' novizi casinensi: con nel fine di questa 2a impressione una aggiunta di alquante considerazioni giaculatorie sopra la passione di nostro Signore distribuite per i giorni della settimana e dedicate alle novizie della stessa congregazione* (A brief and methodical instruction for the mental prayer of D. Celidaro Nonciano (an anagram of Cornelio Codanini) dedicated to the novices at Monte Cassino: with at the end of this 2nd impression the addition of several aspirations on the passion of our Lord distributed for the days of the week and dedicated to the novices of the same congregation) (Padua, 1674). A.S.P., Corporazioni Soppresse, S. Giustina, b. 77, fasc. 1, f. 11; Padua, Biblioteca Universitaria, ms. 1412, ff. 14–15 (19 old file); Padua, Biblioteca del Monumento Nazionale di S. Giustina, ms. b. 36, n. 8, f. 43r-v; Armellini, *Bibliotheca benedictino-Cassinensis*, 139–40. Codanini was never abbot of S. Nazario in Verona and did not die there in 1685, as François erroneously writes (*Bibliothèque générale*, 1:209).

17. Bacchini, *Helenae Lucretiae*, 16; Deza, *Vita di Helena*, 42; Pynsent, *The Life*,

34–35; De Santi, "Elena Lucrezia," V, 434; Dalmazzo, *Lucrezia Cornaro*, 90.

18. The *conversi*, who even before St. Benedict constituted a particular type of devotee, living in the world and united around the patriarch, are considered by some authors as a seed of the future oblates, having developed gradually alongside the rule and the Benedictine order. Leccisotti, "Gli oblati benedictini in Italia," 157.

19. Du Cange, "Oblati monasteriorum," in *Glossarium*, 4:1282–1288; Salvi, "Gli oblati benedittini in Italia," 90; Mannocci, "Gli oblati benedittini dell'abbazia di S. Giovanni Evangelista in Parma," 61.

20. Salvi, "Gli oblati benedettini," 91. To these oblates one can add the "religious" oblates of today, priests and lay persons, welcomed in some monasteries after a simple promise to live according to the rule of St. Benedict.

21. Salvi, "Gli oblati benedettini," 93; Mannocci, "Gli oblati benedettini," 62. The "secular" oblates of today, who have nothing in common with the earlier ones, follow the statutes approved in 1904 and are likened by jurisdiction to the third order of other religious orders (*Codex iuris canonici*, can. 702 ss).

22. St. Thomas Becket (1117–1170), archbishop of Canterbury, continuously wore under his outer clothing a reduced form of the habit; Guglielmo Lungaspada (d. 943), duke of Normandy, had a habit and a tunic which he wore on special occasions; Gérard d'Aurillac (ninth century), a layman and great gentleman, led a religious life in the world, with a monk's habit under his other clothes and his tonsure hidden under his thick head of hair. Simon, *La règle de s. Benoît*, XXI–XXIII.

23. See the examples in Mannocci, "Gli oblati benedettini," 51, 54, 57, 61–62.

24. Simon, *La règle de s. Benoît*, XXIII–XXIV.

25. In the seventeenth century there were people who lived as oblates without abandoning either their own social condition or the clothes which fit their state, but were satisfied to wear under their ordinary clothes some symbol of the Benedictine order (Simon, *La règle de s. Benoît*, XXIV). For more information on Benedictine oblates, see Chauvin, *L'oblature de l'ordre de saint Benoît*; Deroux, *Les origines de l'oblature bénédictine*; Penco, *Storia del monachesimo in Italia*.

26. Delatte, *Commentaire sur la règle de saint Benoît*, 469, note 1.

27. Bacchini, *Helenae Lucretiae*, 16; Deza, *Vita di Helena*, 42; Lupis, *L'eroina veneta*, 26; Pynsent, *The Life*, 34–35; Valery, *Correspondance inédite de Mabillon*, 2:36; Dalmazzo, *Lucrezia Cornaro*, 90.

28. François, *Bibliothèque générale*, 218–19.

29. He writes: "testimonium authenticum, quo in numerum oblatarum a patribus nostris suscepta est anno 1665." Mabillon and Germain, *Iter Italicum*, 35–36. Federici commits a double error when, in attributing to himself the information of the chronicler of the monastery of S. Giustina, he writes that Codanini in 1673, while abbot of S. Giustina, gave the Benedictine habit to Elena, who supposedly professed the solemn vow of chastity in that very abbey (Federici, *Della biblioteca di S. Giustina*, 71). The chronicler from whom Federici drew the information is Giovanni Battista Della Torre, prior of the monastery of S. Giustina of Padua, who wrote (c.

1740) *Matricula sive series chronologica monachorum omnium congregationis Cassinensis.* The erroneous information given by Federici is found in f. 43v.

30. Comneno Papadopoli, *Historia Gymnasii Patavini*, 2:316–317.

31. Bacchini, *Helenae Lucretiae*, 26; Pynsent, *The Life*, 34–35. Dalmazzo accepts a double act of profession: a private one at home at the hand of Abbot Codanini, the other performed later in the Church of S. Giorgio Maggiore before this same abbot (Dalmazzo, *Lucrezia Cornaro*, 90).

32. De Santi, "Attività letteraria nel monastero Sancti Benedicti de Urbe," 705.

33. Bacchini, *Helenae Lucretae*, 16–17; De Santi, "Attività letteraria," 705.

34. Scardova, *Vita compendiosa di Elena*, 28; Simon, *La règle de s. Benoît*, XXV. Here Simon confuses the Benedictine Abbey of S. Giorgio Maggiore (Venice) with a nonexistent abbey of San Giacomo.

35. Dalmazzo, *Lucrezia Cornaro*, 131.

36. Remember the abbot scholar Giuliano Girardelli who, during his leadership of the abbey (1607–1611), to spur the monks on in the study of philosophy, often invited Cesare Cremonini, a professor from the University of Padua, to visit the monastery and to continue, notwithstanding his shaky theories, the teaching of professor Francesco Piccolomini. Cavacius, *Historiarum*, 304.

37. Among those of the S. Giustina Abbey I mention Leonello Crocecalle, Pierantonio Pezzoli, Marino Bellini, Vittorio Batti, Francesco Maria Dotto, Antonio Barisoni, all doctors of theology; Cesare Bonfio, instructor of philosophy; and Modesto Albanese, librarian, writer, and artist. Padua, Biblioteca Universitaria, ms. 1412, ff. 84v, 86v, 88v, 89r-v; François, *Bibliothèque générale*, 1:228; Federici, *Della biblioteca di S. Giustina*, 72–74.

38. Those from other monasteries included Girolamo Bendandi (Ravenna), later abbot of S. Giustina; Leone Matina (Cava dei Tirreni); Giangirolamo Testoris (Savigliano). François, *Bibliothèque générale*, 1:107–108, 2:223, 3:121–22; Federici, *Della biblioteca di S. Giustina*, 70-72.

39. Gloria, *Lucrezia degli Obizzi*, 29; Borgherini Scarabellin, *La vita privata a Padova*, 190.

40. Deza, *Vita di Helena*, 94–95.

41. Quietism is the mystical-religious concept which attempts to achieve perfection primarily with human effort and exonerates the perfect from making use of the sacraments and from obedience to divine and human laws. Rahner and Vorgrimler, "Quietismo," 556. See also: Pourrat, "Quiétisme," 1537–81; Petrocchi, *Il quietismo italiano nel Seicento*; Taverneaux, "Il cattolicesimo post-tridentino," 331–33, 335–36.

42. Scardova, *Vita compendiosa di Elena*, 28; Bacchini, *Helenae Lucretiae*, 45; Simon, *La régle de s. Benoît*, XXV.

43. Berlière, *L'ascèse bénédictine des origines à la fin du XIIe siècle*, 159–160; Delatte, *Commentaire sur la règle*, 152–53, 155–56. The appropriate books for this type of prayer were abundant in Elena's library, such as: the *Breviario* (the Breviary), in various editions, the *Diurnale* (Diurnal), the *Sacerdotale* (Priests' prayerbook), the *Razionale* (Rational) of the divine office, the *Martirologio* (Martyrology), the *Messale* (Missal), comments on the *Ordinario* (Ordinary), the *Canone* (Canon) and the ceremonies of the Mass, treated under the rites of

the church, etc.

44. Besse, *Le moine bénédictin*, 168–70; Berlière, *L'ascèse bénédictine*, 170; Delatte, *Commentaire sur la règle*, 348–49; Gautier, *La spiritualità cattolica*, 45. For *lectio divina* Elena had at her disposal in her library a vast collection of biblical texts with and without commentary, meditations and biblical paraphrases, the complete works of all the major Latin and Greek Fathers of the Church, various subsidiary treatises regarding the Bible, the Fathers, theology, the liturgy, etc.

45. Besse, *Le moine bénédictin*, 172–73; Berlière, *L'ascèse bénédictine*, 236–45; Schmitz, *Histoire de l'ordre de saint Benoît*, 6:188–92.

46. Besse, *Le moine bénédictin*, 111–12; Berlière, *L'ascèse bénédictine*, 247–48; Schmitz, *Histoire de l'ordre de saint Benoît*, 6:192–93.

47. Besse, *Le moine bénédictin*, 108; Berlière, *L'ascèse bénédictine*, 246–47; Schmitz, *Histoire de l'ordre de saint Benoît*, 6:1. II, c. 2 passim.

48. Barbus, *Modus meditandi et orandi*. Barbo (1381 or 1382–1443), a monastic reformer and noted ascetic writer, was abbot of S. Giustina in Padua (1408–1437), then bishop of Treviso (1437–1443). During his episcopate at Treviso he wrote this work, which although it was addressed to the monks of the congregation of S. Giustina, exercised great influence elsewhere. Some scholars debate the influence of the devotio moderna on the spirituality of Ludovico Barbo. Tassi, *Ludovico Barbo*, 95–139; Picasso, "La preghiera nel movimento spirituale di S. Giustina," 733–69; Guarnieri, *Il movimento del Libero spirito*, 351-708; Picasso, "L'imitazione di Cristo nell'epoca della devotio moderna," 11–31; Pesce, *Ludovico Barbo vescovo di Treviso*, 1:252–77.

49. Blosio wrote *Speculum monachorum* (Louvain, 1538), *Paradisus animae fedelis* (Louvain, 1540), *Psychagogia ex ss. Patribus collecta* (Louvain, 1549), *Collyrium haereticorum* (Louvain, 1549), *Institutio spiritualis* (Louvain, 1553), *Consolatio pusillanimum* (Louvain, 1555), *Margaritum spirituale* (Louvain, 1555), *Conclave animae fidelis* (Louvain, 1558).

50. Caro, *Oratio parentalis*, 5.

51. Rinaldini, *Commercium epistolicum*, 86.

52. Simon, *La règle de s. Benoît*, XXXV. In the eighteenth century, oblates followed the destiny of the Benedictine order and agonized with it. It was revived in the nineteenth century by the work of Fr. Prosper Guéranger, first abbot of Solesmes (France); Leo XIII established the privileges of the oblates (1898); Pius X approved their statutes (1904) according to the Code of Canon Law; the Congregation for Religious and Secular Institutes permitted (1975) the oblates' use of the statutes elaborated for the necessary adaptation to the spirit of Vatican Council II.

53. Their rules were compiled by Fr. Virgilio Cepari (1564–1631), a Jesuit and hagiographer who published among other things: *Vita di S. Luigi Gonzaga, primogenito di d. Ferrante Gonzaga, prencipe dell'imperio, marchese di Castiglione* (The life of St. Aloysius Gonzaga, firstborn of Sir Ferrante Gonzaga, imperial prince, marquis of Castiglione) (Rome, 1606); *Regole comuni delle Vergini di Gesù nel collegio di Castiglione* (Common rules of the Virgins of Jesus in the College of Castiglione) (Bologna, 1622).

54. A.S.P., Corporazioni Soppresse, s. Giustina, 384, f. 131 (ducale November 9,

1605); f. 137 (ducale May 24, 1619); f. 99 (ducale September 1, 1601); f. 146 (ducale December 11, 1627).

55. Scardova, *Vita compendiosa*, 12; Deza, *Vita di Helena*, 43; Lupis, *L'eroina veneta*, 28–29; Pynsent, *The Life*, 42–43; Dalmazzo, *Lucrezia Cornaro*, 94–96, 97–98.

56. Boldrin, *Maria Alberghetti*, 28.

57. Bernareggi, "Dimesse," 526; Boldrin, *Maria Alberghetti*, 28–32.

58. Scardova, *Vita compendiosa*, 29; Deza, *Vita di Helena*, 76–77; Lupis, *L'eroina veneta*, 70–71; Pynsent, *The Life*, 99; Dalmazzo, *Lucrezia Cornaro*, 134. Pynsent and Dalmazzo err when they give to the Monastery of the Hermits the title of S. Giovanni Battista (St. John the Baptist). In fact, at its foundation in 1612, by Graziosa Cecchini, in the section of the city known as *Pozzo della vacca* (The Well of the Cow), it was immediately given the name of S. Bonaventura (St. Bonaventure) and professed the rule of S. Chiara (St. Clare), the Franciscan rule (Portenari, *Della felicità di Padova*, 485). From 1400 to 1700 it was the first part of the present day Via Ospedale Civile up to Via S. Francesco, which was called Pozzo della Vacca.

59. I draw this information from three octaves (62–64) of a manuscript work (101 octaves) entitled, *Operette in ottava rima nella quale s'intende la traslazione fatta delle reverende madri eremite della città di Padova l'anno 1682 dal luogo di Ponte Corbo al luogo di Vanzo. Composta per consolazione e ricreazione di tutte quelle religiose che sono e succederanno in detta religione* (Small works in octave rhyme being the translation by the hermit reverend mother of the city of Padua in the year 1682 from Corbo Bridge Place to Vanzo Place. Composed for the consolation and recreation of all those religious sisters who are in and will succeed to said religion), Padova, Biblioteca del Museo Civico, B.P. 680/X.

60. *Memorie di alcune religiose francescane illustri per santità vissute nel monastero delle vergini eremite di S. Bonaventura di Padova in Vanzo* (Memoirs of some of the famous Franciscan religious sisters on saintliness lived in the Monastery of the Hermit Virgins of St. Bonaventure in Padua at Vanzo), 180–82.

61. Bacchini, *Helenae Lucretiae*, 5; Deza, *Vita di Helena*, 10, 18; Lupis, *L'eroina veneta*, 10.

62. Oliva, *Lettere*, Venetian edition, letter 7 (this letter was probably written at Christmas time 1665, the year Elena became an oblate); De Santi, "Elena Lucrezia," V, 438.

63. Oliva, *Lettere*, Roman edition, 2:316, letter 866.

64. The "privileged altar" is one that enjoys a general pardon and plenary indulgence to be applied to the deceased for whom the Mass is being celebrated. This privilege is granted only to the fixed altar and can be perpetual or temporary, daily or not (*Codex iuris canonici*, can. 918).

65. Oliva, *Lettere*, Roman edition, 2:69–70, 218–219, letters 641 and 777.

66. Bacchini, *Helenae Lucretiae*, 47; Deza, *Vita di Helena*, 45; Lupis, *L'eroina veneta*, 66. De Santi, "Elena Lucrezia," V, 443; Dalmazzo, *Lucrezia Cornaro*, 143.

CHAPTER 8. THE END OF A LIFE

1. Rinaldini, *Commercium epistolicum*, 81; De Santi, "Elena Lucrezia," V, 184.

2. Rinaldini, *Commercium epistolicum*, 82.

3. Ibid.

4. Ibid., 84.

5. Ibid. At that chapter, in which Rotondi also participated, dissensions had arisen among the electors regarding the choice of the new minister general. To calm them, Pope Innocent XI had presented seven candidates, and the delegates elected Antonio Aversani from Aversa, who was the seventy-fifth successor of St. Francis (Benoffi, *Compendio di storia minoritica*, 299).

6. Deza, *Vita di Helena*, 65.

7. Bacchini, *Helena Lucretiae*, 33.

8. A.S.V., Riformatori dello Studio di Padova, b. 490.

9. Bacchini, *Helena Lucretiae*, 33; Deza, *Vita di Helena*, 71; Dalmazzo, *Lucrezia Cornaro*, 126.

10. Bacchini, *Helena Lucretiae*, 33; Deza, *Vita di Helena*, 66–67; Dalmazzo, *Lucrezia Cornaro*, 125–26.

11. Bacchini, *Helenae Lucretiae*, 34; Deza, *Vita di Helena*, 72–73; Dalmazzo, *Lucrezia Cornaro*, 129–30.

12. Bacchini, *Helenae Lucretiae,* 152.

13. Lupis, *L'eroina veneta*, 115–16; Scardova, *Vita compendiosa*, 43; Dalmazzo, *Lucrezia Cornaro*, 144.

14. Domenico Marchetti, anatomist and physiologist, son of the physician Pietro, was born in Padua in 1626 and died there in 1688. In 1662 he was a professor at the University of Padua. He was the first to demonstrate with intravenous injections the connection between the most subtle arterial and venous ramifications. In 1686, he was the first to execute in Venice a nephrotomy for kidney stones. He wrote *Anatomia* (Padua, 1652). He was buried with his father in the Basilica of the Saint. Facciolati, *Fasti Gymnasii*, 354, 393, 396; Wernich, "Marchetti Domenico," 128.

    Giorgio Calafatti, son of Stefano, was born in 1652, in Canea on the island of Crete to a rich family descended from the imperial Byzantine family. He became professor of theoretical and practical medicine in 1679 at the University of Padua and a member of the Accademia dei Ricovrati in Padua in 1692. He wrote *Trattato sopra la peste* (Venice, 1682, in 40). He died in Padua on February 9, 1720, and was buried in the Basilica of the Saint along with his wife Alba Caterina Muazzo, a noble woman of Venice, who died on May 28, 1716. A.C.P., *Parrocchia S. Giorgio*, Liber mortuorum 1614–1746, by date; A.S.P., Ufficio di sanità, 490, by name; Padua, Biblioteca del Museo Civico, ms. B.P. 124-XXIV, f. 45; Facciolati, *Fasti Gymnasii*, 373; Wernich, "Calafatti Giorgio," 643.

15. Bacchini, *Helenae Lucretiae*, 32; Deza, *Vita di Helena*, 75; Lupis, *L'eroina veneta*, 115; De Santi, "Elena Lucrezia," V, 441; Dalmazzo, *Lucrezia Cornaro*, 126.

16. The child was baptized by Fr. Giovanni Antonio Pisani, pastor of S. Lorenzo; Giovanni Cigala, a professor at the University of Padua, was the godfather. A.C.P., *Parrocchia S. Lorenzo*, Battesimi (luglio 1683–dicembre 1696), f. 14v.

17. Oliva, *Lettere*, Roman edition, 2:9, letter 575; 2:35–36, letter 605. Oliva alludes to Elena's 1669 translation of Lanspergio's *Colloquio di Cristo nostro Redentore all'anima devota*.

18. Deza, *Vita di Helena*, 80-81.

19. Caro, *Oratio parentalis*, 11.

20. Deza, *Vita di Helena*, 80; Dalmazzo, *Lucrezia Cornaro*, 135.

21. Deza, *Vita di Helena*, 82; Lupis, *L'eroina veneta*, 118; Dalmazzo, *Lucrezia Cornaro*, 146.

22. Dalmazzo, *Lucrezia Cornaro*, 137.

23. Deza, *Vita di Helena*, 81; Lupis, *L'eroina veneta*, 116–17; Dalmazzo, *Lucrezia Cornaro*, 145–46. The Blessed Elena was Elena Enselmini (1207–1231), of the noble Enselmini family. Czestochowa (Jasna Gòra = clear mountain) is Poland's principal holy place, where the image of the *Vergine nera* (Black Madonna) is venerated; the devotion is also linked to the so-called *diluvio* (flood) of Swedish Protestant forces in 1655 from which the Madonna saved Poland.

24. Deza, *Vita di Helena*, 82–83; Lupis, *L'eroina veneta*, 119–20; Dalmazzo, *Lucrezia Cornaro*, 146–47.

25. De Santi, "Elena Lucrezia," V, 440; Dalmazzo, Lucrezia Cornaro, 136.

26. Lupis, *L'eroina veneta*, 117; Scardova, *Vita compendiosa*, 48.

27. Parma, Archivio di Stato, Fondo S. Giovanni, b. 201, May 31, 1687; Bacchini, *Helenae Lucretiae*, 47–48; Deza, *Vita di Helena*, 66; Dalmazzo, *Lucrezia Cornaro*, 143.

28. Caro, *Oratio parentalis*, 11; Bacchini, *Helenae Lucretiae*, 34; Deza, *Vita di Helena*, 83; Lupis, *L'eroina veneta*, 120; Scardova, *Vita compendiosa*, 49; De Santi, "Elena Lucrezia," V, 442.

29. Venice, Biblioteca Nazionale Marciana, ms. It. VII, 15 (=8304), ff. 328v–32v.

30. Venice, Biblioteca Nazionale Marciana, Arbori, III, ms. April 29–July 6 1743, ff. 17–27.

31. Nestler, *Analecta literaria*, 19.

32. Pynsent, *The Life*, 110; Dalmazzo, *Lucrezia Cornaro*, 147. Both these writers erroneously give 1685 as the date of Codanini's death.

33. A.S.P., Ufficio di sanità, 483, by date and name. A cachectic state is the result of serious or chronic illness over a prolonged period; it is characterized by progressive weight loss and deterioration of strength, a state observable in tuberculosis and cancer patients (Casalini, "Cachessia," 225).

34. A.C.P., Parrocchia S. Lorenzo, Morti, n. 31, f. 114v–115r; Treviso, Biblioteca Comunale, ms. 1000/21.

35. A.A.U., ms. 366, f. 113v.

36. Ibid.

37. Ibid., f. 113v–15.

38. Deza, *Vita di Helena*, 86–87; Lupis, *L'eroina veneta*, 124; Valery, *Correspondance inedite*, 37; Dalmazzo, *Lucrezia Cornaro*, 150.

39. "Et semper usque ad ecclesiam divae Iustinae astiterunt apud feretrum per viam." A.A.U., ms. 366, f. 115).

40. Bacchini, *Helenae Lucretiae*, 35; Deza, *Vita di Helena*, 85; Lupis, *L'eroina veneta*, 122; Dalmazzo, *Lucrezia Cornaro*, 149.

41. Giuseppe Maria Barbieri from Vicenza, who had been abbot for little more than a month, had professed at S. Giustina (1657) and was elected abbot of that monastery for the first time in 1684 and a second time in 1708. A prudent and zealous prelate, he was an arbitrator in the dispute between the bishop and the canons of Padua (1687), abbot primate in Rome, then abbot of S. Nicolò of the Lido in Venice, then titular abbot of Zara. He died in the Abbey of S. Giustina on August 12, 1715. Padua, Biblioteca Universitaria, ms. 1412, ff. 84v–85.

42. Bacchini, *Helenae Lucretiae*, 35; Deza, *Vita di Helena*, 86; Lupis, *L'eroina veneta*, 122–123; Valery, *Correspondance inédite de Mabillon*, 37; Pynsent, The Life, 107–108; De Santi, "Elena Lucrezia," V, 442; Dalmazzo, *Lucrezia Cornaro*, 149.

43. Deza, *Vita di Helena*, 86; Dalmazzo, *Lucrezia Cornaro*, 121, 149; Borgherini Scarabellin, *La vita privata a Padova*, 120.

44. Francesco Caro had been a member of the Accademia dei Ricovrati in Padua since January 23, 1681 (Padua, Biblioteca del Museo Civico, ms. B.P. 124-XXIV, f. 37). Campolongo, a Paduan, born in 1657, on March 31, 1683, became professor of philosophy in the University of Padua (A.A.U., ms. 664, f. 357r; ms. 669, f. 313r). Papadopoli defines him as "vir doctus et rei medicae quam privatim et publice ingerebat studiosae iuventuti, inter paucos sciens" (Commeno Papadopoli, *Historia Gymnasii Patavini*, 2:186). He died on April 23, 1716, in Padua, in the Parish of S. Tommaso, after being ill five days (A.S.P., Ufficio di sanità, 490, by name and by date).

45. Caro, *Oratio parentalis*, 4. The full Latin title is *Oratio parentalis ad cenotaphium illustrissimae ac excelentissimae dominae dominae Helenae Lucretiae Corneliae Piscopia, patritiae Venetae, philosophia laureatae, a patre domino Francisco Caro clericorum regularium congregationis e Somascha elucubrata; Issu sacri Collegii dominorum philosophorum atque medicorum ab illustrissimo domino Campolongo Campilongio coram eodem habita in templo Sanctae Iustinae patrum Cassinensium* (Patavii anno 1684 die iulii 28, typis Petri Mariae Frambotti).

The Italian translation was printed in 1684 with the date of the funeral (July 28) and with the title: *Orazion funebre al catafalco dell'illustrissima et eccellentissima signora Elena Lucrezia Cornara Piscopia patrizia veneta e filosofa laureata, composta da don Francesco Caro chierico regolare della congregazione di Somasca, detta per ordine del sacro Collegio de' filosofi e medici dall'illustrissimo signor Campolongo nel tempio di S. Giustina de padri cassinesi, in Padoa l'anno 1684, li 28 di luglio, stampato con l'assenso di superiori da Pietro Maria Frambotto* (Funeral oration at the catafalque of the illustrious and most excellent Lady Elena Lucrezia Cornaro Piscopia, Venetian patrician and graduate in philosophy, composed by Father Francesco Caro, religious clergyman of the Somaschan Congregation, given by order of the Sacred College of

Philosophers and Physicians by the illustrious Sir Campolongo in the temple of S. Giustina of the Cassanese Benedictines, at Padua on July 28, in the year 1684, printed with the consent of the superiors by Pietro Maria Frambotto).

46. He observes that at 11:00 p.m. the twenty candles weighing eight pounds each still burned around the catafalque. A.C.P., Parrocchia S. Lorenzo, Morti, n. 31, f. 115; Treviso, Biblioteca Comunale, ms. 1000/21.

47. Deza, *Vita di Helena*, 87; Lupis, *L'eroina veneta*, 118; Valery, *Correspondance inédite de Mabillon*, 37.

48. Deza, *Vita di Helena*, 82; Lupis, *L'eroina veneta*, 118; Barbiera, *Italiane gloriose*, 256; Dalmazzo, *Lucrezia Cornaro*, 146. This tomb, like those of the monks, had a bottom of pressed clay and was a single grave, while in each of the others several bodies were placed.

49. The chapel is rectangular (8.65 meters x 8 meters) with a pentagonal apse of acute arched lunettes in the second and fourth of which single openings are found, one of which was later walled up. The vault of the span is crossed and that of the apse is in cordoned plumes. The walls, before the pavement was raised (3 m), measured 13 m to the top. Ronchi, *Guida storico-artistica di Padova*, 172–73; Moschetti, "Gli affreschi di Giovanni Storlato in Santa Giustina," 411–19; Pepi, L'abbazia di Santa Giustina, 111.

50. Deza, *Vita di Helena*, 88; Lupis, *L'eroina veneta*, 127; Scardova, *Vita compendiosa*, 60; Valery, *Correspondance inédite*, 37–38; Pynsent, *The Life*, 109. This tombstone (115 cm x 70 cm), made of black friable marble, was in pieces and with few traces of the inscription at the time of the verification of the body (September 1895); it was set into the west wall of the chapel and a substitute was installed, also of black marble and engraved with the same writing as the first. This slab, also broken in several places, was put on the southern wall of the chapel during the restoration (at the beginning of 1977) and was replaced with another in black Belgian marble, bearing the same inscription.

51. Bacchine, *Helenae Lucretiae*, 35–36. Giangirolamo Testoris was born in 1639 in Nice in Provence. Educated at the Savoy Court, he professed as a Benedictine in 1656 in Savigliano and became a professor at the University of Padua in 1678; he taught there until his death, refusing various appointments as bishop offered to him by the pope. He was a member of the Accademia dei Ricovrati (June 30, 1678) and a consultant to the tribunal of the inquisition of Padua (1705). He died on September 11, 1710, in the locality of Bissuola near Mestre (Venice). A.S.P., Corporazioni Sopresse, Santa Giustina, n. 446; Padua, Biblioteca del Museo Civico, ms. B.P. 124-XXIV, f. 34; Facciolati, *Fasti Gymnasii*, 270; François, *Bibliothèque générale*, 3:121–122; Federici, *Della biblioteca di S. Giustina*, 71–72.

52. Borgherini Scarabellin, *La vita privata a Padova*, 104; Venice, Biblioteca Nazionale Marciana, ms. It. VII, 15 (=8304), f. 328v ; Spreti, "Cornaro Piscopia Elena," 541; Zimmerman, *Kalendarium benedictinum*, 499.

53. The same custom applied to the funeral of Princess Brigida Pico della Mirandola. She died in Padua in the Parish of San Lorenzo, but her funeral took place in the Basilica of the Saint. Fr. Battista Gallo, pastor of San Lorenzo at the time, registers the name of the deceased and notes, "and I brought back half of the funeral." A.C.P., Parrocchia S. Lorenzo, Liber

defunctorum, B (at the back) 32, f. 154v.

54. Cechin ruspio, also called *cechin de paèla* (pan) is the newly coined gold (ruspio = ruff) and therefore the right weight. Boerio, *Dizionario del dialetto veneziano*, 588.

55. A.C.P., Parrocchia S. Lorenzo, Morti, n. 31, ff. 115r-v–116; Treviso, Biblioteca Comunale, ms. 1000/21. Father Giuseppe Pisani, who was for forty years pastor of S. Lorenzo in Padua, was a lawyer of the ecclesiastic tribunal and for some time served as diocesan chancellor. He died at about age 74, on April 9, 1710, and was buried in the church of S. Lorenzo. A.C.P., *Parrocchia S. Lorenzo*, Liber defunctorum, B (on the back) 32, f. 116.

56. Borghi, in a petition to the pope, March 17, 1685, qualifies himself as "Andrea Borghi, priest, more than seventy years old, forty of which were consumed in the service of the Holy See in the position he still exercises as secretary of the nunzio's office in Venice" (Vatican City, Archivio Segreto Vaticano, Nunziatura di Venezia, vol. 128, f. 118). Giacobelli is incorrect in affirming that Elena died at the age of forty instead of thirty-eight (ibid., vol. 127, f. 533v).

57. Padua, Archivio dell'Accademia Patavina, Giornale A, 343. Count Alessandro de' Lazzara, a canon of the cathedral of Padua, died on December 3, 1705, and was buried in the cathedral in back of the Chapel of S. Daniele (A.C.P., *Parrocchia S. Lorenzo*, Liber defunctorum, B 32, f. 90).

58. Padua, Archivio dell'Accademia Patavina, *Giornale* A, 342.

59. Ibid., 343. It bears the title *Compositioni degli accademici Ricovrati per la morte della nobile donna signora Elena Lucretia Cornaro Piscopia dedicata all'Eccellenza del signor Gianbattista suo padre procuratore di S. Marco dal conte Alessandro abate de Lazzara principe dell'Accademia* (Compositions of the Ricovrati Academy Members on the death of the noble woman, Lady Elena Lucrezia Cornaro Piscopia dedicated to his excellency Sir Gianbattista, her father, procurator of St. Mark's by Count Alessandro, abbot of Lazzara, prince of the Academy) (Padua, Frambotto, 1684).

60. Guyonnet De Vertron, *La nouvelle Pandore*, 398–400, 401. We must wonder that de Vertron, a member of the Paduan Accademia dei Ricovrati, commits the error of calling it the Venice academy.

61. Tommaso Cardano, a painter and engraver from Rome in the middle of the seventeenth century, painted and then engraved five tablets for *l'Apparato nel mortorio della dottoressa Helena Lucretia Cornelia Cornara Piscopia*. Corna, "Cardano Tommaso," 194; Thieme-Becker, "Cardano Tommaso," in *Kunstler Lexicon*, 5:583; Pelliccioni, "Cardano Tommaso," in *Dizionario degli artisti incisori italiani dalle origini al XIX secolo*, 53; Benezit, "Cardano Tommaso," 310.

62. Pietro Vito Ottoboni, later Pope Alexander VII. Born in Venice in 1610, son of Marco, he graduated in Padua in both laws (canon and civil), became cardinal in 1652, bishop of Brescia in 1654, and was elected pope on October 6, 1689. He died in Rome on February 1, 1691, and was buried in the Basilica of St. Peter. Dalla Torre, "Alessandro VIII," 803–805.

Febei was born in Urbania (Pesaro) in 1623. Doctor in both laws, auditor over the nunciature in Spain, and bishop of Acquapendente (Viterbo) (1683);

he died in 1688. Ritzler and Serfrin, "Febei Aquaependen(tis)," in *Hierarchia catholica*, 5:92, note 5.

63. Giuseppe Berneri, born in Rome in 1634 and died there in 1701, was a playwright and poet, a director and actor in language and in dialect. He was noted above all as author of the poem *Meo Patacca* (1695), in which he allows the audience to relive the memorable plebeian events of Rome in the seventeenth century. "Berneri Giuseppe," in *Dizionario biografico degli autori*, 1:247.

64. Rome, Archivio di Stato, Archivio Cartari Febei, ms. 92, ff. 184–186. The full title is *Le pompe funebri celebrate da' signori accademici Infecondi di Roma per la morte dell'illustrissima signora Elena Lucrezia Cornaro Piscopia* (The funeral ceremonies celebrated by the academic gentlemen of the Infecondi of Rome on the death of the illustrious Lady Elena Lucrezia Cornaro Piscopia) (Padua, Cadorino, 1686).

65. I found this unpublished letter without a date, but traceable to 1686, pasted to the inside cover of the copy of *Le pompe funebri celebrate* (see note 64), preserved in Venice in the Biblioteca Nazionale Marciana and marked: 146. D. 40. In my opinion, this is the copy sent as a gift to the Doge Giustinian by Cardinal Rospigliosi.

66. A.S.P., Ufficio di sanità, 483; A.A.U., ms. 566, f. 115.

67. A.S.V., Notarile, reg. 11212; A.S.V., Notarile, Testamenti, b. 773, nos. 163–164.

68. Venice, Archivio Parrocchiale di S. Marco, Morti (1691–1736), V, f. I; A.S.V., Necrologio a. 1692, Provveditori alla sanità, n. 898; A.S.P., Ufficio di sanità, 486, by name.

69. A.S.P., Notarile, b. 6057, ff. 69r–70v.

70. Bacchini, *Helenae Lucretiae*, 36–37. Up until the present time, the basilica of S. Giustina is one of the few Benedictine churches in Italy not marred by tombs and funereal monuments.

71. A.S.P., S. Antonio Confessore [St. Anthony, Confessor], vol. 200, ff. 160–161 - particular.

72. Tabacco died in Bassano on February 15, 1729. Brentari, *Storia di Bassano*, 721; Thieme-Becker, "Tabacco Bernardo," in *Kunstler Lexicon*, 32:386.

73. Deza, *Vita di Helena*, appendix [1–4]. I express my cordial acknowledgment to the Paduan geometrician Andrea Calore to whose competence I owe this reconstruction.

74. Mabillon and Germain, *Iter Italicum*, 36.

75. Valery, *Correspondance inédite de Mabillon*, 37; Bacchini, *Helenae Lucretiae*, 36; Lupis, *L'eroina veneta*, 127.

76. Lupis, *L'eroina veneta*, 128; De Santi, "Elena Lucrezia," V, 444. De Vertron errs when affirming that this mausoleum was erected to Elena in the Church of S. Giustina (Guyonnet De Vertron, *La nouvelle Pandore*, 388–89).

77. Vergilius, *Aeneidos*, 2:65; Ferrazzi, *Di Bassano e dei bassanesi illustri*, 233.

78. Brentari, *Storia di Bassano*, 721.

79. I cite among these the Venetians Marco Beltrame, Giovanni Battista

Fattoretto, Giuseppe Ziminiani, and the man from Trevigiano, Giovanni Comin (or Comino) and the Genovese, Filippo Parodi.

80. Venice, Biblioteca del Civico Museo Correr, cod. Cicogna 2017, part I, 49, number 414; part II, 51, on the inscription 414. This slab disappeared during the different destinations and frequent changes of property of the palace.

81. Salonomius, *Inscriptiones Patavinae*, 132.

82. Bacchini, *Helenae Lucretiae*, 37; Deza, *Vita di Helena*, 124–26; Lupis, *L'eroina veneta*, 129–31; Scardova, *Vita compendiosa*, 60–61. The coining of the medallion consisted of the profiled image of Elena, with the laurel crown a bit elevated on her head, the doctoral emblem of the ermine stole on her shoulders, and with writing as a double cornice: *Hel.*[ena] *Luc.*[retia] *Cornelia Piscop.*[ia] *Fil.*[ia] *Io.*[annis] *Ba.*[ptistae] *D.*[ivi] *M.*[arci] *P.*[rocuratoris] *Sep.*[tem] *Lin.*[guis] *Orn.*[ata] *Laurea Philosoph.*[iae] *Donata Patavii A.*[nno] *S.*[alutis] *1678.* The reverse side shows an open seashell floating on the waves of the sea and nourished by drops of dew which rain on it from the sky; the surrounding motto reads *Non sine foenore* (Not without fruit) and under the waves are the words *Patav.*[ini] *Phil.*[osophorum] *Colleg.*[ii] *decreto.*

83. Nicolò Frescada was then the procurator of the college. A.A.U., ms. 366, f. 130.

84. Bacchini, *Helenae Lucretiae*, 38–39; Deza, *Vita di Helena*, 120–21; Lupis, *L'eroina veneta*, 133; Scardova, *Vita compendiosa*, 54.

85. Lupis, *L'eroina veneta*, 132–33; Scardova, *Vita compendiosa*, 54. Tommaso Giuseppe Farsetti, a priest from a noble Tuscan family well known in the history of Venetian letters, wrote elegantly in verse and in prose. In the family's palace, still called the palazzo Farsetti, he had gathered a vast collection of plaster reproductions of the most celebrated classic sculptures. This collection, integrated with a rich library, formed the noted Accademia Farsetti where young artists studied. Mutinelli, *Lessico veneto*, 62; Molmenti, *Storia di Venezia*, 3:84, 258; Lorenzetti, *Venezia e il suo estuario*, 485.

CHAPTER 9. EPILOGUE: SURVIVAL

1. Caro, *Oratio parentalis*, 9, 11.

2. Deza, *Vita di Helena*, 85; Lupis, *L'eroina veneta*, 121; Pynsent, *The Life*, 106; De Santi, "Elena Lucrezia," V, 442; Dalmazzo, *Lucrezia Cornaro*, 148.

3. Deza, *Vita di Helena*, 14; Dalmazzo, *Lucrezia Cornaro*, 151.

4. The "note" is incorrect even in indicating the registration of the death certificate in the Parish of S. Giorgio instead of S. Lorenzo. A.C.P., Fondo processi per beatificazioni e canonizzazioni, b. II, [f. 6-7].

5. Rios, *Corona sanctorum*, 77. The author is imprecise in affirming that Elena "maxima cum laude publice docuit in Universitate Patavina" (with highest public praise taught in the University of Padua).

6. Toffanin, *Il dominio austriaco in Padova*, 5, 33–42, passim.

7. Ibid., 57–58, 66, 77–79.

8. Ibid., 99-100.

9. Stella, "Esperienze agrarie e sociali dei benedettini padovani," 281–309; Stella, "I beni fondiari di S. Giustina prima e dopo la secolarizzazione, 93–105.

10. Pepi, *L'abbazia di Santa Giustina*, 68–70.

11. Dolfin's Rime [Rhymes] were published in a collection edited by G. B. Vicini in honor of Virginia Rangoni Morani, entitled Egeria (Paris, 1764). Also published were: *Sonetti in morte di Gian Antonio Dolfin* (Sonnets upon the death of Gian Antonio Dolfin), her father, followed by *Sonetti di diversi autori sopra lo stesso argomento* (Sonnets of several authors on the same hypothesis) (Padua, 1767); *Sonetto, ode, capitolo* (Sonnet, Ode, Chapter), in *Raccolta di poesie per la monacazione di una dama veneta di casa Widman* (Collection of poems for the claustration of a Venetian lady of the Widman House) (Venice, n. d.).

12. Molmenti, *La dogaressa*, 367; E. Musatti, *La donna in Venezia*, 143–44; Brunelli, "I libri di Caterina Dolfin," 2.

13. The inscription reads: *Statuam Helenae Lucretiae Corneliae / Piscopiae Laurea Philosoph.*[iae] *In Patav.*[ino] / *Gymnasio Unico Exemplo Donatae / Catherina Delphina Andreae Troni / Equit.*[is] *Et Aed.*[is] *D.*[ivi] *M.*[arci] *Procur.*[atoris] *Uxor H.*[anc] *P.*[onendam] *C.*[uravit] / *III Viri* [triumviri] *Rei Lit.*[erariae] *Loc.*[o] *Ded.*[icaverunt] *A.*[nno] *MDCCLXXIII.*

14. Damerini, *La vita avventurosa di Caterina Dolfin*, 293, note 15.

15. It is not correct to write that a monument to Elena was erected in the cloister of the university ("Piscopia [Lucrecia Cornelia Helena]," 47), nor that part of the monument existing in the basilica, after its dismemberment, was transferred to the university (Checchi, Gaudenzio, and Grossato, *Padova, guida ai monumenti*, 325). It is more precise to speak of a single statue. Clarification is also needed about Dolfin, whom one author calls a "noble" and "merciful" woman (De Santi, "Elena Lucrezia," V, 446). She was, on the contrary, quite different. She was jubilant, for example, when the Venetian Republic on September 3, 1773, the year after her marriage to Tron, and especially on his advice, resumed its oppressive policies against religious orders, suppressing numerous monasteries and convents considered useless to society and confiscating their property (Molmenti, *Storia di Venezia*, 3:398, note 2; Gullino, *La politica scolastica veneziana*, 16–17).

16. Pynsent, *The Life*, 118–21.

17. A.C.P., Fondo processi per beatificazioni e canonizzazioni, b. II, [f. I].

18. Campeis wrote the petition on officially stamped paper with a sixty-cent revenue stamp and turned it over to the V division of the municipal building. Ibid., b. II, [f. 2].

19. The inscription was published by Pynsent, *The Life*, 123.

20. A.C.P., Fondo processi per beatificazioni e canonizzazioni, b. II, [f. 3–5].

21. According to De Santi, the words added would be these: Domina Mechtildis Pynsent Angla / Eiusdem Ordinis Abbatissa / Restituit Anno MDCCCXCV. "Elena Lucrezia," V, 447.

22. Twelve small zinc cases were moved: ten contained the mortal remains of the

Benedictine monks buried there from 1590 to the end of the eighteenth century, the eleventh contained the bones of abbots, the twelfth those of Fortunato Morosini (1666–1727), Venetian senator, later a monk of S. Giustina, then bishop of Treviso and Brescia, who died in the abbey of S. Giustina. On September 25, 1975, the cases were returned to the funeral chapel, Morosini's to his tomb, and the other eleven to the first tomb on the left entering into the chapel.

23. Being present at that transfer, I can attest that the coffin was buried more *sacerdotali*, that is, with the head turned toward the altar, a privilege which the Roman Ritual concedes to prelates, priests, princes, and sovereigns (*Rituale Romanum*, titulus VI, cap. I, no. 18). She had probably been put in a similar position even in 1684. In fact, the inside of the tomb is not rectangular but wider toward the altar, a sign that the more spacious part of the tomb was reserved for the wider part of of the corpse (shoulders, abdomen).

24. Giovanni Romagnoli (1893–1966) painter, sculptor, and student of the Accademia di belle arti (The Academy of Fine Arts) in Bologna under Ferri and Mariani, established himself later in this city. In 1914 he began to participate in art shows. In 1915, he taught drawing in public schools. Later, he became a professor at the Accademia di belle arti of Modena and of Bologna. He won medals in national competitions in painting and, in 1924, second place in the competition of the Carnegie Institute of Pittsburgh where he taught in 1926, 1930–1931, 1938, and again in 1949; he also gave painting and fresco lessons in the University of Pittsburgh's Cathedral of Learning. He was a member of various Italian art academies and his works are preserved in the "Pasquale Revoltella" Museum in Trieste, in the modern art galleries of Rome, Florence, Milan, and Bologna. In Bologna, a monographic exhibition of Romagnoli was set up and 150 of his works were exhibited. Corna, "Romagnoli Giovanni," in *Dizionario della storia dell'arte*, 2:784; Benezit, "Romagnoli Giovanni," in *Dictionnaire critique*, 7:324; Bottari and Raimondi, "Romagnoli Giovanni," 47–48.

25. This information was furnished to me by Ruth Crawford Mitchell in two meetings, September 14 and 18, 1976, during her visit to Padua.

26. Padua, Municipio, *Delibere anno 1954*, n. 229 (protocollo n. 43531), Toponomy, n. 28, of the order of the day in public session. The little street, situated in the Parish of the Cuore Immacolato di Maria, Madonna Pellegrina (Immaculate Heart of Mary, Pilgrim Virgin), is the first on the right from via dei Giacinti. It is about one hundred meters long, currently has only eight houses and ends abruptly near the bank of the Canale scaricatore, where a metal screen stretches across it.

27. She is called erroneously a third order Franciscan by Saggiori in whose writing there is also a *lapsus calami*: Elena, that is, would have received her degree at the age of two (1648). Saggiori, *Padova nella storia delle sue strade*, 277–78.

28. Tonzig, "Elena Lucrezia Cornaro," 183–192.

BIBLIOGRAPHY

DOCUMENTS AND MANUSCRIPTS

Codevigo, Parrocchia, Archivio, *Battesimi* 1654–1673.

Modena, Archivio di Stato

    Cancelleria ducale. Lettere e documenti di particolari, C. 373/25.

    Carteggi particolari, b. 624.

Padua, Accademia Patavina, Archivio, *Giornale A*.

Padua, Archivio di Stato

    Testamento di Isabella Cornaro Piscopia, fu Giovanni. Archivio Notarile, b. 2199.

    Testamento (I) di Alvise Cornaro. Archivio Notarile, b. 4847.

    Testamento (II) di Alvise Cornaro. Archivio Notarile, b. 4823.

    Girolamo Cornaro Piscopia, fu Giovanni Battista, restituisce ai frati del Santo la porzione del loro orto tenuta in affitto. Archivio Notarile, b. 6057.

    Causa dei frati del Santo contro Girolamo Cornaro Piscopia, fu Giovanni Battista, loro debitore. Archivio Notarile, b. 6061.

    Alvise e Veronica Cornaro rogano atti notarili nella «casa nuova» a Padova. Archivio Notarile, vol. 1996.

    Donazione di Isabella Cornaro Piscopia, fu Giovanni, al fratello Giacomo Alvise e nipoti. Archivio Notarile, vol. 3465.

    Alvise Cornaro prende in affitto dai frati del Santo parte del loro orto. Archivio Notarile, vol. 4166.

    Debito di Girolamo Cornaro Piscopia, fu Giovanni Battista, con la parrocchia di S. Giorgio in Padova. Corporazioni Soppresse, S. Giorgio, no. 5.

    Miscellanea sul monastero di S. Giustina di Padova. Corporazioni Soppresse, S. Giustina, 77.

    Scritture estere del monastero di S. Giustina di Padova. Corporazioni Soppresse, S. Giustina, 384.

    Permesso per l'erezione di un monumento funebre a Elena Cornaro Piscopia nella basilica del Santo a Padova. Sant'Antonio confessore, vol. 200.

    Tomo dove sono delineati tutti i beni del venerando convento di S. Antonio di Padova. Sant'Antonio confessore, vol. 320.

    Ufficio di sanità, nos. 466, 469, 486, 490.

Padua, Biblioteca Antoniana

    Collezione autografi.

        Miscellanea, ms. XXII, 588.

Padua, Biblioteca Antoniana, Archivio Antico dell'Arca del Santo

    Atti e parti. vol. 28 (XXVII secondo la vecchia numerazione).

Opuscula varia Latina et Italica. ms. XXII-588.

Padua, Biblioteca del Monumento Nazionale di Santa Giustina

Della Torre, G. B. *Matricula sive series chronologica monachorum congregationis Cassinensis.* ms. b. 36, no. 8.

Padua, Biblioteca del Museo Civico

Registro de' nomi degli accademici Ricovrati di Padova. B. P. 124-XXIV.

Scardova, G. *Vita Compendiosa di Elena Lucrezia Cornaro Piscopia.* B. P. 125-I.

Ottaviani Cantù, G. *Descrizione della funzione di conferimento della laurea a Elena Cornaro Piscopia.* B. P. 126-XIV.

Gennari, G. *Saggio storico sopra le accademie di Padova.* B. P. 617-I.

Libro d'oro di Venezia. C. M. 16.

Dizionario delle venete famiglie patrizie. C. M. 232.

Genealogia di tutte le famiglie fatte del veneto Consiglio dall'anno 900 fino al presente. C. M. 247.

Annali di Venetia, et origine delle famiglie nobili. C. M. 651-12.

Origine di tutte le famiglie fatte nobili in virtù d'offerte dall'anno 1646 sino all'anno 1669. C. M. 715.

Matricola dell'Arte dei Capelleri di Venezia. ms. 208.

Padua, Biblioteca Universitaria

Raccolta di poesie varie, epigrammi, pasquinate. ms. 186.

Suppliche di Giambattista Cornaro Piscopia per il riconoscimento del vecchio titolo di cavaliere di Cipro. ms. 255.

Appunti storici intorno a Peschiera colla serie dei provveditori. ms. 295.

Leggi intorno alla nobiltà veneta. ms. 340.

Magistrati, reggimenti e officii veneti. ms. 730.

Origine ed aggregazione de famiglie alla nobiltà veneta. ms. 822.

Quadro delle famiglie patrizie che sono estinte dall'anno 1714 al 1792. ms. 882-II.

Filippi, F. *Series abbatum monachorumque catalogus congregationis Cassinensis.* ms. 1412.

Padua, Curia Vescovile, Archivio

Parrocchia S. Giorgio, *Liber mortuorum* (1614–1746).

Parrocchia S. Lorenzo:

Battesimi (luglio 1683–dicembre 1696)

Morti II (1599–1617)

Morti B (sul dorso 32).

Diversorum II. ms. 81.

Fondo processi per beatificazioni e canonizzazioni. b. II.

Visitationes. vol. LI.

Padua, Municipio, *Delibere anno 1954.*

Padua, Università, Archivio Antico

> *Laurea in filosofia di Elena Cornaro Piscopia e sua aggregazione al Collegio dei filosofi e medici di Padova.* ms. 365.

> *Partecipazione del Collegio dei filosofi e medici di Padova al funerale di Elena Cornaro Piscopia.* ms. 366.

> *Professori di Filosofia ordinari e straordinari. Istituzione e cambiamenti di tali cattedre.* ms. 664.

> *Cattedre e professori di logica e metafisica dei libri di Avicenna e di medicina teorica straordinaria.* ms. 669.

> *Partecipazione del Collegio dei filosofi e medici di Padova al funerale di Elena Cornaro Piscopia.* ms. 707.

> *Lettera dei Riformatori allo Studio di Padova ai rettori di Padova per la laurea di Elena Cornaro Piscopia.* ms. 716.

Parma, Archivio di Stato, Fondo S. Giovanni, b. 201.

Rome, Archivio del Collegio Greco, t. XIV.

Rome, Archivio di Stato, Archivio Cartari Febei, ms. 92.

Rome, Compagnia di Gesù, Archivio Romano

> *Epistolae nostrorum.* no. 10, no. 14.

> *Schede Biografiche.*

Treviso, Biblioteca Comunale, *Parti delle famiglie aggregate alla patritia nobiltà veneta nel tempo della guerra di Candia MDCLXVIII.* ms. 774.

Vatican City, Archivio Segreto Vaticano

> *Dispensa papale a Zanetta Boni.* Secr. Brevia, vol. 1310.

> *Contributi finanziari della S. Sede alla repubblica veneta per la guerra contro i Turchi.* Secr. Brevia, vol. 1359, 1392, 1409.

> *Dispense papali a Elena Cornaro Piscopia.* Secr. Brevia, vol. 1454, 1543.

> *Contributi finanziari della S. Sede alla repubblica veneta per la guerra contro i Turchi.* Secr. Brevia, vol. 1564, 1581, 1693, 1694.

> *Lettera di Carlo Airoldi, nunzio a Venezia, alla Segreteria di Stato.* S. S. Venezia, no. 119.

> *Rapporto del nunzio Luigi Giacobelli ad Andrea Borghi in Roma.* S. S. Venezia, no. 127.

Vatican City, Biblioteca Vaticana

> *Discorso accademico di Elena Cornaro Piscopia per l'Accademia degli Infecondi di Roma.* Barb. lat. 4502.

> *Lettere di Elena Cornaro Piscopia al cardinale Francesco Barberini.* Barb. lat. 6462.

> *Sussidio finanziario del vescovo di Treviso alla repubblica veneta per la guerra contro i Turchi.* Ott. lat. 2351.

> *Disputa filosofica di Elena Cornaro Piscopia a Venezia.* Ott. lat. 2479 (I).

> *Corrispondenza tra Alessandro VII e Bertuccio Valier, doge veneziano, per il ritorno dei Gesuiti a Venezia.* Vat. lat. 10419.

Venice, Archivio di Stato

Testamento di Girolamo Cornaro Piscopia, fu Giacomo Alvise. Archivio Notarile, b. 57, no. 335.

Testamento di Iacopo Tintoretto. Archivo Notarile, b. 157, no. 483.

Girolamo Cornaro Piscopia, fu Giacomo Alvise, nomina suo procuratore Guglielmo Thilmans. Archivio Notarile, b. 587.

Girolamo Cornaro Piscopia, fu Giacomo Alvise, acquista un livello a Padova. Archivio Notarile, b. 594.

Divisione dei beni tra Francesco e Girolamo Cornaro Piscopia, fu Giacomo Alvise. Archivio Notarile, b. 595.

Girolamo Cornaro Piscopia, fu Giacomo Alvise, acquista case a Padova. Archivio Notarile, b. 598.

Girolamo Cornaro Piscopia, fu Giacomo Alvise, prende in affitto una parte del palazzo di S. Luca a Venezia. Archivio Notarile, b. 605.

Testamento di Caterina Thilmans. Archivio Notarile, b. 756.

Testamento di Giovanni Battista Cornaro Piscopia. Archivio Notarile, b. 773, nos. 163-164.

Inventario delle suppellettili nella casa di Caterina Thilmans. Archivio Notarile, b. 10780.

Consegna di beni a Baldassare Cornaro Piscopia, di Girolamo, divenuto maggiorenne. Archivio Notarile, b. 10802.

Giovanni Battista Cornaro Piscopia acquista dei beni a Este. Archivio Notarile, b. 11191.

Rinuncia di beni di Caterina Cornaro Piscopia, di Giovanni Battista. Archivio Notarile, b. 11192.

Giovanni Battista Cornaro acquista una casa a Padova (in contrada Pontecorvo). Archivio Notarile, b. 11200 (142).

Zanetta Boni estingue un debito del defunto marito Giovanni Battista Cornaro Piscopia. Archivio Notarile, b. 11212.

Francesco Cornaro Piscopia, di Giovanni Battista, libera un carcerato. Archivio Notarile, b. 11214.

Contratto dotale di Caterina Cornaro Piscopia, di Giovanni Battista, e Antonio Vendramin. Archivio Notarile, b. 11215.

Giovanni Battista Cornaro intima ad Antonio Dandolo di riparare il ponte di Codevigo. Archivio Notarile, b. 11221.

Giovanni Battista Cornaro esige il risarcimento di danni da due suoi mandriani (per la morte di bestiame al pascolo). Archivio Notarile, b. 11221.

Ius patronatus dei Cornaro Piscopia sulla chiesa di Codevigo. Archivio Notarile, b. 11224.

Zanetta Boni manda la disdetta ad un inquilino. Archivio Notarile, b. 11225.

Lascito di Guglielmo Thilmans. Archivio Notarile, f. 10788.

Rinuncia di beni di Isabella Cornaro Piscopia, di Girolamo. Archivio Notarile, f. 10789.

Sostituzione di tutore dei figli di Girolamo Cornaro Piscopia. Archivio Notarile, reg. 10784.

Matrimoni (1600–1647). Avogaria de Comun, b. 82. 2.

Note sulle nascite e matrimoni dei nobili veneti (1675–1684). Avogaria da Comun, b. 83. 3, fasc. XXIII.

Note sulle nascite e matrimoni dei nobili veneti (1703–1714). Avogaria de Comun, b. 84. 4, fasc. XXVI.

Matrimoni (1658–1677). Avogaria de Comun, b. 100. 4, fasc. XVI.

Indice delle nascite. Avogaria de Comun, cassetta 168.

Matrimoni (1506–1554). Avogaria de Comun, ms. 68.

Parti prese per dar la nobiltà a diverse famiglie. Avogaria de Comun, reg. 15.

Matrimoni (1506–1554). Avogaria de Comun, reg. 143.4.

Barbaro M., *Arbori di patrizi veneti.* III, ms. 29 aprile–6 luglio 1743.

Necrologio (a. 1641). Provveditori alla sanità, no. 870.

Necrologio (a. 1692). Provveditori alla sanità, no. 898.

Necrologio (a. 1697). Provveditori alla sanità, no. 901.

Lettera dei Riformatori ai rettori di Padova per il dottorato di Elena Cornaro Piscopia. Riformatori dello Studio di Padova, b. 75.

Lettera di Giovanni Battista Cornaro Piscopia a un professore di Padova. Riformatori dello Studio di Padova, b. 490.

Venice, Biblioteca del Civico Museo Correr

Contratto d'affitto tra Girolamo Cornaro Piscopia, fu Giovanni Battista, e Antonio Farsetti. ms. B.P.C., fasc. 17. 11.

Origine delle famiglie aggregate alla nobiltà veneta per offerte assieme con le suppliche. ms. Cicogna 1213.

Per il dottorato di Elena Cornaro Piscopia. ms. Cicogna 1216.

Estratto dell'atto di battesimo di Elena e Girolamo Cornaro Piscopia. ms. Correr 2039.

Miscellanea Correr. 1108.

Collezione Gherro. XXII (2970–3049).

Onorificenza del «Cavalierato del silenzio». cod. Gradenigo 49.

Esame storicopolitico di cento soggetti della repubblica veneta. Codd. Grimani 15.

Lettera di Elena Cornaro Piscopia ad Antonio Grimani, procuratore di S. Marco. Codd. Morosini-Grimani, b. 442. XVII.

Prestito finanziario di Girolamo Cornaro Piscopia, fu Giacomo Alvise, a Gabriele Cornaro della Ca' Grande. ms. P D – C. 755. 51 (pergamena originale).

Testamento e codicillo di Caterina Cornaro Piscopia relitta di Antonio Vendramin. ms. P D – C. 1324. 2.

Scritture di Giovanni Battista Cornaro Piscopia per il patronato sulla chiesa di Codevigo. ms. P D – C. 2377. XXVI.

Venice, Biblioteca Nazionale Marciana

Capellari Vivaro, *Arbori di patrizi veneti*. ms. It. VII, 15 (=8304). ms. It. VII, 1522 (=8825).

Arbori. III, ms. 29 aprile–6 luglio 1743.

Venice, Curia Patriarcale, Archivio, *Liber collationum beneficiorum*. ms. senza segnatura.

Venice, Parrocchia S. Luca, Archivio

Battesimi II (1633–1647).

Battesimi III (1648–1718).

Matrimoni III (1647–1683).

Matrimoni IV (1683–1732).

Morti I.

Morti III (1638–1665).

Morti IV (1668).

Morti VI (1697).

Morti VII (1733–1752).

Venice, Parrocchia S. Marco, Archivio, *Morti V*.

Venice, Parrocchia S. Polo, Archivio (nell'archivio parrocchiale ai Frari), *Battesimi 1624–1641*.

Venice, Parrocchia di S. Sofia in S. Felice, Archivio, *Matrimoni no. 3*. lettera C.

PRINTED SOURCES

Note: For old works, I have selected historically appropriate editions even when later editions are available.

Alessi, G. *Vita del B. Gregorio card. Barbarigo vescovo di Padua.* 1897.

Amore, A. "Apostolicità delle chiese." In *Enciclopedia cattolica*, I, pp. 1695–1697. Vatican City, 1948.

Angelini, G. B. *Catalogo cronologico de' rettori di Bergamo.* Bergamo, 1742.

Angiolgabriello di S. Maria (Paolo Calvi). *Biblioteca e storia di quegli scrittori così della città come del territorio di Vicenza che pervennero fin' ad ora a notizia*, 6 vols. Vicenza, 1772-182.

Applausi accademici alla laurea filosofica di Elena Lucrezia Cornaro Piscopia, accademica Infeconda composti e raccolti dall'Accademia stessa. Rome, 1679.

Armellini, M. Bibliotheca benedictino-Cassinensis sive scriptorum Cassinensis congregationis, alias s. Iustinae Patavinae operum ac gestorum notitiae. 2 vols. in 1. Assisi.

Autore, S. "Lansperge." In *Dictionnaire de théologie catholique*, VIII, pp. 2606–2609. Paris, 1947.

Bacchini, B. *Helenae Lucretiae Corneliae Piscopiae opera quae quidem haberi potuerunt.* Parma, 1668.

Bandiera, G. N. *Trattato degli studi delle donne in due parti diviso. Opera d'un accademico Intronato.* Venice, 1740.

Bandini Buti, M. *Poetesse e scrittrici.* Rome, 1941–42. 2 vols. Enciclopedia biografica e bibliografica italiana, s. VI.

Barbiera, R. *Italiane gloriose.* Milan, 1923.

Barbus, L. *Modus meditandi et orandi.* Venice, 1523; Rome, 1605; Coloniae, 1644.

Battaglia, S. *Grande dizionario della lingua italiana.* Vol. 1. Turin, 1961.

Battisti, C., and Alessio, G. *Dizionario etimologico italiano.* 5 vols. Florence, 1950–57.

Becci, G. B. *Veritas anagrammate explorata ad varia texenda encomia.* Padua, 1668.

Bellinati, C. S. *Gregorio Barbarigo, "un vescovo eroico" (1625–1697).* Padua, 1960.

Belloni, A. *Il Seicento.* 2d ed. Milan, 1955.

Belotti, B. *Storia di Bergamo e dei bergamaschi.* 7 vols. Bergamo, 1959.

Beltrami, D. *Forze di lavoro e proprietà fondiaria nelle campagne venete dei secc. XVII–XVIII.* Civiltà veneziana: Studi, 12. Venice and Rome, 1961.

Benedictus (Sanctus). *Regula monachorum. Textus critico-practicus secundum codicem Sangallensem 914.* Maredsous, 1955.

Benezit, E. *Dictionnaire critique et documentaire des peintres, sculpteurs, dessinateurs et graveurs de tous les temps et de tous les pays.* 8 vols. Paris, 1966.

Benoffi, F. A. *Compendio di storia minoritica.* Pesaro, 1829.

Benzoni, G. *Venezia nell'età della controriforma.* Problemi di storia, 22. Turin, 1973.

Bergalli, L. *Componimenti poetici delle più illustri rimatrici d'ogni secolo*. 2 vols. Venice, 1726.

Berlière, U. *L'ascèse bénédictine des origines à la fin du XIIe siècle*. Paris, 1927.

Bernareggi, A. "Dimesse." In *Enciclopedia ecclesiastica*, II, p. 526. Milan and Turin, 1944.

"Berneri, Giuseppe." In *Dizionario biografico degli autori*, I, p. 247. Milan, 1956.

Berruti, A. *Patriziato veneto. I Cornaro*. Turin, 1952.

Besse, J. M. *Le moine bénédictin*. Ligugé (Vienna), 1898.

Bianchi-Giovini, A. *Biografia di fra Paolo Sarpi*. 2 vols. Brussels, 1836.

Biasuz, G. "Carlo Patin medico e numismatico." *Bollettino del Museo Civico di Padova*, XLVI–XLVII (1957–1958): 67–114.

Blaise, A. *Lexicon latinitatis medii aevi*. Thurnolti, 1975.

———. *Dictionnaire latin-français des auteurs chrétiens*, by H. Chirat. 4th ed. Thurnholt, 1975.

Boerio, G. *Dizionario del dialetto veneziano*. 2d ed. Venice, 1856. Reprint: Milan, 1971.

Boldrin, S. *Maria Alberghetti (1578–1664): Vita e opere*. Tesi di laurea, relatore prof. A. Vecchi. University of Padua, Istituto di storia delle religioni, anno accademico, 1967–1968.

Borgherini Scarabellin, M. *La vita privata a Padova nel sec. XVII*. Miscellanea di storia veneta, s. III, XII. Venice, 1917.

Borsetti, F. *Historia almi Ferrariae Gymnasii*. 2 vols. Ferrara, 1735. Reprint: Bologna, 1970 (Atheneum, 3).

Boschini, M. *Carta del navegar pitoresco*. Venice, 1660.

Bosmin, P. "Cornaro." In *Enciclopedia italiana di scienze, lettere e arti*, XI, pp. 418–19. Rome, 1950.

Bottari, S., and Raimondi, G. *Romagnoli Giovanni. Mostra monografica. Catalogo della mostra (Bologna 24 settembre–29 ottobre 1961)*. Bologna, 1961.

Brentari, O. *Storia di Bassano e del suo territorio*. Bassano, 1884.

Brenzoni, R. *Dizionario di artisti veneti*. Florence, 1972.

Bresciani Alvarez, G. "L'opera di Giov. Bonazza al Santo nel quadro della sua attività." *Il Santo*, IV (1964): 25–40.

Brignole-Sale, A. G. *Il satirico innocente*. Genoa, 1648.

Briois, P. *Voyage littéraire de Paris à Rome en 1698*, by H. Omont. Paris, 1904.

Bronckhorst, O. *La dama di lettere: applausi ad Elena Cornaro Piscopia accademica Ricovrata, dedicata alle dame di Padova*. Padua, 15 July 1678.

Brunati, G. *Uomini illustri della riviera di Salò*. Milan, 1837.

Brunelli, B. "I libri di Caterina Dolfin." *Marzocco*, XXXI (1926): no.. 6–7, 2.

Caccia, E. "Cultura e letteratura." In *Storia di Brescia*, II, pp. 477–535. Brescia, 1963.

Calcaterra, C. "Il problema del barocco." In *Questioni e correnti di storia letteraria*, ed. U. Bosco, pp. 405–501. Problemi e orientamenti critici di lingua e di letteratura italiana, ed. A. Momigliano. Milan, 1968.

Canepari, C. "Secentismo." In *Grande dizionario enciclopedico*, XI, pp. 673–74. 2nd ed. Turin, 1961.

Cantù, C. *Storia di Milano*. Grande illustrazione del Lombardo-Veneto, I. Milan, 1857.

———. *Storia di Venezia*. Grande illustrazione del Lombardo-Veneto, II. Milan, 1858.

Capone-Braga, G. *La filosofia francese e italiana del Settecento*. 2 vols. 2nd ed. Padua, 1942.

Cappelletti, G. *Storia della Chiesa di Venezia*. 3 vols. Venice, 1849–53.

Caro, F. *Oratio parentalis ad cenotaphium Helenae Lucretiae Corneliae Piscopia, patritiae Venetae, philosophia laureatae*. Padua, 1684.

Casalini, G. "Cachessia." In *Dizionario di medicina per medici e famiglie*, I, p. 225. 3rd ed. Turin, 1951.

Catoni, G. "Bandiera, Giovanni Nicola." In *Dizionario biografico degli italiani*, V, pp. 686–88. Rome, 1963.

Cavacius, I. *Historiarum coenobii d. Iustinae patavinae libri sex*. 2nd ed. Padua, 1696.

Cepari, V. *Vita di s. Luigi Gonzaga, primogenito d. Ferrante Gonzaga, prencipe dell'Imperio, marchese di Castiglione*. Rome, 1606.

———. *Regole comuni delle Vergini di Gesù nel Collegio di Castiglione*. Bologna, 1622.

Cessi, R. "Cipro." In *Enciclopedia di scienze, lettere e arti*, X, pp. 396–398. Rome, 1950.

———. *La Repubblica di Venezia e il problema adriatico*. Naples, 1953.

———. *Storia della repubblica di Venezia*. 2 vols. Milan and Messina, 1968.

Chauvin, P. *L'oblature de l'ordre de saint Benoît*. Paris, 1921.

Checchi, M., Gaudenzio, L., and Grossato, L. *Padova, guida ai monumenti e alle opere d'arte*. Venice, 1961.

Cherubini, F. *Vocabolario milanese-italiano*. 5 vols. Milan, 1839.

Chevalier, J., and Gheerbrant, A. *Dictionnaire des symboles*. Paris, 1969.

Cicogna, E. A. *Delle inscrizioni veneziane*. 6 vols. Venice, 1824–53. Reprint: Collana di bibliografia e storia veneziana, 3. Bologna, 1969–70.

———. *Saggio di bibliografia veneziana*. Venice, 1847. Reprint: Collana di bibliografia e storia veneziana, I. Bologna, 1967.

Cistellini, A. "Estrées César." In *Enciclopedia cattolica*, pp. 652–53. Rome, 1950.

Claudiani, C. *Opera quae extant interpretatione et annotationibus illustravit Gulielmus Pirrho ad usum Delphini*. Paris, 1677.

Cocchetti, C. *Brescia e la sua provincia*. Grande illustrazione del Lombardo-Veneto, III. Milan, 1858.

Codex iuris canonici Pii X pontificis maximi iussu digestus Benedicti papae XV auctoritate promulgatus praefatione cardinalis Petri Gasparri. Rome, 1949.

Cognasso, F. *L'unificazione della Lombardia sotto Milano*. Storia di Milano, V. Milan, 1955.

Colomies, P. *Opera*. Hamburg, 1709.

Comneno Papadopol, N. *Historia Gymnasii Patavini*. 2 vols. in 1. Venice, 1726.

Comparoni, P. G. *Storia delle valli Trompia e Sabbia*. Salò, 1805.

Compositioni degli accademici Ricovrati per la morte della nobile donna signora Elena Lucrezia Cornaro Piscopia dedicate all'Eccellenza del signor Gianbattista suo padre procuratore di S. Marco dal conte Alessandro abb. De Lazzara principe dell'Accademia. Padua, 1684.

Congar, Y. M. J. "Théologie." In *Dictionnaire de théologie catholique*, XV, pp. 341–502. Paris, 1946.

Contarini, P. *Dizionario tascabile delle voci e frasi particolari del dialetto veneziano*. Venice, 1852.

Corna, P. A. *Dizionario della storia dell'arte in Italia*. 2 vols. Piacenza, 1930.

Cornaro, A. *Discorsi intorno alla vita sobria*. Ed. P. Pancrazi. Florence, 1942.

Cornaro, M. *Scritture sulla laguna*. Ed. G. Pavanello. Antichi scrittori d'idraulica veneta, I. Venice, 1919.

Cornelius, F. *Ecclesiae Venetae antiquis monumentis illustratae*. 15 vols. Venice, 1749.

Coronelli, V. *Isolario dell'atlante veneto*. 2 vols. Venice, 1696.

Corradi, G. "Cipro." In *Grande dizionario enciclopedico*, III, pp. 625–626. Turin, 1955.

Cracco, G. *Società e Stato nel medioevo veneziano (secc. XII–XIV)*. Civiltà veneziana. Studi, 22. Florence, 1967.

Croce, B. "Appunti di letteratura secentesca inedita o rara." *La critica*, s. III, XXVII (1929): 468–80.

Croce, F. "Critica e trattatistica del barocco." In *Storia della letteratura italiana. Il Seicento*, ed. E. Cecchi and N. Sapegno, V, pp. 471–518. Milan, 1967.

Crollalanza, G. B. *Dizionario storico-blasonico delle famiglie nobili e notabili italiane estinte e fiorenti*. 3 vols. Bologna, 1965.

Dalla Torre, P. "Alessandro VIII." In *Enciclopedia cattolica*, I, pp. 803–805. Vatican City, 1948.

Dalmazzo, F. *Lucrezia Cornaro Piscopia oblata benedettina*. Subiaco, 1943.

Damerini, G. *La vita avventurosa di Caterina Dolfin Tron*. Milan, 1929.

David, Abraham. "Aboab Samuel Ben Abraham." In *Encyclopaedia Judaica*, II, pp. 94–95. Jerusalem, 1971.

D'Ayala, M. *Bibliografia militare italiana antica e moderna*. Turin, 1854.

De Bernardin, S. "La politica culturale della repubblica di Venezia e l'Università di Padova nel XVII secolo." *Studi veneziani*, XVI (1974): 443–502.

Delatte, P. *Commentaire sur la règle de saint Benoît*. 10th ed. Paris, 1931.

Della Corte, A., and Pannain, G. *Storia della musica*. 3 vols. Turin, 1942.

De Morembert, T. "Estrées César d'." In *Dictionnaire d'histoire et géographie ecclésiastique*, pp. 1087–88. Paris, 1963.

Deroux, M. P. *Les origines de l'oblature bénédictine*. Paris, 1927.

De Santi, A. "Attività letteraria nel monastero Sancti Benedicti de Urbe." *La civiltà cattolica*, s. XVII, II (1898): 702–10.

———. "Elena Lucrezia Cornaro Piscopia. Nuove ricerche." *La civiltà cattolica*, s. XVII, IV (1898): 172–86, 421–40, 678–89; V (1899): 176–93, 433–47.

Desio, A. "Piscopi, l'isola meno nota del Dodecaneso." *Le vie d'Italia*, XXX (1924): 49–56.

Devoto, G. *Avviamento alla etimologia italiana. Dizionario etimologio.* Florence, 1967.

Devoto, G., and Oli, G. C. *Vocabolario illustrato della lingua italiana.* 2 vols. Milan, 1967.

Deza, M. *Vita di Helena Lucretia Cornaro Piscopia.* 2nd ed. Venice, 1692.

La diocesi di Padova 1972. Padua, 1973.

Discorsi accademici di vari autori viventi intorno agli studi delle donne la maggior parte recitati nell'Accademia de' Ricovarati di Padova. Padua, 1729.

Distichon ad sapientissimam virginem Helenam Corneliam philosophiae laurea in Patavino Collegio inauguratam. Padua, 1678.

Dizionario musicale Larousse. Ed. D. Nava. 3 vols. Milan, 1961.

Dolfin Tron, C. *Sonetti in morte di Gian Antonio Dolfin.* Padua, 1767.

Dragoni, A. *Oratione di A. D. e componimenti d'altri soggetti in lode di Giovanni Cornaro, luogotenente della patria del Friuli.* Udine, 1683.

Du Cange, Ch. *Glossarium ad scriptores mediae et infimae latinitatis.* 6 vols. Paris, 1733–36.

Enciclopedia filosofica. 6 vols. 2d ed. Florence, 1968–69.

Epantismatologia overo raccoglimento poetico de più forti ingegni nella solenne coronatione in filosofia e medicina del signor Angelo Sumachi nob. di Zante. Padua, 1668.

Fabronius, A. *Historia Academiae Pisanae.* 3 vols. Pisa, 1791–95.

Facciolati, I. *Fasti Gymnasii Patavini.* Padua, 1757.

Falaschi, P. L. "Procuratori di S. Marco." In *Novissimo digesto italiano*, XIII, pp. 1261–1262. 3d ed. Turin, 1966.

Fano, A. *Sperone Speroni.* Padua, 1909.

Favaro, A. *L'Università di Padova.* Padua, 1922.

———. *Galileo Galilei e lo Studio di Padova.* 2 vols. Contributi alla storia dell'Università di Padova, 3–4. Padua, 1966.

Federici, F. *Della biblioteca di S. Giustina.* Padua, 1815.

Federazzi, G. I. *Di Bassano e dei bassanesi illustri.* Bassano, 1847.

Fiocco, G. *Alvise Cornaro il suo tempo e le sue opere.* Venice, 1965.

———. "La Casa di Alvise Cornaro." *Bollettino del Museo Civico di Padova*, LVIII (1968): 7–16.

Fiorelli, G. *Detti e fatti memorabili del Senato e patritii veneti.* Venice, 1672.

Fontana, G. I. *Cento palazzi di Venezia storicamente illustrati.* Venice, 1934.

François, J. *Bibliothèque générale des écrivains de l'ordre de saint Benoît.* 4 vols. 1777–78. Reprint: Louvain-Héverlé, 1961.

Gaeta, F. *S. Lorenzo.* Fonti per la storia di Venezia. Sez. II. Archivi ecclesiastici. Diocesi Castellana. Venice, 1959.

Galilei, G. *Opere.* 20 vols. Ed. A. Favaro. Florence, 1929–39.

Gamba, C. M. "L'educazione della donna." In *Storia della scuola italiana nel Seicento e nel Settecento*, VII, pp. 237–329. Milan, 1972. (La pedagogia.)

Gar, T. "I codici storici della collezione Foscarini conservati nella Imperiale Biblioteca di Vienna." *Archivio storico italiano*, s. I, V (1843): 281–476.

Garin, E. *L'educazione in Europa: 1400-1600*. Rome and Bari, 1976.

Garzoni, T. *L'hospitale de' pazzi incurabili*. Venice, 1601.

Gautier, G. *La spiritualità cattolica*. Milan, 1956.

Gennari, G. *Memorie inedite sopra le tre chiese in Padova: Cattedrale, S. Giustina e Santo*. Padua, 1842.

Getto, G. "La polemica sul barocco." In *Letteratura italiana. Le Correnti*, pp. 417–504. Orientamenti culturali, I. Milan, 1972.

Geymonat, L. *Storia del pensiero filosofico e scientifico*. 7 vols. Milan, 1970–1976.

Giulini, G. *Memorie della città e campagna di Milano*. 9 vols. Milan, 1855.

"Gli *Intronati* di Siena." *L'Osservatore Romano*, 6 December 1953, p. 5.

Gloria, A. Lucrezia degli Obizzi e il suo secolo. Padua, 1853.

———. "Nuovi documenti intorno la abitazione di Galileo Galilei in Padova." *Atti e memorie della R. Accademia di scienze, lettere ed arti in Padova*, n. s., IX (1892–93): 127-48.

Gonzati, B. *La basilica di S. Antonio di Padova descritta ed illustrata*. 2 vols. Padua, 1852.

Graziani, C. "L'educazione della donna." In *Storia della scuola italiana nel Seicento e nel Settecento*, I, pp. 790–840. Milan, 1970. (La pedagogia.)

Guarnieri, R. "Il movimento del Libero spirito. Testi e documenti." In *Archivio italiano per la storia della pieta*, IV, pp. 351–708. Rome, 1965.

Guasco, G. *Storia litteraria del principio e progresso dell'Accademia di belle lettere in Reggio*. Reggio, 1711.

Gullino, G. *La politica scolastica veneziana nell'età delle riforme*. Deputazione di storia patria per le Venezie. Miscellanea di studi e memorie, XV. Venice, 1973.

Guyonnet, C. Ch. De Vertron. *La nouvelle Pandore ou les femmes illustres du siècle de Louis le Grand*. Paris, 1698.

Hoefer, M. *Nouvelle biographie générale*. 46 vols. Paris, 1855–66.

Hommetz-Patina, M. *Riflessioni morali e cristiane cavate per lo piú dall'epistole di s. Paolo*. Padua, 1680.

Ivanovich, C. *Minerva al tavolino*. 2 vols. Venice, 1688.

Jedin, H. *Storia della Chiesa: Riforma e controriforma*. Vol. 6. Milan, 1975.

Journal des Sçavans, de l'an 1678. Amsterdam, 1679.

Journal des Sçavans, pour l'an 1679. Paris, 1728.

König, G. M. *Bibliotheca vetus et nova*. Altdorf, 1678.

Lavagnini, B. "Erotocrito." In *Dizionario letterario Bompiani delle opere e dei personaggi*, III, p. 204, VIII, pp. 305–306. Milan, 1947, 1950.

———. "Cornaro, Vincenzo." In *Dizionario letterario Bompiani degli autori*, I, p. 591. Milan, 1956.

Laymann, P. Theologia moralis. Venice, 1662.

Leccisotti, T. "Gli oblati benedettini in Italia." *Benedictina*, VII (1953): 153–60.

Legrand, E. *Bibliographie hellénique siècle XVIIe.* 4 vols. Paris, 1894–96.

Le pompe funebri celebrate da' signori accademici Infecondi di Roma, per la morte dell'illustrissima sig. Elena Lucrezia Cornaro Piscopia, accademica, detta Inalterabile, dedicate alla serenissima repubblica di Venezia. Padua, 1686.

Lesort, A. "Bouillon Emmanuel." In *Dictionnaire d'histoire et géographie ecclésiastique*, X, pp. 43–45. Paris, 1938.

Lestocquoy, J. *Aux origines de la bourgeoisie: les villes de Flandre et d'Italie sous le gouvernement des patriciens (XI–XV siècles)*, Paris, 1952.

Leti, G. *L'Italia regnante.* 4 vols. Genoa, 1676.

Lettere d'uomini illustri che fiorirono nel principio del secolo decimosettimo. Venice, 1744.

Loewe, R. "Hebraists Christian (1100–1890)." In *Encyclopaedia Judaica*, VIII, pp. 9–71. Jerusalem, 1971.

Lorenz, H. *Analecta literaria ad Helenae Lucretiae Corneliae Piscopiae liberalium artium magistrae vitam.* Altenburgi, [1872].

Lorenzetti, G. *Venezia e il suo esturario.* 2nd ed. Rome, 1956.

Lucanus, M. A. *Pharsalia cum appositis Italico carmine interpretationibus ac notis.* 2 vols. Milan, 1781–82.

Lupis, A. *L'eroina veneta, overo la vita di Elena Lucretia Cornaro Piscopia.* Venice, 1689.

Luzzatto, G. *I prestiti della Repubblica di Venezia (sec. XIII–XV).* Padua, 1929.

Mabillon, I., and Germain, M. *Museum Italicum.* 2 vols. Luteciae Parisiorum, 1687.

Macedo, F. *Myrothecium morale.* Padua, 1675.

———. *Panegyricus dominae Helenae Corneliae.* Padua, 1679.

———. *Pictura Venetae urbis.* Venice, 1681.

Magagnò, Menòn, and Begotto. *Rime in lingua rustica padovana.* Venice, 1610.

Malaguzzi-Valeri, V. *L'innocente riconosciuta.* Bologna, 1660.

Malusa, L. *Dall'umanesimo alla controriforma.* Storia del pensiero occidentale, 3. Milan, 1975.

Manfredi, F. *Dignità procuratoria di S. Marco.* Venice, 1602.

Mannocci, I. "Gli oblati benedettini dell'abbazia di S. Giovanni Evangelista in Parma." *Rivista storica benedettina*, XXIII (1954): 47–62, 132–49.

Manuel de bibliographie biographique et d'iconographie des femmes célèbres. Turin and Paris, 1882.

Manzoni, A. *I promessi sposi.* Ed. L. Gessi. Rome, 1953.

Marini, E. *Venezia antica e moderna.* Venice, 1905.

Mazzotti, G. *Le ville venete.* 3rd ed. Treviso, 1954.

Memorie di alcune religiose francescane illustri per santità vissute nel monastero delle vergini eremite di S. Bonaventura di Padova in Vanzo. Venice, 1773.

Menegazzo, E. "Altre osservazioni intorno alla vita e all'ambiente del Ruzante e di Alvise Cornaro." *Italia medioevale e umanistica*, IX (1966): 229–63.

Meneghini, A. *Padova e sua provincia.* Grande illustrazione del Lombardo-Veneto,

IV, Milan, 1859.

Menin, L. *Cenni storici della r. Accademia di scienze, lettere ed arti in Padova*. Padua, 1842.

Mercure Galant. Lyon, 1678.

Michel, A. "Trente (Concile de)." In *Dictionnaire de théologie catholique*, XV, 1414–1508. Paris, 1946.

Migliorini, B. "Onomastica." In *Enciclopedia italiana di scienze, lettere e arti*, XXV, pp. 378–381. Rome, 1950.

Milano, A. *Storia degli ebrei in Italia*. Turin, 1963.

Molmenti, P. G. *La Dogaressa*. Turin, 1884.

Molmenti, P. *Storia di Venezia nella vita privata dalle origini alla caduta della repubblica*. 3 vols. Bergamo 1927. Reprint of 1880 edition: Trieste, 1973.

Morelli, G. *Della pubblica Libreria di S. Marco. Dissertazione storica*. Venice, 1774.

Morery, L. *Le grand dictionnaire historique, nouvelle édition revue et corrigée par M. Drouet*. 10 vols. Paris, 1759.

Moroni, G. *Dizionario di erudizione storico-ecclesiastica*. 103 vols. Venice, 1840–1861.

Moschetti, A. "Gli affreschi di Giovanni Storlato in Santa Giustina di Padova." *Atti del r. Istituto veneto di scienze, lettere, arti*, LXXXV (1925-1926): 411-19.

Moschini, G. *Guida per la città di Padova*. Venice, 1817.

Muratori, L. A. *Lettere inedite scritte a toscani*. Florence, 1854.

Musatti, E. *Storia d'un lembo di terra ossia Venezia ed i Veniziani*. Padua, 1886.

———. *La donna in Venezia*. Padua, 1891.

Musatti, G. *Storia di Venezia*. 2 vols. 3d ed. Milan, 1936.

Muti, A. M. *La penna volante*. Venice, 1681.

Mutinelli, F. *Lessico veneto*. Venice, 1852.

Neocorus, L., and Sikius, H. *Bibliotheca librorum novorum anni 1698*. Traiecti ad Rhenum, 1698.

Nouvelle biographie universelle. 46 vols. Paris, 1862–1877.

Occioni Bonaffons, G. *Brevi cenni sulle Accademie in Venezia. L'Ateneo veneto nel suo primo centenario*. Venice, 1912.

Oliva, G. P. *Lettere*. 2 vols. Rome, 1681.

———. *Lettere*. Venice, 1681.

Olivieri, D. *Toponomastica veneta*. Venice, 1961.

Patin, G. *Dissertation sur le phénix d'une médaille d'Antoine Caracalla*. Venice, 1683.

Patin-Rosa, C. *Mitra ou la démone mariée, nouvelle hébraïque et morale*. Demonopolis, 1688.

———. *Tabellae selectae ac explicatae*. Padua, 1691.

Patinus, C. *Lyceum Patavinum sive icones et vitae professorum Patavii, MDCLXXXII publice docentium*. Padua, 1682.

Patriarchi, G. *Vocabolario veneziano e padovano co' termini e modi corrispondenti toscani*. Padua, 1775.

Penco, G. *Storia del monachesimo in Italia dalle origini alla fine del medio evo*. Vol. 1. Tempi e figure, 31. Rome, 1961. Vol. 2. Tempi e figure, 52. Rome, 1968.

Pepi, R. *L'abbazia di Santa Giustina. Storia e arte*. Padua, 1966.

Pesce, L. *Ludovico Barbo vescovo di Treviso (1437–1443)*. 2 vols. Italia Sacra, 9–10. Padua, 1969.

Petrocchi, M. *Il quietismo italiano nel Seicento*. Storia e letteratura, XX. Rome, 1948.

Picasso, G. M. "La preghiera nel movimento spirituale di S. Giustina." In *La preghiera nella Bibbia e nella tradizione patristica e monastica*, pp. 733–69. Rome, 1964.

———. "L'imitazione di Cristo nell'epoca della devoltio moderna e nella spiritualità monastica del sec. XV in Italia." *Rivista di storia e letteratura religiosa*, IV (1968): 11–31.

"Piscopia (Lucrecia Cornelia Helena)." In *Enciclopedia universal ilustrada europeo-americana*, XLV, p. 47. Barcelona, 1921.

Poesie de' signori accademici Infecondi di Roma. Venice, 1684.

Pompeati, A. Storia della letteratura italiana. 4 vols. Turin, 1953.

Poppi, A. *Causalità e infinità nella Scuola padovana dal 1480 al 1513*. Saggi e testi, 5. Padua, 1966.

———. *La dottrina della scienza in Giacomo Zabarella*. Saggi e testi, 12. Padua, 1972.

Portenari, A. *Della felicità di Padova*. Padua, 1623.

Pourrat, P. "Quiétisme." In Dictionnaire de théologie catholique, XIII, pp. 1537–81. Paris, 1937.

Prati, A. Etimologie venete. Venice, 1968.

Prodi, P. "Riforma cattolica e controriforma." In *Nuove questioni di storia moderna*, I, pp. 357–418. Milan, 1970.

Pychowska, L. D. "A Learned Woman." *Catholic World*, LII (1890–1891): 660–674.

Pynsent, M. *The Life of Helen Lucretia Cornaro Piscopia Oblate of the Order of St. Benedict and Doctor in the University of Padua*. Rome, 1896.

Raner, K., and Vorgrimler, H. "Quietismo." In *Dizionario di teologia*. Rome and Brescia, 1968.

Ravenna, A. "Aboab, Samuele." In *Dizionario biografico degli Italiani*, I, 54–55. Rome, 1960.

Richard, Ch., and Giraud, J. J. *Dizionario universale delle scienze religiose*. 10 vols. Naples, 1843–53.

Ridolfi, C. *Le meraviglie dell'arte*. 2 vols. Venice, 1648. Reprint, ed. D. von Hadeln: Berlin, 1914–24.

Rinaldini, C. *De resolutione et compositione mathematica libri duo*. Padua, 1668.

———. *Geometra promotus*. Padua, 1670.

———. *Commercium epistolicum*. Padua, 1682.

Rios, R. *Corona sanctorum anni benedictini*. Ramsgate, 1948.

Rituale Romanum Pauli V pontificis maximi iussu editum atque auctoritate Pii papae

XI ad normam codicis iuris canonici accomodatum. Rome, 1925.

Ritzler, R., and Sefrin, P. *Hierarchia catholica medii et recentioris aevi.* 7 vols. Monasterii-Patavii, 1913–68.

Roberti, M. *Le magistrature giudiziarie veneziane e i loro Capitolari fino al 300.* 3 vols. Monumenti storici della r. Deputazione veneta di storia patria, s. II, Statuti II-III. Venice, 1907–1911.

Romanin, S. *Storia documentata di Venezia.* 10 vols. Venice, 1853–61. Reprint: Bologna, 1972.

Ronchi, O. *Guida storico-artistica di Padova e dintorni.* Padua, 1922.

Rossetti, L. *L'Università di Padova: Profilo storico.* Milan, 1972.

———. "Francescani del Santo docenti all'Università di Padova." In *Storia e cultura al Santo di Padova*, pp. 169–207. Fondi e studi per la storia del Santo a Padova, III. Studi, I. Padua, 1976.

Rossi, E. "Rodi." In *Enciclopedia italiana di scienze, lettere e arti*, XIX, pp. 547–57. Rome, 1949.

Roth, C. *Gli ebrei in Venezia.* Trans. D. Lattes. Tivoli, 1933.

Ruysschaert, J. "Cornaro." In *Dictionnaire d'histoire et géographie ecclésiastique*, XIII, pp. 886–90. Paris, 1956.

———. "Delfino, Pietro." In *Dictionnaire d'histoire et géographie ecclésiastique*, XIV, pp. 179–80. Paris, 1960.

Saggiori, G. *Padova nella storia delle sue strade.* Padua, 1972.

Salomonius, I. *Inscriptiones Patavinae sacrae et prophanae.* Padua, 1708.

Salvi, G. "Gli oblati benedettini in Italia." *Rivista storica benedettina*, XXI (1952): 89–169.

Sambin, P. "I testamenti di Alvise Cornaro." *Italia medioevale e umanistica*, IX (1966): 296-385.

Sandri, M. G., and Alazraki, P. *Arte e vita ebraica a Venezia: 1516–1797.* Florence, 1971.

Sansovino, F., and Martinioni, G. *Venetia città nobilissima con aggiunta di tutte le cose notabili fatte et occorse dall'anno 1580 fino al presente 1663.* Venice, 1663.

Sapegno, N. *Disegno storico della letteratura italiana.* 13th ed. Florence, 1959.

Savini Branca, S. *Il collezionismo veneziano nel '600.* Università di Padova. Pubblicazioni della facoltà di lettere e filosofia, XLI. Florence, 1965.

Schmitz, Ph. *Histoire de l'ordre de saint Benoît.* 7 vols. Maredsous, 1942–49.

Seconda corona intrecciata da varii letterati co' fiori de' loro ingegni, per coronar di nuovo il molto reverendo padre Giacomo Lubrani della Compagnia di Gesù. Venice, 1675.

Selvatico, P. *L'architettura e scultura in Venezia dal medio-evo sino ai nostri giorni.* Venice, 1847.

Serena, S. *Lettere inedite del beato Gregorio Barbarigo a Giulio Giustinian.* Padua, 1932.

———. *S. Gregorio Barbarigo e la vita spirituale e culturale nel suo seminario di Padova.* 2 vols. Padua, 1963.

Simon, G. A. *La règle de s. Benoît commentée pour les oblats de son ordre.* Paris, 1947.

Sommervogel, Ch. *Bibliothèque de la Compagnie de Jésus.* 12 vols. Brussels and Paris, 1890–1932.

Soppelsa, M. "Un dimenticato scolaro galileiano: il padre Girolamo Spinelli." *Bollettino del Museo Civico di Padova*, LX, no. 2 (1971): 97–114.

———. *Genesi del metodo galileiano e tramonto dell'aristotelismo nella scuola di Padova.* Padua, 1974.

Spicilegium benedictinum. 4 vols. Rome, 1896–99.

Spini, G. *Ricerca dei libertini. La teoria dell'impostura delle religioni nel Seicento italiano.* Rome, 1950.

Spreti, V. "Cornaro Piscopia Elena." In *Enciclopedia storico-nobiliare italiana*, II, p. 541. Milan, 1929.

Stella, A. "Esperienze agrarie e sociali dei benedettini padovani nella prima metà del '700." *Benedictina*, III (1959): 281–309.

———. "I beni fondiari di S. Giustina prima e dopo la secolarizzazione." *Memorie della Accademia patavina di scienze, lettere e arti*, LXXVI (1963–64): 93–105.

Storia di Brescia. 5 vols. Brescia, 1963.

Sumachi, A. *Enypnionsophiae panagrypnon, overo, sapientia in somno ad virtutis stimulum omnino vigilans.* Padua, 1668.

Tabacco, G. *Andrea Tron (1712–1785) e la crisi dell'aristocrazia senatoria a Venezia.* Trieste, 1957.

Tagliaferri, A.,ed. *Relazioni de rettori veneti in terraferma. Vol. 4: Podestaria e capitanato di Padova.* Milano, 1975.

Tanquerey, A. *Compendio di teologia ascetica e mistica.* 2d ed. Rome, 1930.

Tassi, I. *Ludovico Barbo (1381–1443).* Uomini e dottrine, I. Rome, 1952.

Tassini, G. *Alcuni palazzi ed antichi edifici.* Venice, 1879.

Taveneaux, R. "Il cattolicesimo post-tridentino." In *Storia delle religioni*, ed. H.-Ch Puech, III, pp. 305–402. Bari, 1977.

Temanza, T. *Vite dei più celebri architetti e scultori veneziani che fiorirono nel secolo decimosesto.* Venice, 1778.

Tentori, C. *Saggio sulla storia civile, politica, ecclesiastica della repubblica di Venezia.* 12 vols. Venice, 1785.

Tiraboschi, G. *Biblioteca modenese.* 6 vols. Modena, 1783–86.

———. *Storia della letteratura italiana.* 30 vols. Milan, 1826–29.

Toffanin, J. *Il dominio austriaco in Padova dal 20 gennaio 1798 al 16 gennaio 1801.* Padua, 1901.

Tommaseo, N., and Bellini, B. *Dizionario della lingua italiana nuovamente compilato.* Vol. I, pt. 2. Turin, 1865.

Tonzig, M. "Elena Lucrezia Cornaro Piscopia (1646–1684) prima donna laureata." *Quaderni per la storia dell'Università di Padova*, 6 (1974): 183–192.

Tron, E. *Tributo d'ossequio nella partenza dal felicissimo reggimento di Girolamo Cornaro podestà, e capitano di Trevigi.* Treviso, 1685.

Tua, C. "Marinali, scultori." In *Enciclopedia italiana di scienze, lettere e arti*, XXII, p. 345. Rome, 1950.

Vaglia, U. *Storia della valle Sabbia*. 2 vols. Brescia, 1964.

Valery, M. *Correspondance inédite de Mabillon et de Montfaucon avec l'Italie*. 3 vols. Paris, 1846.

Vedova, G. *Biografia degli scrittori padovani*. 2 vols. Padua, 1836.

Ventura, A. *Nobiltà e popolo nella società veneta del' 400 e del' 500*. Bari, 1964.

Vicini, G. B. *Egeria*. Paris, 1764.

Viviani, A. "Rinaldini, Carlo." In *Enciclopedia filosofica*, V, pp. 788–89. Florence, 1967.

Wernich, A. "Calafatti Giorgio." In *Biographisches Lexicon der Hervorragenden Aertze aller Zieten und Völker*, I, p. 643. Vienna and Leipzig, 1884.

———. "Marchetti Pietro." In *Biographisches Lexicon der Hervorragenden Aertze aller Zieten und Völker*, IV, p. 128. Vienna and Leipzig, 1886.

Zannandreis, D. *Le vite dei pittori scultori e architetti veronesi*. Verona, 1891. Reprint: Bologna, 1971.

Ziegelbauer, M. *Historia rei literariae ordinis s. Benedicti*. 4 vols. Augustae Vindelicorum, 1754.

Zimmerman, A. *Kalendarium benedictinum*. 2 vols. Metten, 1934.

INDEX

A

Aboaf, David, 235; patron, 235

Aboaf, Jacob, (Father), 55

Aboaf, Jacob, Rabbi of Venice, (d. 1727), 56, 235

Aboaf, Joseph, Rabbi of Venice, 235

Aboaf, Shemuel, Rabbi of Venice, (1610-1694), 55-57, 235; asceticism, 56; academy, 55; burial, 56; charitable activities, 55; death, 56; linguistic skills, 56; persecution, 56, 235; scholar, 55-56; tutor, 55, 57; Venetian community, 56

academic academies, 83-84, 86, 93-94, 96, 125, 241

Académie Française, Paris, (1635-1793, 1803-present), 242

Academy of Geography, Venice, 48

Accademia Affettuosi, Amatori, Arditi... Padua, (c. 1550), 241

Accademia Agraria, Padua, (suppressed 1779), 241

Accademia de Belle Arti, Bologna, 260

Accademia de Belle Arti, Modena, 260

Accademia del Cimento, Pisa, (founded 1657), 49-50

Accademia Dodonea, Venice, 84

Accademia degli Erranti, Brescia, (founded 1619), 84

Accademia Eterei, Padua, (founded 1564), 241

Accademia Farsetti, Venice, 258

Accademia Giustiniani, Padua, (founded 17th c.), 241

Accademia Incogniti, Infiammati, Padua, (founded 1540), 241

Accademia degli Infecondi, Rome, (founded early 17th c.), 39, 84, 95-96, 126, 179, 244, 257

Accademia degli Intronati, Siena, (founded 13th c.), 84

Accademia Invigoriti, Orditi, Serafici..., Padua, (founded early 17th c.), 241

Accademia dei Pacifici, Venice, 84, 93-94, 241

Accademia Patavina, Padua, 189, 240, 241

Accademia dei Ricovrati, Padua, (founded 1599), 46, 50, 54, 77, 83-84, 86, 96-98, 124-126, 240-241, 244-245, 254, 255, 256; Cornaro patronage, 125; registry, 240

Accademia di Scienze, Lettere e Arti, Padua, 241

Accademia degli Unanimi, Salò, (founded 1564),12

Accademia Veneziana dei Delfici, Venice, (1647-1690), 40

Achillini, Alessandro, Philosopher, Physician, (1463-1512), 51

Acqua, Antonio dall', 207

Acquapendente, Italy, 126, 256

acrostic, 93

Addormentati, (Academic Name), 241

Adriatic Sea, 236

Aedes Monetaria, (17th c.), 40

Aegean Islands, 5, 24, 55

Agiati, (Academic Name), 241

Agostini, C., 162

Agusti, Alvise, 202

Agusti, Marin, 202

Airoldi, Carlo, 75

D

O

Z

ABOUT THE AUTHOR

Francesco Ludovico Maschietto, O.S.B. (1909-2000), was a monk of the Monastery of Santa Giustina in Padua, where he served as librarian for over twenty years. He was the author of numerous studies about the monks of Santa Giustina and various people associated with this historic Benedictine abbey. He is buried in the municipal cemetery of Padua, although plans are underway to transfer his remains to the Cornaro Chapel near the tomb of Elena Lucrezia Cornaro Piscopia.

CONTRIBUTORS

Jan Vairo and William Crochetiere teach Italian at Duquesne University. Catherine Marshall is a retired Senior Editor at the University of Pittsburgh Press.